The Dreaming Brain

THE

DREAMING

BRAIN

J. Allan Hobson

Basic Books, Inc., Publishers   *New York*

Figures 7.4, 7.6, and 9.3 copyright 1977, The American Psychiatric Association. Reprinted by permission.

Dreams are rough copies of the waking soul
Yet uncorrected of the higher will,
So that men sometimes in their dreams confess
An unsuspected, or forgotten, self;
—Since Dreaming, Madness, Passion, are akin
In missing each that salutory rein
Of reason, and the grinding will of man.

— Pedro Calderon de la Barca
(1600–1681)

CONTENTS

PART I
EARLY DREAM SCIENCE

PART II
DREAMING AND NEUROBIOLOGY

PART III
A NEW MODEL OF THE DREAMING BRAIN

Contents

PART IV

DREAM FORM: THE JOURNAL OF THE ENGINE MAN

PART V

THE FUTURE OF DREAM SCIENCE

LIST OF ILLUSTRATIONS

ACKNOWLEDGMENTS

I was born with mixed cerebral dominance: being left-handed and right-eyed, at age fifteen I attracted the attention of the Hartford dyslexia specialist, Page Sharp, because I did not have the difficulty with reading, writing, and spelling predicted by such a brain-wiring diagram. Sharp became my mentor, confidant, and role model. As his research assistant, I learned psychometric methods and an optimistic view of the prospects of neuropsychology. As his adopted son, I learned good reasons for expecting more of myself and of life.

I am tempted to attribute the neurobehavioral anomaly to my mother's early encouragement of my literary and artistic interests. If anyone's nurture could have overcome nature, it was my mother's. My natural penchant for spatial analysis, design, and engineering was amplified by my father and his inventor friends, whose clever machines he helped to patent. Together we built a laboratory for the microscope, chemicals, and anatomical specimens that I began collecting at the age of eight.

To these three people who gave me the basics, I dedicate this book. I hope they will not be too embarrassed by it.

Many of the teachers who shaped my thinking and direction are naturally acknowledged in the book itself through my account of their own scientific contributions. But Squirrel Norris of The Loomis-Chaffee School (Connecticut) is not. And neither is Wesleyan University's Rudy Haffner. In high school and in college, they taught me neuroanatomy and spurred my drive to investigate the brain as a structure. Without their help I might have accepted my classmates' diagnosis of my penchant for the dissection of brains as weird, perverted, and disgusting. And I might have succumbed to their pressure to play more football, to drive faster, to drink more martinis, and thus to court the brain damage that disabled and even killed many of us.

As a cerebral and educational oddball, I was naturally inclined to cross disciplinary lines early and often. Against the almost deafening call to specialization were the clear and articulate interdisciplinary voices of Fred Millett and Nobby Brown at Wesleyan. In their garden of earthly delights, the Russell House, this academic odd couple first quenched my thirst for psychology by dunking me into the Freudian depths. Then I would run to the other end of the Wesleyan campus for a good scientific toweling-down. Vince Cochran gave me my first appetizing taste of analytic and dynamic biological science, which became my deeper hunger for neurophysiology in medical school. These teachers represent the best of the liberal arts tradition, and I hope this book's wide reach will not make them regret their tolerant enthusiasm.

The marriage of mind and brain was a clear, if shimmering, mirage in the sky above the solid ground of the Harvard Medical School. Like the ivy of its Vermont-marble palaces, my science took root in the classical neurophysiology of Elwood Henneman and the dynamic biochemistry of Manfred Karnovsky. The ghost of Walter Cannon hovered above the laboratories and the amphitheaters. Dan Funkenstein, who personified lions and rabbits, made psychophysiology seem both possible and important. The propeller in my integrative skullcap was spun by that loving visionary, Mark Altschule. He knew psychiatric history and was critical about the present state of the art; loose-thinking Freudians got no quarter from Mark.

My mission set, I wanted only in guidance and sponsorship to get off the ground. Chiefs Lewis Thomas (medicine) and Jack Ewalt (psychiatry) were both charismatic and permissive. Both within and without its walls, the National Institute of Mental Health was consistently generous in providing training and research support. Even the National Science Foundation chipped in. Launched, I was lucky to have the feisty crew of co-workers whose names appear with mine in papers. The theory presented here grew out of my sixteen-year collaboration with Bob McCarley and is at least half his. It is impossible to describe how awful and how wonderful it all was. I offer ambivalent thanks to my competitors, those crucial antagonists in a continuing dialectic: Freud and his legion of diehard disciples; Michel Jouvet and his tenacious serotonin theory of sleep; the group of behavioral physiologists at the University of California at Los Angeles who, with the speed of a monosynaptic reflex, still seem to doubt everything I say. Dear colleagues all, there must be truth on both sides of any interesting debate!

When it came to telling this story, I was helped to think and to write by various invited lectureships and fellowships. "La Machine à Rêver" was my 1973 lecture title in Bordeaux, at the instigation of my dear friend, the surrealist-physiologist Jean-Didier Vincent. That same year, the reciprocal-interaction model was fleshed out in response to invitations from Vern Johnson and Eliot Weitzman to address the eighth annual meeting of the

Sleep Research Society in San Diego. Ian Oswald made me the Sandoz Lecturer at Edinburgh University in 1975: "The Brain as a Dream Machine" was the title of that address to a very nervous psychoanalytic audience in the David Hume tower!

Research on the book itself began in the summer of 1977 when a grant from the Commonwealth Fund allowed me to hide out in Riolo, an abandoned hill town in Tuscany. Giuseppe Moruzzi lent me a trunkful of books each week when I descended a perilous mule track to his precious library at the Physiology Institute in Pisa. My escape that summer was timely since the exhibit "Dreamstage: An Experimental Portrait of the Sleeping Brain" had just touched off, in the United States, a media explosion that both turned my head and made me lots of enemies. It also seduced me into theater. But even that diverting project, supported by Roche Laboratories, ultimately helped the book by its emphasis on a visual representation of sleep and dream research. I hope Paul Earls, Ragnhild Karlstrom, and Ted Spagna, my artistic collaborators in that Hard Day's Night, take no offense at this more verbal rendering. They helped me to recognize and begin even to reach the wide lay audience for whom this book is intended.

Progress on the book itself was slow in part because I kept getting sidetracked. In 1980 and 1986, two major writing projects, both with Mircea Steriade of Laval University in Quebec, allowed the neurophysiology presented here to be integrated within comprehensive reviews of the world literature. Meanwhile, I also needed to study dreaming itself as well as further to test the sleep model in the laboratory. Upstairs, Rita Helfand, Steve Hoffman, Delia Kostner, and Helene Porte studied dreaming. Downstairs, Ralph Lydic, Helen Baghdoyan, Cliff Callaway, and Tony Monaco mined the physiological salt. My staff was thus burdened by more projects and more manuscripts than was reasonable. Thank you Noreene Storrie, Selma Nechin, Andrew Galdins, Lynn DiMatteo, and Eve Melnechuck for being so good-humored and resolute. Chris Lindsey finally pulled us into the computer age and word-processed all 575 pages of my first draft!

Once it was written, I received helpful suggestions from encouraging editors and colleagues, including Linda Chaput and Jonathan Cobb at W. H. Freeman Company, E. O. Wilson and Howard Boyer at Harvard, and Martin Kessler and Jo Ann Miller at Basic Books. In her capacity as developmental editor, Phoebe Hoss has done her best to liberate my prose from jargon's straitjacket and to bring textual order to chaos. My friend, the Washington attorney George Denney, helped us obtain permission to reproduce the text and drawings of the Dream Journal so that we could illustrate our new method of analyzing dream form.

To the reader who may become impatient with technical details, let me say that the nervous system is so complicated that only such laborious quests as this will penetrate its mysteries. As I have pointed out earlier, studying the simple nervous systems of invertebrates may lead relatively quickly to relatively conclusive evidence—but simple systems will never answer questions that depend upon complexity. The fact that experimental programs such as ours are still inconclusive after twenty years of work must not be taken as proof that the approach is wrong. For the preceding 2,500 years, humanity speculated in vain about the relationship of the mind to the brain. Rather than become impatient with these two decades of slow and halting progress, we must continue carefully to build up our pictures of mind-brain states, neuron by neuron, and to construct our theory hypothesis by hypothesis. We will not jump to premature conclusions. By regarding *any* progress as adequate recompense, we will slowly but surely solve the age-old problem.

It is impossible to express enthusiasm for one's own ideas without sounding boastful. In writing this way, I hope somehow to communicate the ineffable aesthetic pleasure that a scientist feels as an explanatory concept crystallizes.

Critical feedback and support for my thinking about the book's subject grew out of two related groups. On the inside was the New Psychiatry Seminar, a quasi-revolutionary band of young psychiatric malcontents who creatively complained to and quarreled with me from 1983 to 1986 in the New Psychiatry Seminar. Willard Quine wryly dubbed us "Freudians Anonymous." Ned Hallowell, John Ratey, and David Mann were the ringleaders of this band. On the outside was the still evolving discussion among a group of critics that includes Charles Brenner, Frank Sulloway, Adolf Grunbaum, Paul Roazen, and Frederick Crews. By inviting them to speak at our grand-rounds lecture series, we were able to establish dialogues of soul and substance.

Such a wild agenda was possible only within a circle of loving friends that was centered on a deeply committed family. My wife, Joan, with whom I have slept, and dreamed—over ten thousand nights—has patiently salved my body and piqued my mind. For the past fifteen years, Chantal Rode has helped us hold it all together in a frame whose grace and style are her great gifts. I hope that our children—Ian, Christopher, and Julia— may one day feel that the baseball games, camping trips, and TV dinners they missed were compensated by the models of intense passion and insane absorption with work they witnessed in our house. Maybe they will have sense enough to cultivate more peaceful lives.

The Dreaming Brain

Introduction

A Brain-Based Approach

to Dreaming

A man dreamt that he flayed his own child and made a wineskin out of him. On the following day, his little child fell into the river and drowned. For a wineskin is made from dead bodies and is capable of receiving liquids.

—Artemidorus
The Interpretation of Dreams (A.D. 150)

Sleep affords the opportunity, within certain limits, for the brain to act of itself, and dreams are the result.
—Edward Clarke
Vision: A Study of False Sight (1878)

OVER THE CENTURIES and even today, dreams have been looked at subjectively and as experiences whose significance is cryptic, needing to be decoded in some way. A new way of viewing dreams, as transparent, their significance available to the dreamer unaided by prophet or psychoanalyst, derives from the objective studies of modern sleep science and neurobiology. How the study of the brain has come to help us understand dreaming in this straightforward manner is the subject of this book.

The Nature of Dreaming

I am in my car (or so it seems) on the third and highest of three parallel, shelflike levels. The level just below (about 30 or 40 feet) is a uniquely modern service station designed to handle up to 1,000 cars at a time. (Fill gas tanks, change oil and tires, perform pitstop repairs.) There are two long ribbonlike lanes on either side of the service station; and as I gaze down upon them, I am aware that they are having the finishing touches put on them. Heavy laminae of plywood are being surfaced with blue formica (in the manner of a kitchen or bathroom surface).

My task is to get (my car?) from level 3 to level 2 where the services can be performed. It is not obvious how this can be done since the levels are discontinuous. (Nor is it even made clear what is on level 1!)

I find myself hazardously close to the edge. Without transition or explanation, I am no longer (if ever I really was) in my car. "Good God!" I say. "This is a precarious perch." And I decide to swing my brown leather JAH briefcase up and over the edge so as to free my left hand for the job of sticking to the shelf edge. As the bag swings up, its contents spill, and myriad papers flutter down. I resist the impulse to drop off the edge to rescue them.

"Hobson," cry my colleagues, suddenly assembled below on level 2, "can we help you?" And they begin to gather up my scattered papers.

"Don't bother with the papers," I exclaim. "Come up and help me off this ledge."

Now my hold becomes increasingly tenuous, and the edges of the blue formica shelf begin to fold down, like the hinged levers of a dinette. When all seems lost, I awake in terror. [JAH Dream Journal, Entry II, 7 November 1984]

In this dream, terror has so strongly seized me as to reverse the time-honored professorial axiom of "Publish or perish!"—and interrupt my sleep. In these respects, this dream exemplifies at least two of the five most characteristic features of dreaming: emotion so intensely felt that it may fracture or terminate the dream state; and illogical content and organization, in which the unities of time, place, and person do not apply, and natural laws are disobeyed. Included in this dream also are a third and fourth aspect of dreaming: the experience of formed sensory impressions, however bizarre; and uncritical acceptance, as though the experience were a normal, everyday one, of the strange things that I am seeing, hearing, and feeling. The fifth feature of dreaming—the difficulty of remembering a dream once it is over—did not hold for me, since I keep a dream journal in which, upon waking, I record my dreams, and thus generally am able to obviate their elusiveness.

These five cardinal features of dreaming are, moreover, familiar to us all. For every one of us dreams every night, even though for centuries people have believed that dreams occur only when one is upset or in the instant before awakening, or are caused by indigestion, or that good sleep is dreamless. Since the discovery of REM sleep in 1953, research has demonstrated the unreliability of such subjective experience as well as of one's capacity to estimate the frequency and duration of dreams based upon waking recall. Even the best dream recallers do not remember all their dreams. And some people never remember any dreams at all. Thus, we all dream in a regular and predictable way every night of our lives, whether we are upset or not. And we usually dream for periods as long as one hour without waking up. In fact, good sleep has just as much dreaming in it as does poor sleep—if not more. In a normal life span of seventy years, an individual devotes at least 50,000 hours to dreaming: that is, 2,000 days or 6 full years of dream time. Dreaming must therefore be not only psychologically intriguing but biologically important.

Sustained dream scenarios occur only after sleep is well established. Dreaming then alternates with thoughtlike mentation at intervals of 90 to 100 minutes throughout the night. Recall of dreams and other forms of mental activity in sleep depend upon one's prompt awakening from the sleep state in which the mental activity occurs; retention of such recall further depends upon the instrumental act of verbally reporting or transcribing the dream narration.

Waking fantasy, which often shares the self-indulgence and the scenario structure of dreaming—and can be equally difficult to recall—is usually less perceptually vivid and less cognitively bizarre than dreaming.

Dreams are characterized by vivid and fully formed hallucinatory imagery with the visual sense predominant; auditory, tactile, and movement sensations are also prominent in most dream reports. Compared with the intense involvement of these sensorimotor domains, taste and smell are underrepresented and reports of pain are exceedingly rare. The rarity of pain experience is the more surprising given the frequent involvement of dreamers in frightening and even physically mutilating scenarios.

Dreaming is properly considered delusional because most subjects have virtually no insight regarding the true nature of the state in which they have these unusual sensory experiences. During a dream, one tends to consider dream events as if they were completely real, even though, upon waking, one promptly recognizes them as fabrications. This loss of critical perspective is doubly significant since one believes in the reality of dream events in spite of their extreme improbability and even physical impossibility. Contributing to this state of credulity in dreaming is the fact that one lacks the reflective self-awareness that helps us test reality during the waking state. Instead, the dreamer is of but one mind, and that mind is wholly absorbed by the dream process.

The lack of insight that makes the whole dream experience delusional is part of a broader set of characteristic cognitive disturbances. These include: discontinuities (with unexplained changes of subject, action, and setting); improbabilities and impossibilities (with frank defiance of physical law); incongruities (with plot or scene features that do not fit together); and uncertainties (with explicit vagueness of explanation). Dream characters and dream objects may be of an everyday nature or altogether fantastic and physically impossible collages of existing reality; they may behave normally or indulge in the most absurd, improbable, or impossible actions in settings either familiar or bearing only the faintest resemblances to those of real life. To explain these unique and remarkable dream features, illogical thought processes—such as non sequiturs, post-hoc explanations, and symbolic, mythical, or metaphorical constructions—are the norm.

The following dream account by a colleague of mine contains a characteristic dream mishmash of two common boyhood aspirations—to be a great baseball player and to be a great scientist:

I was in a rather large auditorium, the whereabouts of which I am unsure. I am a member of a large audience, and up on the stage is a man whom I had just been told by someone standing next to me had just won the Nobel Prize. He is about to give an acceptance speech, and I am very surprised as he begins to speak that he identifies himself as Ken (Someone) and that I have some familiarity with his name, but remain unsure of exactly who he is until I learn that he is a baseball player. He has not earned the Nobel Prize for Peace for playing baseball specifically, but rather because of the fact that he is a famous baseball player who has also performed some civic duty, the nature of which is unclear to me. He begins to give a slide show detailing the last thirty years of his career, showing us what he had done. There is a long narrative that explains certain kinds of baseball events but also other kinds of civic events with all sorts of buildings and different stadiums and large crowds. Somehow he has been involved with each of these events, and I thought, "He must be the first baseball player to ever win the Nobel Prize for Peace. This is strange." I also cannot help noticing that he does not seem very bright at all in explaining what he has done, and wonder to myself, "If he can win the Nobel Prize, why can't I?" [Laboratory Collection]

The wish fulfillment of this dream is blatant and its grandiose power easily overcomes the conflict, confusion, and incompatibility of its dual motives to win the Nobel Prize and to be a baseball star. In accomplishing this feat, the dreaming mind shows a striking neglect of such extreme cognitive abnormalities as disorientation to place ("whereabouts . . . unsure") and to person ("someone standing next to me"; "Ken [Someone]"). The dream character, Ken, is not only vaguely identified but has discontinuous, incomplete, and incongruous attributes:

a baseball player,
with (unclear) civic achievements, he
gives a slide show with all sorts of buildings
and different stadiums, but
is not very bright.

All of these peculiar phenomena relate transparently to the dreamer's self-portrait as an ordinary person who will nonetheless succeed.

One careful self-observer, whose remarkable dream journal is analyzed in Part IV, has spoken of being

impressed time and time again by the extraordinary elusiveness of certain dream episodes which seemed very vivid while happening in the dream, but which lose their richness and character very rapidly, sometimes entirely disappearing as soon as the waking mind takes possession. [Dream Journal of the Engine Man, introduction, 15 July 1939]

After six weeks of concerted and sustained efforts had enhanced his own dream recall to four to five detailed reports each night, a journal entry notes:

One dream entirely lost except for the incident of the new chair (a large wooden one) which was obtained for E. S. at the office. I recall that the chair was being pushed up to the desk. [Dream Journal of the Engine Man, report 45, 3 August 1939]

Memory may thus undergo a paradoxical intensification as well as suppression during dreaming: recall is intensified within the dream as remote characters, scenes, events, and concerns are knitted into the fanciful and evanescent fabric of the dream. The dreaming mind can thus be said to be *hypermnesic;* this increased access to memory *within* the state of dreaming contrasts markedly with the virtual impossibility of recovering the dream product *after* the state has terminated. Thus, there is amnesia for the hypermnesic dream. On awakening, even suddenly, from a dream in full progress, subjects have difficulty holding their vivid experience in short-term memory long enough to give a report or to transcribe the dream scenario in detail. A conservative estimate has it that more than 95 percent of all dream mentation is completely unremembered.

Emotion fluctuates widely in association with the bizarre and vivid mental content of dreaming: anxiety, fear, and surprise are the most common affects to undergo a marked intensification during dreaming. Obsessional concerns are common, with dreamers focusing their worry on nudity, missed trains, unpacked suitcases, and a host of other incomplete arrangements. Depressive affects are markedly underrepresented, with shame and guilt making up a surprisingly small part of dream affect, despite indulgence in shabby behavior that would immediately perturb the waking conscience.

This formal definition of dreaming is exclusive of four other kinds of mental activity that also occur during sleep.

First, pictorial consciousness similar to dreaming may occur at the onset of sleep; but the visual images at sleep onset are more likely than dreams to be either fleeting or unstructured, and far less likely to be integrated into a sustained and episodic narrative frame; and they may be associated with, or terminated by, the abrupt sensation of falling. The similarities and differences between these *hypnagogic* images and dreams, which fascinated such nineteenth-century dream students as Alfred Maury (see chapter 1), are now known to have their own specific physiological underpinnings.

Second, dreamlike experiences occur on arousal from sleep and may be extensions of dream forms into waking. Thus, a sleeper may either see formed visual images set within the real bedroom (these waking visions are called *hypnopompic hallucinations*) and/or be unable to move despite intense efforts to do so (an experience called *sleep paralysis*). When both experiences occur together, the feeling of dread associated with each is multiplied. These arousal experiences are clearly compounded of both waking-state and dream-state features, and occur because the brain cannot instantaneously switch from one state to the other.

Not only does dreaming occupy as much as two hours per night, but mental activity of some sort appears to accompany at least half of our sleep. In fact, the most common form of mental activity in sleep is not dreaming but thinking. Sleep thinking is not accompanied by sensory illusions and is not bizarre. It tends to be commonplace, often concerned with the real-life events of yesterday or tomorrow, and is usually banal, uncreative, and repetitive. It feels as if the mind (and the brain) were idling, running in place, as it were. We become aware of this kind of sleep mentation when we are preparing for an important social event such as an examination, a project deadline, or a decisive meeting.

At another extreme from dreaming is the experience of pure terror or dread, without the accompaniment of visions or a plot. Drenching sweats, palpitations, and throttled vocalizations may accompany these nightmare emotions. It is as if a switch were turned on, releasing all fear's bodily and mental manifestations and thus awakening one. In children, such night terrors may be accompanied by frightening hypnopompic hallucinations, causing a child to behave dementedly for a brief period. Here again, the brain is having difficulty changing state.

The five cardinal characteristics of dream mentation may also be seen in the hallucinations, disorientations, bizarre thoughts, delusions, and amnesias of patients with mental illness. These mental symptoms collectively constitute delirium, dementia, and psychosis. Thus, were it not for the fact that we are asleep when they occur, we would be obliged to say that our dreams are formally psychotic and that we are all, during dreaming, formally delirious and demented.

Indeed, the visual, auditory, tactile, and postural sensory illusions of dreams are as formally impressive as any schizophrenic patient's hallucinations, while the bizarre defiance of temporal, spatial, and personal law that occurs in dreaming is as formally outlandish as the most disoriented utterances of the most demented patient with structural or functional brain disease. The noncritical acceptance of all such bizarre sensory dream events as real is as devoid of insight as the most convinced delusional assertions of the schizophrenic, the manic depressive, or the organically impaired patient. Furthermore, our amnesia for our dreams is as impossible to overcome as is the forgetfulness for recent events that occurs in advanced senility.

Dreaming could thus be the mental product of the same *kind* of physiological process that is deranged in mental illness. This conclusion gives the scientific study of the dream process implications beyond the realm of dreaming itself: since all of the major signs of mental illness can be imitated by normal minds in the normal state of dreaming. The study of dreams is the study of a model of mental illness.

THE INTERPRETATION OF DREAMS

Down through history—at least from Joseph's interpretation of Pharaoh's dreams in Genesis through Freud and the modern psychoanalytic tradition—a variety of soothsayers have sought to find meaning in these vivid and elusive manifestations of the human mind. The details in dreams have, according to the outlook of a particular era, appeared to be symbols indicative, to one who knows the code, of the future or bearing some other hidden meaning.

The time-honored approach to understanding dreams is to regard them as communications from external agencies: gods, angels, or spirits. This fundamentally religious idea can never be either proved or disproved. The best that science can do is to examine the evidence for it and try to account for that evidence with propositions that may be capable of verification.

The reasons for the long and continued popularity of the prophetic tradition are not difficult to discern. Dreams are so strange—and so involuntary—as to challenge and deny the twin notions of rationality and responsibility. To be responsible, I must be rational; but in dreaming I appear irrational. And I lose my sense of volition. How, then, can I be responsible for my dreams? Surely they occur whether I will them or not. If I do not will them, then how can I cause them? And if not I, then who does will or cause them? While clearly involving me, dreams seem to happen to me regardless of my will; and they run their course—with few exceptions—no matter what I say, think, or feel.

Human intelligence has balked at two aspects of this experience. First, common sense says that there can be no effects without causes. Next, the individual sense of personal responsibility—and the freedom that is the basis of one's sense of will, choice, and morality—refuses to be held accountable for unwilled phenomena. One obvious conclusion: dreams are caused by some *external* agency over which we have no control; on the contrary, it is this external agency that during dreams controls the dreamer. Such assumptions have led naturally to religious theories and religious practices, in the effort to placate and appease the forces (or gods) that seem to drive our destiny.

In its simplest form, the hypothesis of prophecy offers only temporary comfort since it does not account for the peculiar nature of the unwilled, externally directed experience of dreaming. While there may be both good and evil gods (angels and devils), they, too, must have their reasons. People are, and have been, unhappy with the idea of gods as insane, and must believe that their nocturnal visitations have a point, however obscure. In other words, we have great difficulty in accepting the irrationality of dreams as a natural phenomenon.

Since it is in the very nature of gods to be invisible as well as omnipotent, many people have supposed that dreams are complex communications whose codes contain the key to gods' future plans. For these seers, dream symbols are the glyphs of a mystical language, and full of prophetic portent. Viewed in this way, the prophetic tradition of dream study can be seen in its modern as well as its antique form. The wise man, the priest, or the psychoanalyst knows the dream code and can thus predict the future while deciphering both the past and the present.

Other aspects of the dream experience give added credence to the prophetic position. Complementing the notion of an external agency is the out-of-body experience that may occur in nocturnal dreams or in the transitional states between waking and sleep. In these states, it seems that a part of the self (the soul or the ego) leaves the body and becomes an external agency. It may even seem that the soul wanders abroad, exert-

ing its action in places remote from the body. In this way, magical interventions can be achieved, and the notion of gods as external agents is
complemented by the sense of being visited by disembodied spirits, with
agency power. Reinforcing the notion of dreams as prophetic symbols is
the idea that dreaming of particular events or objects may actually cause
(or signal the cause) of real-life events.

Dreaming of an anticipated (or unanticipated) event may be followed
by its real-life occurrence. Sometimes the actual event takes place in striking confirmation of a dream. Such precognitive dreams are as frightening
as they are gratifying: they suggest not only that dreams are only the result
of external agencies but that the dreams themselves are agents. In the
precognitive dream, the omnipotence of the gods becomes one with a
person's thoughts. If the dream event is the death of a loved one, the
consequences for the dreamer can be frightening since causality and volition are both implied. It is not uncommon for the dreamer of an anticipated
but unwanted event to feel responsible for willing it in and through the
dream.

In assuming that our dreams may not only signal, but actually cause
real-life events, the prophetic point of view has collapsed and the dreamer
has resumed responsibility for the dream's actions. We humans seem to
have as much difficulty delegating responsibility for important life events
as we do in accepting it. But there is a third way by which we may avoid
the dilemma of unacceptable responsibility for unwilled acts. The scientific
evidence, to be reviewed in Parts III and IV, now suggests that both life
events (such as births, deaths, and accidents) and dream events (such as
out-of-body and precognitive experiences) are all, in essence, unwilled
natural phenomena: they occur according to their own laws, in which both
determinism and chance are statutes, and the associations between them
are as much casual as they are causal. It may thus be as unwise as it is
unnecessary to regard their nonsensical aspects as hypermeaningful, and
as unhealthy as it is unscientific to indulge in symbol interpretation.

Embedded in the notion of dreams as prophecy (where the prophet is
external agent) is the implication that prophetic messages are disguised
either symbolically or metaphorically and therefore need translation or
interpretation. Thus, Joseph read Pharaoh's dream of the seven fat and the
seven lean kine as heralding seven rich years of harvest followed by seven
fallow ones. The most modern manifestation of this interpretive tradition
is the theory of dreams advanced by psychoanalysis.

Because psychoanalysis is so dominant a theory, its critical treatment
is an essential theme of this book. Psychoanalysis is a conceptual advance
over biblical prophecy in doing away with the notion of external agency
and placing the communicator deep within the self. According to psycho-

analysis, this internal agency resides in an occult chamber of the psyche as a constellation of drives, which Freud called the id. Released from restraint during sleep, the id sends its uncensored commands up from the unconscious to perform acts that would be forbidden by the ego-superego in waking consciousness. This internal agency is so unwelcome even to the sleeping mind that its commands must be altered so that they can invade consciousness and disrupt sleep. This is the *disguise-censorship* theory of dreams.

Although the brain-based theory that I will develop runs deeply counter to the psychoanalytic theory of the interpretation of dreams, I do not mean to imply that I disagree with its psychodynamic spirit. But I do mean to propose alternative explanations for all of its important claims. And the result is a radically opposite approach to interpretation.

I differ from Freud in that I think that most dreams are neither obscure nor bowdlerized, but rather that they are transparent and unedited. They reveal clearly meaningful, undisguised, and often highly conflictual themes worthy of note by the dreamer (and any interpretive assistant). My position echoes Jung's notion of dreams as transparently meaningful and does away with any distinction between manifest and latent content.

Dream Science

All the interpretative traditions, including psychoanalysis, rely exclusively upon subjective experience. In every case, the dreamer must recollect his or her own dream without instrumental or experimental help. For this reason, the yield of particular dreams is usually small, and their content unreliable. But there is one tradition—long antedating the modern scientific era—in which experimental accomplices or instrumentation have been used to make the study of dreams more systematic and more objective.

A technical forerunner of modern dream science was dream incubation, practiced by the classical Greeks. Ill patients came to sleep in a temple and, during sleep, were awakened by priests who elicited reports of their dreams. These dreams were then used as a basis for an arcane medical diagnostic system in which certain dream elements represented certain body parts and the action in a dream represented pathological conditions of those parts. However fatuous and outmoded this idea may seem to us today, the ancient priests at least recognized that access to dreams and accuracy of reporting could be increased by performing experimental awakenings.

Closer to our own time were two nineteenth-century French scholars, the Marquis d'Hervey de Saint-Denis and Alfred Maury, who both resorted to instrumental means of dream access, practicing self-awakening and sometimes using accomplices (see chapter 1). Although working at home, they are the true predecessors of the modern sleep laboratory scientist.

In his introductory chapter to *The Interpretation of Dreams* (1900), Freud buried these and other proponents of the objective tradition beneath an avalanche of polemical discourse against such studies which he decried together with the medical science tradition that inspired them.

Meanwhile we shall feel no surprise at the overestimation of the part played in forming dreams by stimuli that do not arise from mental life. Not only are they easy to discover and even open to experimental confirmation; but the somatic view of the origin of dreams is completely in line with the prevailing trend of thought in psychiatry. [1900, p. 75].

It is ironic that Freud, while proclaiming a scientific approach to dreams, relied exclusively upon subjective reports and failed utterly to protect himself, or his subjects, from the effects of dream distortion via suggestion.

In so clearing the decks for his own psychoanalytic dream theory, Freud nonetheless recognized the promise that brain science held for psychology, and maintained that ultimately his theories would be replaced by the findings of neurobiology. Building on the neuron doctrine of Freud's contemporary, Santiago Ramón y Cajal, brain science has grown in parallel with objective approaches to sleep and dreaming. The current merger of these fields yields a theory of dreaming with surprisingly different features from those that Freud imagined.

With the discovery in 1953 of the bursts of *rapid eye movements* (REM) that occur during sleep and accompany brain activation, the study of dreaming became both more objective and more systematic. Using sleep laboratory techniques, it became possible to establish the general psychological nature of dreaming by collecting thousands of reports from hundreds of subjects. It was further possible to show the strong correlation between dreaming and rapid-eye-movement sleep and to distinguish, in a statistical way, that correlation from other kinds of mental activity in other kinds of sleep. Finally, the discovery that REM sleep occurs in all mammals provided both an animal model for a deeper analysis of the brain physiology of REM sleep than was possible in humans, and clear evidence that human dreaming is tied to a brain process of broad biological significance. (See figure I.1.)

It is my aim in this book to present a psychophysiological theory of

FIGURE I.1

Sleeping man and cat

Modern dream research involves the simultaneous study of human subjects (who can report their subjective experience in REM sleep) and animals (whose brain activity in REM sleep can be characterized at the level of individual cells). The basic architecture of the brain and its sleep physiology is the same in the two species. This and the following drawings were inspired by the time-lapse photographic and video studies of sleep by Theodore Spagna and the author. *Drawing by Barbara Haines.*

how dreams are formed: specifically, that the form of dreams is related to the form of brain activity in sleep; and that the brain is first turned on (activated) during sleep and then generates and integrates (synthesizes) its own sensory and motor information. The sensory and motor signals that the brain automatically generates are both the driving force and the directional vector for the dream plot, which is synthesized in light of an individual's past experiences, attitudes, and expectations.

The activation-synthesis hypothesis thus proposes a specific brain mechanism that is both necessary and sufficient for dreaming to occur. This mechanism is both more and less deterministic than previous theories of dreaming have been.

More deterministic because the automaticity and the fixed quality and quantity of dreaming that it produces make dreaming an integral part of vegetative life rather than a mere reaction to life's vicissitudes. Dreaming is seen, by activation synthesis, as an endogenous process with its own genetically determined dynamics. There may be no covert informational meaning to this process; on the contrary, information processing may be just one of the many functions served by dreaming.

Less deterministic because the activation-synthesis theory supposes an open system of information processing, which is capable not only of repro-duction and distortion of stored information but of the elaboration of novel information. Activation synthesis thus includes creativity among its assumptions. This theory sees the brain as so inexorably bent upon the quest for meaning that it attributes and even creates meaning when there is little or none to be found in the data it is asked to process. In this sense, the study of dreaming is the study of the brain-mind as an autocreative mechanism.

In using physiology to understand dreaming, I aim to show that the most remarkable property of mind—an aspect that is most essentially human, the capacity to imagine, to hope, and to create—is physically given and physically based. The brain is neither a closed system with its own set of fixed determinancies nor a slave to information received from the out-side world. It is a dynamic and self-sustaining organ capable of generating its own information. It is designed to deal with the external world by having ideas about the external world. The brain therefore constantly imposes its own truth upon the external world.

The activation-synthesis model can account for dream nonsense and for dream meaning in terms of an extremely simple and economical set of principles, without recourse either to the collective unconscious or to a dynamically repressed unconscious in accounting for either the occurrence of dreams or for their unique properties. While activation synthesis cannot, of course, disprove such mechanisms, it proposes a much simpler model to explain an equally rich variety of experience. It has, thus, the virtue of economy and is also congruent with what is now known about the activity of the brain during dreaming sleep.

So strong is the relationship between the form of mental activity in dreaming and the form of brain activity in REM sleep that we may begin to entertain a unified theory of mind and brain. To that end, I use the hybrid term *brain-mind* to signal my conviction that a complete description of either (brain or mind) will be a complete description of the other (mind or brain). At some future time, the two words may well be replaced by one.

THE TRANSPARENCY AND CREATIVITY OF DREAMS

Freud's dream theory necessitated interpretation: unwelcome wishes from the unconscious are assumed to be transformed by the sleeping mind so as to make the experienced dream a pale, obscure, or even unrecognizable copy of its underlying impulse. This copy is what Freud called the *manifest* dream content to distinguish it from the true instigator and meaning of the dream, the *latent* content. To make the translation from manifest to latent, an interpreter was needed, since (by definition) the latent content was unacceptable to the dreamer's consciousness.

In describing the rules for this translation, Freud vacillated between an extremely rigid position in which certain dream objects were regarded as specific symbols (especially symbols of sexual parts) to a position of relative flexibility and openness. Some dreams needed no interpretation, and others a great deal. But he never formulated the rules by which one could tell the difference.

The view of dreams as transparent with respect to personal meaning changes radically the approach to dreaming taken in self-exploration or psychotherapy. In shifting the emphasis from the opaque to the transparent aspect of dreaming, activation synthesis regards the dream process as more progressive than regressive; as more positive than negative; as more creative than destructive. In sum, as more healthy than neurotic.

In dreams, problems are not only posed but sometimes even solved. These problems may be perceptual as well as emotional and thus provide hints of interest to both one's aesthetic and one's psychological self. In the dream state, plasticity and visual-sensory perception are both heightened and enriched. When Leonardo da Vinci asked, "Why does the eye see a thing more clearly in dreams than the mind while awake?" he was calling attention to the hyperreal, the hypervivid aspect of dream experience, which I ascribe to increased activation of the visual brain during dreaming sleep.

While sleep persists, our brains are more active in dreams than in some states of waking—one of the many paradoxes uncovered by modern sleep science. But I would call attention not only to this heightened intensity but also to the increase in the variety of forms that one may perceive during the dream state. Some contemporary psychologists claim that dream mentation is not uniquely bizarre since waking fantasy may contain all the elements present in dreams. But dreams put these bizarre elements together with a convincing reality, a pictorial clarity, sometimes even an artistic talent that are difficult for most of us to achieve in the waking state.

It is this hyperreal quality, with mutually incompatible, bizarre elements effortlessly combined, to which I apply the term *autocreative.* (See figure I.2.) These most extraordinary dream "tableaux" are made by the sleeping brain-mind without access to external cues; the composition uses only the traces of experience that are stored in memory. This imaginative quality of dreaming fascinated the European artists who, under the conceptual leadership of the poet and essayist André Breton, called themselves *surrealists.* This school, which was founded in 1924 and flourished through the 1930s, included the artists Max Ernst, Salvador Dali, and René Ma-

FIGURE I.2

The autocreativity and bizarreness of dreaming

This desktop computer is the dream work of the Engine Man, a scientist who recorded 233 dreams in the summer of 1939 (see chapters 10–14). At the dawn of the age of electronic computation, his brain-mind invented a mechanized information retrieval device that is as charming as it is impossible. What connection it may have to its dream user—a fat Frenchman in a hospital nightgown—is the sort of question that has prompted elaborate psychological speculation. Brain science provides new explanations for both the sense and the nonsense of such dreams. *Source:* The dream journal of the Engine Man, Report 38, 30 July 1939.

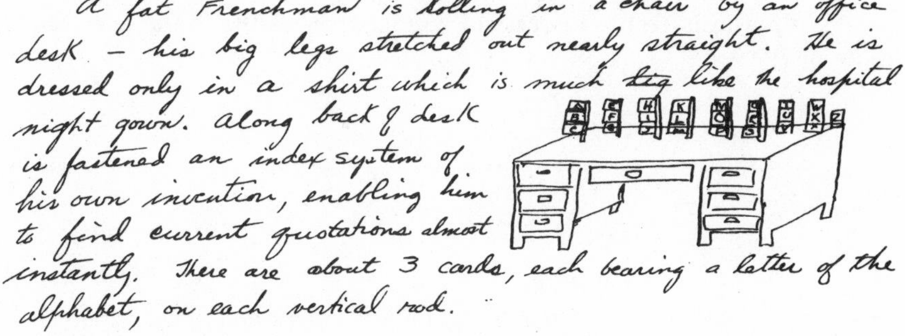
A fat Frenchman is lolling in a chair by an office desk – his big legs stretched out nearly straight. He is dressed only in a shirt which is much ~~big~~ like the hospital night gown. Along back of desk is fastened an index system of his own invention, enabling him to find current quotations almost instantly. There are about 3 cards, each bearing a letter of the alphabet, on each vertical rod.

gritte. As part of our scientific analysis of dreams, my colleagues and I have studied the drawings that illustrate the remarkable journal of an artistic scientist whom I call the Engine Man (see Part IV).

Since dreaming is universal, it stands as testimony to the universality of the artistic experience. In our dreams, we all become writers, painters, and film makers, combining extraordinary sets of characters, actions, and locations into strangely coherent experiences. In this creative aspect of the dream experience, interpretation is actually unwelcome since analytic interpretation involves a reduction of wholes into component parts. I thus strongly object to any implication that the artistic experiences of waking or dreaming are fundamentally pathological, defensive, or neurotic. I believe that neither state can be reduced to instinctual elements. Such reduction does gross disservice to the synthetic capabilities of the brain-mind. Analysis may show us the way in which certain motivational propensities shape or color the mental product, but the new science of dreaming shows us that the creative process is an independent given. It is an integral part of healthy brain-mind activity, whether one is asleep or awake.

Not only have artists called attention to the creative aspect of dreaming, but scientists also have been impressed with it. One example is the dream of the German biochemist August Kekule von Stradonitz (1829–96), in which the Jungian archetypal snake was taken as a clue to the ring structure of benzene rather than as a wish to return to the garden of Eden. Another example is that of the German-born biochemist Otto Loewi (1873–1961), who reported (1921–26) that the crossed frog-heart perfusion experiment—which led to the postulations of chemical neurotransmission and won him the 1936 Nobel Prize for Physiology or Medicine, shared with Sir Henry Dale—occurred to him in a dream (see pages 117–23).

It is in its plastic aspect that the dream state can sometimes serve the creative scientist. But many analytic solutions that occur during sleep are accepted by the uncritical dreaming mind, only to be seen in the light of day as illusory, fanciful, and useless. The reason is that during dreaming many integrations of disparate cognitive elements are tried, a process akin to the hypothesis-testing process of science that results in the rejection of most of them.

THE DREAMING BRAIN: AN OVERVIEW

In Part I, the parallel development of neurobiology and psychoanalysis is traced, with special emphasis upon the shared interests and sharp divergence in the careers of Sigmund Freud, the founder of psychoanalysis, and his contemporary Santiago Ramón y Cajal, the founder of modern neurobiology. Both men studied the brain in the conviction that it is the physical basis of mind. While Freud abandoned neurobiology, its concepts shaped his dream theory and so came to permeate all of psychoanalysis. While Ramón y Cajal abandoned his early interest in the practice of psychology, his neurobiology was consistently functional and dynamic in its conceptual orientation. I will show that following the publication of *The Interpretation of Dreams* in 1900, the fields of psychiatry and neurology followed separate tracks for half a century.

The discoveries of modern sleep and dream research, which have both provided the building blocks of my integrated brain-mind theory of dreaming and vindicated the original philosophical convictions of Ramón y Cajal and Freud, are described in Part II. In 1953, the correlation of dreaming with REM sleep by Eugene Aserinsky and Nathaniel Kleitman initiated an era of intense psychophysiological investigation of dreaming. Simultaneous studies of the brain led to Michel Jouvet's localization, in 1959, of a trigger zone for REM sleep and dreaming in the brain stem.

Since 1960, the capacity to study the functional activity of individual nerve cells in the brain stem has allowed Robert McCarley and me to construct a model of brain-mind state control. This model, described in Part III, not only specifies the brain cells and the molecules that trigger REM sleep and dreaming, but describes the dynamics of their reciprocal interaction as the brain changes its mind from the waking to the dreaming mode. The most recent validation of the model is the triggering of REM sleep and dreaming by the experimental manipulation of a brain chemical, acetylcholine. It is upon this reciprocal interaction that the activation-synthesis theory of dreaming is based.

Part IV presents the preliminary results of a new, formal analysis of dreaming inspired by the activation-synthesis hypothesis, and designed to test its predictions. By comparing the mental states depicted in home-based journals and in laboratory dream reports, I sketch the spectrum of hallucinoid sensations, movements, and thought processes that typify dreaming. Much of the data of Part IV comes from the Dream Journal of the Engine Man, who recorded—in copious detail and without interpretation—233 accounts of this dream experience in the summer of 1939. Even though the content of each dream is highly personalized, the form of dreaming is shown to be analogous to organic dementia with its visual hallucinations, its disorientation, its confabulation, and its memory loss.

Having interpreted the form of dreams in terms of physiology, the book concludes, in Part V, with a review of the functional theories that dream science must now test to complete its agenda. In concert with the emphasis that the new psychological theory lays upon transparency and creativity is evidence suggesting that the purpose of REM sleep and dreaming includes both the development and the active maintenance of the functional integrity of the human brain-mind. Much more than recovery from the wear and tear of today, tonight's sleep may be an active and dynamic preparation for the challenges of tomorrow.

PART I

EARLY
DREAM SCIENCE

1

The Study of Dreaming in the Nineteenth Century

True, I talk of dreams,
Which are the children of an idle brain,
Begot of nothing but vain fantasy.
—WILLIAM SHAKESPEARE
Romeo and Juliet

The characteristics of sleep, favorable to dreams, are
first, and most important, the predominance in the cerebral machinery of automatic over volitional control.
—WILHELM WUNDT
Grundzuge der Physiologischen Psychologie (1874)

THE RISE OF SCIENCE AND THE STUDY OF DREAMING

The success of science on a broad intellectual front encouraged optimism
in many nineteenth-century thinkers that the elusive nature of human
consciousness—including its unique manifestations in dreaming—might
finally be understood. By mid-century, Europe was a ferment of speculative and experimental inquiry regarding the brain-mind question. The
yeast of this brew was physiology, and it gave rise to three lines of work:
experimental psychology, psychoanalysis, and neurobiology.

Physiological theories of dreaming abounded as knowledge of the
brain advanced from a superficial and static anatomical level to a deeper

and more dynamic analysis of the nervous system. The emerging neuro-physiological data was seized upon by those bent upon constructing a material basis of mind. Nowhere was this "bottom-up" approach more optimistically pursued than in Germany and Austria where it led, directly, to the birth of experimental psychology (at the hands of Wilhelm Wundt) and of psychoanalysis (through the work of Sigmund Freud). The main-stream of this tradition became modern cellular neurobiology and flows into the brain-based study of dreaming that is the main subject of this book (see Parts II and III).

Simultaneously, the psychological study of dreaming assumed a proto-scientific character through the persistent and systematic self-obser-vations of two Parisians, Alfred Maury and the Marquis d'Hervey de Saint-Denis. Both of these meticulous French phenomenologists were in-spired by developing science and technology but believed that their "top-down" introspective approach was as indispensable as neurology to clearly define and better understand the mental aspects of dreaming. By testing hypotheses through interventions upon their own sleep and dreams, they long anticipated the instrumental, objective paradigm of the human sleep laboratories of our day, and set in motion a mode of observation that was widely taken up in the psychophysiology of the early twentieth century (see chapter 6).

It was owing to the initially slow growth of neurobiology that psy-choanalysis diverged from the experimental tradition. And it is owing to the currently explosive growth of the brain sciences that a reunification of psychoanalysis and experimental psychology may now be contemplated in a new, integrated field called cognitive neuroscience.

The Physiological Approach

Helmholtz and Internal Perception

> I cannot see how it would be possible to refute a system
> of even the most extreme subjective idealism, which
> would consider life as a dream.
> —Hermann von Helmholtz

A germinal figure in the scientific movement of the nineteenth century was Johannes Müller (1801–58). Despite his brilliance as a scientist, Müller was a vitalist and a nativist, in the spirit of the romantic era in which he grew up. His law of specific nerve energies states that whenever a nerve is stimulated it gives rise to sensations appropriate to the organs served by that nerve. This concept was an important antecedent to the psychophysics of Gustav Fechner (1801–87), making Müller thus a father of the most strictly reductionistic psychophysical theories. Yet, for his students, his thinking was plagued by the unacceptably Platonic postulation of pre-existing forms.

In 1845, four students in Müller's laboratory signed a pact against *vitalism*, the notion of a life force unexplainable through analytic science. They were Carl Ludwig (1816–95), then twenty-nine years old, who was later to become professor in Leipzig and the teacher of Fechner; Emil du Bois-Reymond (1818–96), then twenty-seven, who was to become a professor in Berlin where he developed the concept of the electrical excitation of muscle; Ernst Brücke (1819–92) twenty-six, who was to become a professor in Vienna and the teacher of both Breuer and Freud; and the youngest and most versatile of the four, Hermann von Helmholtz (1821–94), then only twenty-four (see figure 1.1).

For Helmholtz, the law of the conservation of energy implied that the body is a machine, and his brilliant experimental career based upon this faith enabled him to accomplish such feats as the invention of the ophthalmoscope (1851); the determination of nerve-conduction velocity (1850); and the firm proof that nerve fibers are an extension of the cell body (an idea he owed to Müller).

By means of the opthalmoscope, Helmholtz was able to observe directly the interior chamber of the eye and its light-sensitive neural lining, the retina. This technique allowed one to see into the brain. Helmholtz's discoveries regarding the nerve cell and its capacity to conduct impulses were cornerstones of cellular neuroscience that later supported Ramón y Cajal's neuron doctrine and Sherrington's reflex concept (see chapter 4).

For the subject of dreaming, Helmholtz's most important work was in the theory of perception; and his ideas on this subject are contained in his great work, *The Physiological Optics,* published in 1856. This was followed by his work on the auditory system and the publication of a related volume entitled *Sensations of Tone* (1863) in which he enunciated the place theory of audition, which states that tones of various frequencies activate different loci in the inner ear. Furthermore, Helmholtz discovered—or at least put on the map, by his brilliant use of it—the ophthalometer, by which one is able to measure the diameter of the pupil of the eye. He also measured the reaction time of reflex responses and estimated the added duration

FIGURE 1.1
Hermann von Helmholtz

A member of the "pact against vitalism" and the father of modern perceptual physiology, Helmholtz was also the first scientist to suggest that the brain might actually command movement in dreaming and thus give rise to sensory images appropriate to those commands. This idea is echoed in the modern finding that information about the rapid eye movements of sleep reaches the visual centers of the brain (see chapters 8 and 9).

When Helmholtz died in 1894, the English magazine *Punch* published this poetic epitaph:

> When emperors, kings, pretenders shadows all,
> Leave not a dust trace on our whirling ball,
> Thy work, oh, grave-eyed searcher shall endure,
> Unmarked by faction, from low passion pure.

Source: Rare Books and Print Department, Francis A. Countway Library of Medicine, Harvard Medical School. Dick Wolfe, Director.

incurred by subjective consciousness.* Helmholtz is thus a father not only of modern physiology but of psychophysiology as well.

Helmholtz was a hero for the English because he followed the empirical tradition of John Locke and John Stuart Mill. Helmholtz believed that perceptions are acquired through a process of hypothesis testing regarding the nature of form and space and involving the senses of touch and sight. As an empiricist, he stood in contrast to the then-dominant nativistic school (represented by Leibnitz and by Kant), which asserted that images must be intrinsic to the nervous system and are only evoked by external forms, an idea taken up in the collective unconscious theory of Jung and echoed by some assumptions of the activation-synthesis hypothesis. In his perception theory, Helmholtz was particularly interested in the relationship of vision to movement—an important aspect of the modern activation-synthesis hypothesis of dreaming. Most significant is his idea that the individual is continually, through action and use of the senses of touch and sight, testing hypotheses about the world. Whether these hypotheses are innate or acquired is unimportant to this fundamentally forward-looking or anticipatory aspect of perception:

As we have seen, we have not only changing sensory impressions which occur without any action on our part, but we also make observations during our own constant activity, and thereby we arrive at the knowledge that a lawful relationship exists between our innervations and the appearance of different impressions from the range of existing phenomena. Each voluntary movement by which we change the appearance of objects must be regarded as an experiment, by which we test whether we have correctly interpreted the lawful behavior of the phenomenon in question, that is, its postulated existence in a definite spatial arrangement.

Helmholtz went on to emphasize the importance of motor actions in determining the effect of perceptions, in determining, in particular, whether we learn from them:

The persuasive power of such experiments, however, is very much greater than the observation of an event taking place without our own cooperation, mainly because in these experiments the chain of causes runs through our consciousness. One link of these causes, the impulses of our volition, is known to us by internal perception and we know which motives brought it about. Starting with this impulse as from an initial link known to us, at a moment which is likewise known, the chain of the physical causes acts and results in success of the experiment. [1968, p. 223]

---

*Some reflexes (for example, knee jerk) do not go via the cortex and do not involve consciousness. Others (for example, which way to turn to avoid an oncoming car) require discrimination judgment. The latter take longer.

Not only is Helmholtz's formulation important technically, with respect to such relatively esoteric issues as the so-called corollary discharge theory to be elaborated shortly; but he cast motor events in a primary role and not as merely secondary, or reflexive, to stimulation—an idea that makes great sense from an evolutionary point of view. Even the simplest organisms should be capable of action *(motility)*, whether or not they are capable of sensation *(irritability)*. Sensation might well be added to help guide the action. According to Helmholtz, action itself may thus be used to help shape perception. This idea would also allow us to imagine a means by which complex perceptions could arise through activation of motor systems. Since this is exactly what appears to occur during rapid-eye-movement sleep, Helmholtz's prescient comments are of particular interest, as is his curious distinction between the psychic and the physical:

But a prerequisite essential for the conviction to be achieved is that the impulse of our volition has neither been influenced by physical causes which simultaneously determine the physical process, nor that the impulse in its turn has a psychic influence on the perception following it. The latter uncertainty may well be considered to fall within our topic of discussion. The voluntary impulse for a specific movement is a psychic act which subsequently is also perceived as a change in sensation. Now is it not possible that the first act causes the second by purely psychic means? It is not impossible. Something like this happens when we dream. While dreaming, we believe we are executing a movement and we then continue dreaming that what actually happens is a natural consequence of that movement, as would have occurred also during a waking state. We dream that we are stepping onto a boat pushing off from the shore, gliding out on the water and seeing how the surrounding objects change their positions, etc. Here the expectation of the dreamer, that he is going to see the consequences of his activities, seems to produce the dreamed perception in a purely psychic way. Who can say how long and drawn out such a dream could become? If everything in a dream happened extremely regularly, according to the natural order, it would be no different than being awake except for the possibility of waking up, and the interruption of this dreamed sequence of images. [1968, p. 223]

Helmholtz was concerned to make a distinction between the psychic and the physical out of his need to explain the phenomena of dreams, apparently purely psychic acts, by means of his motor perceptual theory and his wish to use the perception of movement in dreams as a way of further shoring up that theory. But if we take the position that the psychic event (like the subjective experience of the dream) reflects underlying neural activity, we need make no qualitative distinction between the two or postulate any causality in the one domain independent of causality in the other.

Helmholtz was correct in postulating that waking perception is an active hypothesis-testing mode of the brain-mind. In waking, feedback from the external world allows a "hypothesis" to be verified or denied; and I believe that such phenomena probably also occur in dreams.

Other kinds of experimental and clinical evidence already indicate that Helmholtz was correct about the neuronal basis of intended movements in dreaming: animals and humans both directly act out their dreams if the brain centers of motor inhibition are damaged. We also know that the motor neurons that normally command movement during waking also command movement during dreaming sleep. Hence, as far as the nervous system is concerned, the physical substrate of motoric intention and all of the mechanisms of movement generation are physically activated during REM sleep. Motor commands thus constitute primary informational elements upon which the dream imagery and story line may be built.

The passages from Helmholtz link perceptual theory to dream theory and demonstrate the opportunities and pitfalls of such a linkage. A strict dualist, Helmholtz posited psychic causes and effects independent of the physiological domain.

In summary, the implications for dream theory of Helmholtz's hypothesis of sensorimotor interaction are several: (1) the movement command actually predicts changes in perception; (2) the changes in perception are, in fact, not only anticipated but specified; (3) in the absence of peripheral input, a perception can be quite actively and accurately specified, simply by activation of a motor-pattern generator; (4) this can occur whether or not "voluntary" motor mechanisms are involved.

Wundt and Reciprocal Interaction

> In reality all which in these phenomena [sleep and dreams] suggest an esoteric explanation can without difficulty be explained psychologically and physiologically; but those things which cannot be explained in this way will always be demonstrated to be, on closer examination, either superstition or auto-illusions.
> —WILHELM WUNDT

Helmholtz did not perform direct observations of sleep and dreams. Nor did his contemporary Wilhelm Wundt (1832–1920), who in Leipzig in 1879 founded the world's first laboratory of experimental psychology and went on to become the first great physiological psychologist (see figure 1.2). Because of his emphasis upon psychological experimentation and his interesting theories of dreaming, Wundt is as least as important as Helmholtz (whose assistant he was at Heidelberg from 1858 to 1871) in shaping the

FIGURE 1.2
Wilhelm Wundt

One of Helmholtz's most distinguished students was Wilhelm Wundt, who founded the world's first laboratory devoted entirely to physiological psychology. Wundt was convinced that the distinctive psychology of dreaming must derive from the distinctive physiology of the brain in sleep. Noting that dreaming is characterized by both deficits (logic, memory, and judgment all being impaired) and enhancements (associative propensity, visual imagery, and emotion all being enhanced), Wundt correctly intuited that some brain regions would show decreases and others increases in their activity, as modern physiology has abundantly confirmed. *Source:* Rare Books and Print Department, Francis A. Countway Library of Medicine, Harvard Medical School. Dick Wolfe, Director.

conceptual orientation and practical approach of the pre-Freudian era. In chapter 18 of his *Compendium of Psychology (1900),* a classic German "warhorse" work, Wundt considered the psychic states. He called attention to two normal states that have an anomalous conscious component: the dream and the hypnotic trance. Wundt thought that the content of dreams arose mainly in response to sensory stimuli. The illusions of dreams were, for him, pure mnemonic responses carried to the level of hallucinations; and also definitive of dreaming were "apperceptive combinations, frequent alternations with the sense of self and errors of judgment" (p. 220). But what distinguished the dream from every other psychic state similar to it was not so much these positive properties but the fact that augmented excitability of sensory structures, as implied by hallucinosis, was paradoxically contrasted with complete inhibition of the external activity of the will. Indeed, the enormous increase in perceptual capability during dreaming with the concurrent decrease in volition capability was, to Wundt, the hallmark of the dream state. He went on to make the following important prediction:

The psychophysiological conditions of sleep, dreams and hypnosis are in all probability essentially alike. Since psychologically, they all appear as particular alterations of sensibility and volition, they can be explained physiologically as alterations in the functions of the underlying central structures. These functional changes have not yet been directly investigated. [p. 221]

Wundt was confident that science would one day be capable of investigating the underlying activity in central structures. We now know that many of his predictions were precisely correct.

Wundt's thoroughgoing adherence to physiology enabled him to develop several hypotheses about the physiology of sleep and dreams which have now been validated. First, he made a general point about strict psychophysical parallelism: "Nevertheless, at the root of the psychological manifestations [of dreams, etc.], I hypothesize that it is a question of an arrest of the function of the central influence on the process of volition and attention, combined with an increase in the excitability of the sensory centers" (1890, p. 222). (This notion, of increases and decreases of various cerebral functions, was one that Freud criticized in setting the stage for his "psychological theory." See chapter 2, pp. 42–51.) Wundt continued:

The internal theory of sleep, dreams and hypnosis is above all the task of physiology. Aside from the general assumption that certain cortical regions decrease activity while others increase, let us deduce from the psychological symptoms according to the general neurological principle that holds in all probability, namely the principle of compensation of function. In the light of this principle, the arrest of function of certain central influences is related to an increase in function of certain other influences which have reciprocal underlying relations with one another. [1890, p. 222]

Wundt came to this statement, which is precisely apt for the present-day reciprocal-interaction hypothesis of sleep-cycle control (see chapter

9), by the application of pure reason. Assuming that a mind state will have a corresponding brain state, Wundt pointed out that, if the mind state of dreams is characterized by heightened sensations and decreased volition, it therefore follows that physiological experiment would one day reveal an increase in activity in sensory centers and a decrease in other nervous centers related to volition or attention. The increases and decreases would be not only concomitant but also reciprocal to one another. He saw thus a deep causal link between the decrease in one function and the increase in the other. As a scientist, Wundt was skeptical of exotic explanations and believed that the mechanism of sleep and dreaming would turn out to be relatively straightforward.

While the neurophysiological techniques necessary to test Wundt's hypothesis on the central neural structures controlling sleep and dreams were not available during his time, some observers undertook direct psychological and behavioral studies of sleep, a tradition to which I shall now turn.

THE PSYCHOLOGICAL APPROACH

The Self as Experimental Subject: Alfred Maury

In 1861, the French scientist Alfred Maury (1817–92) published his book on sleep and dreams (see figure 1.3). Maury may be the first person to have recorded systematic, intentional experiments upon his own sleep and dream states. In order to do this, he enlisted the aid of an accomplice who periodically awakened him so that he could have access to consciousness otherwise not recoverable. Maury was particularly interested in the visual images and the complex dreamlike events that occur at sleep onset, the so-called *hypnagogic hallucinations*. Maury also introduced specific pre-sleep stimuli in an effort to trace their triggering role and their later transformation into the visual images of sleep onset and into the dreams that occur later in the night.

In one of Maury's experiments, the illusion of light perceived when he pressed on his eyeball (the so-called *phosgene phenomenon*) gave rise, in a subsequent hypnagogic state, to the visual image of a maid in a white apron, which was followed by the auditory image of the maid saying, "I cleaned your room." Maury was interested in the possible primacy of the sensory event in triggering the subsequent chain of associations and im-

FIGURE 1.3
Alfred Maury

A pioneer in the descriptive study of sleep and dreams, Alfred Maury was the first scientist to attempt a systematization of self-observation experiments on the effect of external stimuli upon dreaming. To control for the problem of subjectivity and for the loss of awareness experienced at sleep onset, Maury had accomplices awaken him at specified times and after presenting specific sensory stimuli. Although he failed to appreciate that the source of most dream stimuli is within the brain itself, Maury's work shows how much can be learned by simple means, and how well straightforward theories can make dream science understood. *Source:* Bibliothèque Nationale, Paris.

ages. He was impressed that the initial event was "spontaneous"; that is to say, "born of an illusion, due to a false sensation." This, in turn, aroused an impression that had rested strongly inscribed in his brain: "I remembered, in fact, that the picture of my maid with her white apron had struck me several days previously, I had not thought of it, however, since then" (1861, p. 72).

For Maury the essential unit of any hallucinoid process consisted of a stimulus arising in the peripheral nervous system. When this stimulus

reached central nervous structures, it then triggered an illusion of a sensation; and the illusion, in turn, called forth a visual memory. Maury was in
good company in believing in the peripheral origin of such stimuli: such
leading physiologists as Johannes Müller and Jan Evangelista Purkinje
(1787–1869) all shared this idea, and were unaware of the possibility that
sensory stimuli might arise centrally.

Like Maury, the French neurologist Jules Baillarger postulated that
sensory "automatisms" stimulate bizarre sensations that are the origin of
hallucinations (1846). The notion of an automatism was also mirrored in
Maury's conviction that memory is more important than invention in the
elaboration of the hallucinated image. In other words, his view of the
nervous system was like Freud's in being relatively reflex bound. Maury
imagined that the triggering of hallucinations must proceed from the periphery to the center; and that, in the center, the content of the hallucinations would be dictated by previously inscribed experience.

Both ideas of hallucinosis, peripheral origin and memory-bound nature, now appear overly narrow and probably incorrect. Even Maury seems
to have guessed as much, since he imagined that the process could be
reversed in "a phenomenon of spontaneous memory, reacting so strongly
on the senses affected as to simulate external perceptions; a phenomenon
which implies a previously acquired percept and an automatic action of the
spirit, which is graded and has two major divisions; the psychic and the
psychosensory" (1861). Such "automatisms" are more likely to arise when
brain relaxation in sleep is not yet complete but only partial. According to
Maury, at such times parts of the brain are shut off while others are still
active. In this case, continuity of brain activity during sleep was correctly
anticipated by his assumption.

In summary, Alfred Maury was careful in his introspection and ingenious in his use of sleep-onset phenomena as a source of experimental
data. He was also physiologically committed, insisting upon a sensory
genesis for the hallucinosis of dreams. His attribution of the defects and
peculiarities of dreaming to a partial inactivation of brain function also
seems intelligent. Like many others, he was mistaken in looking to peripheral sources for the initiation of all dream imagery.

The Dream Journal of Hervey de Saint-Denis

In one of Maury's self-stimulation experiments, a bright blue spot
served to awaken him. With eyes closed and dozing, he then visualized,
in turn, an illuminated gas lamp and a street (it was, he supposed, the rue
Hautefeuille where he had lived thirty years before, lit up at night by
gaslight). On arousal, Maury thought of his colleague the Marquis Marie

FIGURE 1.4
Hervey de Saint-Denis

Perhaps the most diligent dream journalist of all time, Hervey de Saint-Denis filled twenty-two volumes with his self-observations and hypotheses. Troubled by the moral problem posed by the loss of volitional control in dreams, he set out to show that willpower could be reinstituted by pre-sleep autosuggestion. Like that of many other lucid dreamers, Hervey's success in this endeavor was as striking as it was fleeting. Although scientifically untutored, he used the budding technique of photography to construct a filmic model of memory as replayable in dreaming, and chastised contemporary science for shedding so little light on the nature and cause of dreaming. *Source:* Bibliothèque Nationale, Paris.

Jean Léon Hervey de Saint-Denis (see figure 1.4), who also practiced systematic self-observation. Less scientific but no less persistent than Maury, Hervey was determined to show that volition was not necessarily abolished during dreams. He conducted self-experimentation and recorded his intensive and prolonged observations in a journal of dream reports and drawings.

The Marquis d'Hervey de Saint-Denis was an aristocrat. Raised alone, he spent a great deal of his childhood time drawing and coloring. At the age of fifteen, he decided, apparently on his own, to begin to sketch his own dream imagery, and thereupon initiated an album of dream drawings and descriptions. Having embarked upon a career of dream recording, he soon discovered that he dreamed every night. Next he developed dream consciousness. Thus by simply turning his attention to his own dream process, Hervey was justified in criticizing dream theories as fundamentally unscientific because of their authors' failure to examine dreaming directly: "Most celebrated psychologists and physiologists have hardly shed a ray of light on that which they thought had been the object of direct elucidation" (1867, p. 139).

Hervey was quite right. No one previously had looked directly at the process of dreaming itself. When Maury was beginning to do this, Hervey had already shown that it was possible for individuals to gain greater access to their own dreams simply by paying attention to them. According to the account given in his recently republished *Les Rêves et les moyens de les diriger (1867)*, Hervey's dream journal filled twenty-two notebooks with colored images (see figure 1.5) and represented almost five years of continuous self-observation.* He must thus be the greatest of all auto-experimenters in the history of sleep and dream research.

In order to provoke and control dreams, Hervey stated that one must, first, establish a link between a sensation and an idea or a person, and then try to remember the sensation while asleep, in order to trigger the idea or person. His method for dream control was formally similar to that used by Maury to induce hypnagogic hallucinations. Hervey knew of the latter's work, which was considered to be the classic formulation, at least in French mid-nineteenth-century intellectual circles.

With Maury, Hervey shared the notion of dreaming being a replay of images stored in memory. He defined dreaming as the "representation to the eyes of our spirit the objects which occupy our thoughts." Memory, he thought, was like a mirror covered with collodion "which keeps continually and instantly the impression of images projected onto it by the lens of the dark chamber" (p. 141). In addition, memory can renew itself by its own mechanisms. Fundamental images, stereotyped memories, *clichés-souvenirs,* are stored infinitely in memory and can be called up, often at one's bidding. There is a difference between conscious memory and the

---

*The epitome of the French autodidactic tradition, Hervey was completely self-educated and well acquainted with other leading French intellectuals. He pursued interests in many fields. In two, he achieved distinction: the study of dreaming and Chinese culture, for which he was actually best known. Since Hervey's dream journals cannot be found, we have to rely upon his book for some hint of his illustrative capabilities.

consciousness of something that one finds in thought without knowing that one is remembering it. These *clichés-souvenirs* are a fundamental element in Hervey's dream theory.

By calling attention to the fluidity of the memory process, he also added an important aspect to the developing theory that dreams might be auto-activated. His model was clearly influenced by the then-emerging technique of photography; but it was also plastic:

Life multiplies and modifies the clichés-souvenirs continually. The human imagination runs, glides and invents (insofar as this creation is novel) from the unknown. We find this process continually in the dream. To imagine is to combine, to call up from memory these clichés-souvenirs. Between dreaming and thinking there is only one difference, confirmation by real life. Hallucinations are nothing but the dreams of a waking man. The dream shows us the scaffolding of the mental apparatus as one rarely perceives it in real life, the life of conscious thought. [p. 141]

Hervey de Saint-Denis was thus also aware not only that dreams can be studied directly, but that their study is a unique strategy for understanding such phenomena as the hallucinations of madness. Like Freud, Hervey thought that physiologists were incapable of explaining the way in which associations are organized in dreams: "I do not know what happens at the root of my cerebral fibers, but here is what happens in the open domain of my more modest appreciation" (p. 141).

Hervey's response to dreaming was aesthetic. He believed that dreaming conveys artistic powers to every man; hence, his own indulgence in dream drawing. Like Freud, he believed that the image of the dream is only the copy of an idea. The principal thing, for Hervey, was the idea: the idea was the substance; the vision was accessory. His position on this point is thus in contrast to the theoretical assumptions of many other experimentalists discussed in this chapter.

Hervey also believed that if one understood the ideas and their succession in a dream, one could understand the dream itself. Dreams, he thought, were due to: (1) natural and spontaneous unraveling of a chain of reminiscences; and/or (2) a sudden departure from the chain caused by a physical stimulus; and (3) voluntary influences. With his second point, Hervey was attempting to explain the characteristic scene shifts in dreaming, but this important dream element posed a problem for his other two principles. If the chain of associations were continuous, and if voluntary influences were continuously at work, then why does the dream seem often to change course, and without warning?

Hervey greatly underestimated the differences in the states of waking and dreaming, but his greatest error was to imagine volition to be continuous during the dream. To Maury's previous contention that the "dreamer is not more free than the madman or the drunkard" (1861), Hervey's experiments in dream consciousness and dream control were designed to give the lie.

Hervey advanced strong arguments about the positive powers of the dream process. For example, he thought that the imaginative memory was more extensive in dreams than in waking. Stores of memory were:

immense caves where the light of the mind never penetrates better than when it has ceased to shine outside. Thus, one is not surprised to see in a dream with a marvelous lucidity, people dead or absent for a long time; to discover in the most elaborate detail, places that one has visited to hear songs that one has heard and to see entire pages that one has read years earlier. [p. 156]

He marveled at, but could not explain, the creative imagination of dreaming. He guessed that this, too, could be a state-dependent property of sleep: the product of a hyperintense activation of perceptions, of an increase both in access to old memories and in some endogenous source of patterned stimulation, and of a decrease in patterned stimulation from the outside world. He here forecasts almost precisely the activation-synthesis hypothesis of dreams, leaving out only an account of dream bizarreness.

Hervey wondered whether the creative work of the dream could be attributed to the action of sleep itself or to memory. Like his contemporaries, he struggled with the problem of the increase in certain mental capabilities coupled with a decrease in others. Wundt's early version of our reciprocal-interaction hypothesis would have dealt handily with this paradox, but of Wundt's work Hervey was apparently unaware.

He also believed that in dreaming one could accomplish practical problem solving. Dreaming was to him characterized by a kind of intellectual enhancement in which, for instance, a chess player might find the solution to an otherwise insoluble problem; a poet might come up with the most apt image for a verse; and a mathematician might find the solution to a difficult intellectual problem.

For Hervey the interpretation of dreams was systematic. He believed that dream architecture could be both analyzed and influenced. The method of analysis consisted of classifying the transitions chronologically. He thought that the sequences were determined by the order of memory storage, rather than by associations to them of abstract meaning: "The chain of associations can proceed following the order in which the memories are laid down in memory, outside of any other relationship or abstract

FIGURE 1.5

Two kinds of visual imagery in sleep

The frontispiece of Hervey de Saint-Denis's 1867 book, *Dreams and How to Control Them,* depicts the fully formed and narratively framed visual imagery of dreams *(top)* and the more geometric and fleeting phantasms of sleep onset *(bottom).* Like many other late-nineteenth-century theorists, Hervey ascribed the kaleidoscopic sleep onset imagery to retinal stimuli but assumed that the dream scenarios are somehow read out of memory (as a series of *clichés-souvenirs*). While we do not know whether either of these illustrations is by his own hand, we do know that drawing was his preferred means of recording the irreducibly visual quality of his dreams. *Source: Les Rêves et Comment Les Diriger* (Paris: Amyot, 1867). Courtesy of Library of Yale University School of Medicine.

process" (p. 160). Hervey saw dreaming as fundamentally a reading out of sequences of the *clichés-souvenirs,* or memory snapshots—a fixed order suggesting the rigid sequence of a moving-picture scenario.

It is in his emphasis and documentation of the hypervisual quality of dreams that Hervey may be considered most original. Although he believed ideas to be primary and the visual images a mere copy of them, he devoted more attention than anyone in recorded history to the visual nature of dreams. He was particularly interested in those dreams that he considered to be "supersensual." Such dreams were entirely spontaneous and appeared very bizarre, reflecting the mind's work as seen in abstraction, with symbolization being strikingly clear. Two types of abstraction occurred: the sensible, with direct links to the sensations, the concrete images of the dream; and the moral and the purely abstract beliefs, traditions, and symbols associated in a more remote way with the imagery. There were also transitional examples with qualities of both types.

Some of Hervey's descriptions of specific types of mental activity are admirably detailed and vivid. At sleep onset, mental experience was found to be exclusively visual with fragments of sensations. For example, he drew in his notebook small suns that turned, dots of color that appeared and disappeared over a web of fine threads of silver, gold, purple, and emerald green. There were sometimes geometric figures like arabesques. These sleep-onset phenomena differed from ordinary dreams, which were well formed and had a narrative character. Two detailed examples of Hervey's description of sleep-onset phenomena illustrate his famous contrast between the visual imagery of sleep onset and the dreams that occur later in the night. In the first example:

White smoke passes like a cloud driven before the wind. Flames shoot out in spurts impinging painfully upon my retina. Soon they have dissolved the cloud, their explosiveness subsides. They spin, forming broad blooms, black in the center, orange and red at the edges. After a moment they open gradually from the center becoming a thin golden ring, a sort of frame in which I see the portrait of one of my friends. [p. 162]

Hervey was clearly a forerunner of the modern psychedelic users, although he rarely used drugs to enhance his visual experience. He was also something of a Puritan in his effort to establish the continuation of human will and morality during dreams. With his interest in orientalism, he was undoubtedly aware, as were many intellectuals of his era, of the earlier psychedelic tradition that reached its peak in the work of Blake and Coleridge. Here is a second description of a sleep onset or hypnagogic hallucination:

A crystal green color takes shape in the center of my internal visual field. I make out, little by little, that it is a collection of leaves. It boils like a volcano about to erupt, it swells and expands rapidly owing to its moving forces. Red flowers come out of the crater and make an enormous bouquet. This remains clear for a minute then it all evaporates. [p. 162]

Since he thought that these images were the basic elements from which more complex dreams were made, it is difficult to understand his assertion of the primacy of ideas. Perhaps ideas help to give shape to the succession of visual images; but in the details of these quotes, it is inescapable that Hervey recognized the primacy of pure hallucinoid experience in sleep. In the first example quoted, unformed images become the face of his friend; in the second, a crystal becomes biomorphic and then takes the form of leaves or a bouquet of flowers. The organizing principle—in the first case, a human face, and in the second, a floral pattern—is evoked by and imposed upon the more visual elements, adding to them a succession of associated forms.

Turning his attention to dreams themselves, Hervey argued that ideas merged, that images melded and substituted quickly for one another. Similarly, there could be substitution of personalities, transplantation of the dream locus in the middle of a dream episode, and a transposition of sexes. He noticed the elasticity and bizarreness of dreaming, and, to study these processes, performed the following experiment. He looked at an exotic oriental album for three days while inhaling oriental perfume. This gave rise on subsequent nights to three dreams with album elements mixed with other materials and to two dreams of people associated with the idea of the album. These appeared in his dream as a collection of engravings and watercolors without life or dimension.

Hervey saw immoral dreams as equating the thought with the act: dream events happen too rapidly for the will to stop them. Thus did he acknowledge not only the bizarreness of dreams but also the extraordinary compulsion driving certain acts in a way unacceptable to waking consciousness. Dreaming has its own motive force. He also performed experiments on the effects of hashish on his dreams and found that it produced "morbid modifications" of what he called his "true dreams" (p. 164). He therefore preferred to experiment on healthy phenomena.

The importance of Hervey de Saint-Denis lies in his emphasis on the self as a scientific instrument. His prescription for the study of dreams is as adequate today as at the time it was written: be conscious of sleep and dreams and keep a journal; associate stimuli with memories; and note the idea images that arise from the dream pictures and the way in which they shape the development of the dream. That autosuggestion is the key to dream lucidity is demonstrated in the modern work of Stephen LaBerge (1985). This technique, when combined with the objective method of sleep-lab recording (see chapters 5 and 6), amply validates Hervey's work and his seriousness of purpose.

FREUD ON NINETEENTH-CENTURY DREAM THEORIES

These two French intellectuals—Alfred Maury and the Marquis de Hervey de Saint-Denis—were true scientists in that they observed and recorded observations directly and performed experiments based upon the conclusions drawn from those observations. Both were skeptical and critical of theories that they believed to be superstitious and gratuitous; and both were—in their observation, experimentation, and critical thought—true precursors of the modern science of sleep and dreams.* The works of Helmholtz and Wundt are also modern in method and theory. Reading these nineteenth-century observers, one might well expect that the scientific development of dream theory would have been a continuous line from their work to the present, and that it would be widely recognized—but that line was broken, and that work was not only overshadowed by the dramatic success of psychoanalytic dream theory (which I will review in chapter 2) but discredited by Freud himself.

To clear the way for his radical dream theory, Freud examined the work of his immediate predecessors. A close look at this critique is enlightening in three ways: it sets out clearly the demands of a successful theory by its systematic organization; it details the strengths and weaknesses of his contemporary competition; and it demonstrates Freud's rhetorical skills in effectively discrediting all previous hypotheses, especially those based on physiology. At the turn of the century, study of the physiology of the brain was only beginning. Thus, inadequate physiological data combined with the bold thoroughness of Freud's alternative hypothesis made for a break, which lasted half a century, in the scientific tradition of dream theory.

In *The Interpretation of Dreams,* Freud first reviewed the stance of previous thinkers with respect to the "Relationship of Dreams to Waking Experi-

---

*As an example of Hervey's critical rejection of a gratuitous idea, consider his statement against the commonsense analogy of sleep and death: "Isn't it a strange idea to presume to compare a situation which is hardly known, with another of which one is completely ignorant?" (1867).

ence" (1900, pp. 41–44). Some (like Karl Frederick Burdach [1838] and Johann Gottlieb Fichte [1864]) thought that dreaming contrasts with waking, whereas others (such as Heinz Haffner [1887], Alfred Maury [1878], Wilhelm Weygandt [1893], P. Jessen [1855], and H. S. Maass [1805]) saw dreaming as being formally continuous with waking consciousness. Finding these contrasting views unsatisfactory, Freud introduced a unifying principle to account for the discrepancies: the disguise-censorship principle that became the heart of his dream theory. To the extent that the censor is hard pressed to disguise psycho-noxious wishes, dream mentation is bizarre and thus distinctly different from waking thought. When there is less intrapsychic strain, a dream is banal and like the waking state, Freud made no systematic, quantitative comparisons of the waking and the dreaming states; nor do we today have much data bearing on this important question. A systematic, quantitative study comparing wake-state fantasy to dreaming in the same subjects is sorely needed.

In the second section of chapter 1, the "Material of Dreams and Memory in Dreams," Freud stated: "All the material making up the content of a dream is in some way derived from experience" (1900, p. 44). For Freud, "apparently constructed fragments" could always be traced to antecedent experience (for activation synthesis's approach to experience, see pages 272–77).

Many previous authors had noted the origin of dream themes in preceding experience, however remote. Freud quoted the Belgian psychophysicist Joseph Delboeuf (1855), P. Jessen (1855), Hervey de Saint-Denis (1867), and the English psychic Frederic Myers (1892), all of whom claimed they could trace apparently obscure dream elements to historical experience. F. W. Hildebrandt (1875), Ludwig Strümpell (1877), and others found that experience from even the earliest years of life might be represented in dreams; or, as W. Robert (1886) and J. Nelson (1888) emphasized, dream sources could spring from relatively recent experience. All of these authors, like Freud himself, used anecdotal approaches and offered no systematic evidence for their opinions.

On the other hand, the American psychologist Mary Calkins (1893) found that 11 percent of systematically collected dream reports had *no* evident connection with waking experience (see chapter 3)—an exception Freud saw as only proving his rule. The failure in this 11 percent was only apparent: the apparent novel element must be due to the transformation by the censor of remembered but unacceptable memories. Although Freud's notion of censorial transformation comes close to admitting synthetic capability, it stops just short by emphasizing degradative rather than elaborative aspects of dream formation.

"The way in which memory behaves in dreams is undoubtedly of the greatest importance for any theory of memory in general"—a claim of Freud's with which I agree wholeheartedly, although I cannot accept his conclusion that the way memory behaves in dreams "teaches us that nothing which we have mentally possessed can be entirely lost" (1900, p. 54). The idea that information is never lost is the corollary of Freud's failure to recognize that the nervous system constructs its own information. These two ideas are the Freudian equivalent of Newton's second law regarding the conservation of energy. Experimental evidence now strongly indicates that early childhood memories (which psychoanalysts have judged to be the source of later conflict) are in fact irretrievably lost. Children retain very little memory of any experience before the age of three. Once this dual set of postulates, that information cannot be constructed and that information cannot be lost, is broken, many Freudian arguments founder disastrously.

Many of Freud's predecessors thought that external and/or internal sensory stimuli, both arising outside the brain, might be the source of dreams. After all, the motive force and the information has to come from some place. Freud was later to conclude that it comes from the dynamically repressed unconscious. In contrast, Strümpell (1883) thought that the restriction of external sensory input might make certain internal sensory stimuli more potent in giving rise to dreams; while Jessen (1855) imagined that external stimuli might be incorporated into dreams. Both concepts had experimental support: Maury, Hervey de Saint-Denis, and F. W. Hildebrandt had performed experimental studies showing that external stimuli could indeed be incorporated into dreams. While acknowledging this work, Freud focused on the alterations made in the character of the stimulus as it was incorporated. His emphasis on this transformation is linked to the central notion of disguise and censorship as the principal rule governing information processing during dreaming.

Strümpell (1877) and Wundt (1874) both saw dreaming as related to the conditions favorable to the formation of illusions that characterize the sleeping brain. Under these conditions, an internal or an external stimulus could excite numerous associations—a *facilitation of the associative process of the mind* which impressed Strümpell and Wundt (as it has all students of dreaming). For these German dream theorists, the path of associations chosen was indeterminate. For Freud, by contrast, the path was overdetermined: it led straight to the unconscious. And so he doubted the illusion theory.

Freud was already turning away from the physiological tradition on which his earlier *Project for a Scientific Psychology* (1895) had been so soundly based. Wundt believed that the visual nature of dreams could be related to entopic imagery: by *entopic,* he meant that the visual images arise through stimulation of the visual system itself—most probably, of the retina. Although Freud rejected this notion because it could not be confirmed, it has now been amply and objectively demonstrated that the visual system is indeed autoactivated in REM sleep; the source, however, is the brain and not the retina.

For Johannes Müller, hypnagogic hallucinations (those fleeting visions that occur at sleep onset) also indicated entopic stimulation. This was a specific case of Müller's general law of specific nerve energy: whenever a nerve is stimulated, it gives rise to a sensation appropriate to the organ served (1826). G. T. Ladd, a psychophysiologist who worked at Yale in the 1890s, performed experiments on himself and suggested an intraocular source of stimulation during dreaming: "The changing, perpetually shifting character of the excitation of the idio-retinal light corresponds precisely to the constantly moving succession of images shown us by our dreams" (1892). Of these observations Freud was apparently unaware.

Internal somatic stimuli had long been recognized as one of the sources of dreaming in sick people. Individuals suffering from heart disease would awaken from short terrifying dreams, presumably incorporating into their dream scenarios the pain of angina pectoris. Patients with lung disease often awoke with a sense of suffocation incorporated into a dream—a condition perhaps derived from the now well documented and entirely normal compromise of the respiratory system during REM sleep. Freud reasoned that these explanations were inadequate to account for dreams of healthy individuals. Having considered other normal organic processes, he flatly rejected the theory of the origin of dreams which regarded the "vegetative organic sensation as the constructor of dreams" (1900). In this assumption, he was correct.

Few thinkers of the time imagined that the brain itself might be the source of the dream stimuli. The philosopher Arthur Schopenhauer, writing in 1862, was not far from this view when he stated that, in waking, external stimuli impinge upon the mind and cause it to erect models of time, space, and causality in relation to the realities of the external world. Thus, during the attentive waking state, internal stimuli have relatively little importance. During sleep, by contrast, the sources of external stimulation diminish markedly, allowing the ratio of internal to external stimulation to rise. The internal stimuli are remodeled into forms occupying space and time by rules unique to the brain itself. Freud criticized this point of view because almost any internal information source could be invoked. Furthermore, dream interpretation would be rendered practically impossible if one had to trace each aspect of dream content back to some obscure organic stimulus.

It is true that the task of dream interpretation based on physiology is difficult or even impossible; but while this recognition means only that dream interpretation should be undertaken cautiously, it is certainly not a reason to reject a physiological theory. Physiological theories must rise or fall on their own merits; and, insofar as they survive scientific scrutiny, they compel revision of any psychological theory that denies, ignores, or runs counter to them. The internal-stimulus hypothesis of Schopenhauer must therefore be considered even more sound today than it was when he launched it, nearly forty years before Freud dismissed it.

While writers such as Friedrich Krauss (1859), P. M. Simon (1888), and J. Mourly Vold (1896) all took seriously the notion of specific internal stimuli (see chapter 3), Freud could not. He was impressed with "the apparent absence of determination in the choice of what images are to be produced" (1900, p. 73), and with this lack of determinacy I would agree. During dreaming sleep, the brain-mind system is in so open a mode that determinism may be impossible to establish. In further arguing against the adequacy of physiological theories, Freud posited purely psychic stimuli for "pure" hallucinations—an idea that suggests that there are mental phenomena without physiological correlates. Finding this assertion impossible to accept on logical grounds, I believe that the appropriate position is closer to that of Wundt who, to quote Freud, "takes up a middle position and does not fail to remark that in most dreams somatic stimuli and physical instigators whether unknown or recognized as daytime interests, work in cooperation" (1900, p. 73).

In a key passage, Freud anticipated his attribution of the formation of dreams to an unsuspected psychical source of stimulation and acknowledged the current scientific appeal and ultimate scientific vindication of the organic approach:

It is true that the dominance of the brain over the organism is asserted with apparent confidence. Nevertheless, anything that might indicate that mental life is in any way independent of demonstrable organic changes or that its manifestations are in any way spontaneous, alarms the modern psychiatrist as though a recognition of such things would inevitably bring back the days of the philosophy of nature and of the metaphysical view of the nature of the mind. The suspicions of the psychiatrists have put the mind under tutelage and they now insist that none of its impulses shall be allowed to suggest that it has any means of its own. This behavior of theirs only shows how little trust they have in the validity of a causal connection between the somatic and the mental. Even when investigations show that the primary exciting cause of the phenomena is psychical, deeper research will one day trace the path further and discover an organic basis for the mental event.

But if at the moment we cannot see beyond the mental, that is no reason for denying its existence. [1900, p. 75]

This statement clearly reveals a Freud who was rebelling against an overly organic point of view—an attitude he attributed to the reaction against vitalism, which he himself shared. But he moved dangerously close to an either/or position when he put the psychical in opposition to the physiological. And he echoed vitalism in suggesting that the psychical aspect may operate independently of the physiological. Neither Freud nor his contemporaries could have any idea that dream information is actually generated by the brain itself.

In the fourth part of his historical review in chapter 1, Freud considered why dreams are forgotten after waking. Almost none of his predecessors guessed that a state-dependent change in the mode of operation of memory systems might be at the root of this remarkable phenomenon. Strümpell, writing in 1877, thought that dream images are weak on awakening and also, owing to their bizarreness, unintelligible. For these two reasons, they might therefore be swamped by the stronger, clearer sensations of waking.

According to the Italian F. Bonatelli (1880), there is, in the experience of the sleeping and waking states, an alteration that is unfavorable to reciprocal communication between them—a state difference that manifests itself as a different *arrangement* of ideational material in dreams. Dreaming is thus untranslatable to the language of waking consciousness.* But in reviewing as inadequate the explanations of Strümpell and Jessen, Freud set up his own explanation: namely, that the dream memories are forcibly crammed back down into the unconscious from which they have sprung; they are repressed.

The fifth section of Freud's historical first chapter deals with the unique formal features of dreams, those psychological characteristics that distinguish dreaming from other mental states. Freud began his discussion with reference to the creator of the psychophysical law (which related the strength of a stimulus to the strength of response), Gustav Fechner (1889), who drew a sharp contrast between the mode of operation of the mind during waking and during dreams. The German psychologist claimed that

---

*While admitting that dreams cannot be adequately described in words, we now know that this difficulty cannot explain poor dream recall because instrumental awakenings have little difficulty in eliciting amply detailed reports which confidently describe preawakening mentation. Thus, if recall is instrumentally enhanced, dream ideas may be easily if imperfectly translated from one state to another.

The explanation for dream forgetting now seems to be that unless an awakening occurs, memories of dreaming are simply not laid down.

the scene of action of dreams is different from that of waking ideational life:

If the scene of action of psychophysical activity were the same in sleep and waking, dreams could in my view only be a prolongation at a lower degree of intensity of waking ideational life and moreover would necessarily be of the same material and form. The facts are quite otherwise. [1860]

Expressing surprise about this statement, Freud assumed that Fechner did not mean to imply an anatomical interpretation; nor that he was alluding to reorganization of activity in the cerebral cortex. Freud used Fechner's argument as added support for the necessity of a mental theory. Today, however, it is not quite so easy to dismiss Fechner's suggestion. As a thoroughgoing psychophysicist, he believed that every sensation and every mental experience has a physical substrate. Best known for his work on the appreciation of external sensations during waking, and aware that his psychophysical law was true only under certain conditions, Fechner recognized that it applied only to external stimuli, and not to internal ones. In denying that this transformation could be entirely peripheral and in appealing to what he called the "division of consciousness," Fechner was clearly positing a central variable to explain the differences between the perceptions of dreaming and waking. This statement could be taken to indicate that he was aware of the state-dependent nature of perception, and that he intuited, however dimly, the possibility that a change in the central operating properties of the brain determines the difference between waking and dreaming consciousness.

Freud reviewed previous explanations of the incoherence and absurdity of dreams and summarized the then-prevalent scientific view of the dream process:

Stimuli generated during sleep arouse hallucinations or illusions which become linked according to the laws of association and call up a further series of ideas or images. This material is then worked over by what remains of the organizing faculties of the mind. All that remains undiscovered are the motives which decide whether the calling up of images should proceed along one chain of associations or another. [1900, p. 91]

Beyond explaining how this all can actually occur physiologically, modern science has added little to this story. But this very confirmation of the view that Freud rejected weakens his alternative view of dream formation.

Of all the authors cited by Freud, only Jessen (1855) appears neutral on the issue of dream formation, seeing dreaming as "a more or less mechanical succession of images and ideas provoked by internal impulses" and therefore not necessarily a measure of motivational force (1855). The alternative idea, which intuition affirms and modern dream science does not deny, is that the associative train in dreams is driven by a multitude of personally significant factors: One's appetites (or instincts), one's emotions, one's recent and remote experiences, and one's ways of thinking are all vectors in dream-plot formation. And all these factors can be, in part, conscious and, in part, unconscious. This commonsense view is completely compatible with physiology and saves the dream from the ashbin of cognitive oblivion without postulating convoluted and improbable psychological mechanisms.

Many of Freud's physiologically oriented colleagues held all or part of such a view. Thus Havelock Ellis (1899), the English pioneer in the sociology of sex, acknowledged the primitive, instinctual factors in dream formation; and the English psychologist James Sully (1893) coined the term *regression* to describe this "back to basics" aspect of dreaming. F. W. Hildebrandt supposed that "wishes" play their part, and viewed dreaming as an intensification of the artistic qualities of mind and a simultaneous enfeeblement of the analytic (1875). E. R. Pfaff (1868), Kant (1764), and Fichter (1864) were all impressed with the capacity of dreaming to reveal one's hidden nature truthfully and transparently. However reasonable these views, they were *not* Freud's.

Freud reviewed three classes of theory with respect to dream function:

State Condition Theories.   According to Delboeuf (1885), a change in the state of the brain in sleep causes a change in mental state. In this view, Freud found no explanation of *why* we dream. Delboeuf seemed to be saying, "Look to the brain for your answer." Freud could not accept the implication that dreaming was in any way an epiphenomenon of physiology.

Diminished Capacity Theories.   Karl Binz (1878) likewise ascribed the changes in mental activity during dreaming to a diminished activity of the brain, which allows the brain cells to recover from fatigue and leads to increased coherence of thought in subsequent waking periods (see Part III); and therefore thought that dreaming must be categorized as a somatic process. Freud objected to such radical reductionism. Maury imagined that, in the transition from waking to sleep, brain activity shifts from one anatomical region to another. He thought that dreaming reflects a partial awakening of the brain, and that this partiality is responsible for the meaninglessness of dreams. He likened the operation of the brain during dreaming sleep to "the ten fingers of a man who knows nothing of music wandering over the keys of the piano" (1861). For Robert, dreaming represented "the somatic excretion of incomplete ideas"; again, dreaming was seen as an epiphenomenon, and dreams as "scavengers of the mind" (1886).

Special Capacity Theories. Theories of special capacity ascribed a utilitarian function to dreaming. For the physiologically inclined Burdach, dreaming is "a natural activity of the mind which is not limited by the power of individuality, not interrupted by self consciousness, and which is not directed by self-determination but which is the freely operating vitality of the sensory centers." While we cannot quite be sure that Burdach was correct in calling dreaming "a holiday for the mind" (1838), we may regard dreaming as playing a positive role rather than the merely protective function Freud postulated. The German Romantic poet Novalis (1772–1801) praised the reign of dreams as a "spaceshield against the hum-drum monotony of life"; while Purkinje also saw a reviving and healing function in dreaming (1846).

All these theories are variations on the theme of rest, but add a special dimension in suggesting that it is the mind's positive indulgence in pleasurable activities during dreaming that refreshes it in some special way. A more mystical, even ecstatic version of the same theory is given by Karl Albert Scherner (1861), who accepted the notion of somatic stimuli as the originator of dreaming, but shared with Freud the belief that these stimuli are symbolically transformed into dream images. Freud criticized Scherner's failure to give this symbolic transformation functional significance. Freud's lengthy treatment of Scherner's theory denotes his recognition of its formal similarity to his own. Rather than rejecting the German psychologist out of hand, Freud credited Scherner with seriousness of purpose but chided him for lack of precision. That the state of the mind—in concert with the state of the brain—is *intrinsically fantastic* is the nub of Scherner's position, a position he shared with physiologists such as Binz. His position is summarized by the idea that "ganglion cells can be fantastic too" (quoted in Freud 1900, p. 119). In other words, a fantastic mental state implies a fantastic state of the brain and its constituent neurons.

The essence of Freud's critique is that previous scientists had not only failed to provide an adequate theory of dreaming but were quite wrong to view dreams as the meaningless product of disorganized brain activity. Throughout his review, Freud struggled with a poorly articulated view of the mind-brain relationship. In discounting the brain and crediting the mind, he sometimes appeared to assume them to be independent entities. Yet, as he also recognized, it seems logically clear that brain state and mind state are unified in some deep, as yet undefined way.

The Interpretation of Dreams was antiscientific because Freud so forcefully dismissed all previous writers that he actually aborted an emerging experimental tradition. Psychiatry and psychology have been in Freud's thrall for almost a century; and even within the field of modern sleep research, the tenacity of psychoanalytic views remains impressively obstructive to integrative theorizing.

Freud's dream theory was the cornerstone of his general theory of the mind; both had the same psychopathological slant. In the last section of his historical survey, therefore, Freud turned to the similarities of dreaming to mental illness and reviewed many formal similarities between dreaming and madness: the madman as waking dreamer (I. Kant 1798); insanity as a dream that occurs when the senses are awake (A. Krauss 1858); the definition of dreams as a brief madness versus that of madness as a long dream (A. Schopenhauer 1862); delirium as a dream state induced by illness (F. W. Hagen 1846); almost all phenomena experienced in dreams can be seen in insane asylums (W. Wundt 1890). There were also etiological connections: dreaming was seen as capable of inducing both hysterical paralysis and paranoia; and vice versa, psychosis was seen as a breakthrough of the dream process. Thus many pre-Freudian authors regarded the dream as nocturnal insanity.

Freud concluded his historical survey with the following comparison:

The indisputable analogy between dreams and insanity, extending as it does down to their characteristic details, is one of the powerful props of the medical theory of dream life which regards dreaming as a useless and disturbing process and as the expression of a reduced activity of the mind. Nevertheless, it is not to be expected that we shall find the ultimate explanation of dreams in the direction of mental disorders; for the unsatisfactory state of our knowledge of the origin of these latter conditions is generally recognized. It is quite likely, on the contrary, that a modification of our attitude towards dreams will at the same time affect our views upon the internal mechanisms of mental disorders and that we shall be working towards an explanation of the psychoses while we are endeavoring to throw some light on the mystery of dreams. [1900, p. 124]

While agreeing with many of these Freudian assertions, this book is firmly dedicated to a scientific resuscitation of the "medical theory of dream life," which Freud disdained. Rather than regarding dreaming as useless or disturbing—and certainly not as the simple expression of a reduced activity of the mind—we will come to see that dreaming is the result of a reorganization of brain and mental activity, with intensifications of some faculties mirrored by reduced activity of others, and both serving purposes as yet unclear but as likely to be productive as protective.

2

Psychoanalysis and Dreaming

> Nor is there any doubt that all weapons or tools are used as symbols for the male organ: e.g., hammers, rifles, revolvers, daggers, sabres, etc. In the same way, landscapes in dreams, especially any containing bridges or wooded hills, may clearly be recognized as descriptions of the genitals.
>
> —SIGMUND FREUD
> *The Interpretation of Dreams* (1900)

> I can make nothing in my own case with his dream theories and obviously "symbolism" is a most dangerous method.
>
> —Letter from WILLIAM JAMES to Theodore Fluornoy
> September 28, 1909

IN THE LAST DECADE of the nineteenth century, two men had crucial insights that determined the course of psychology and neurobiology well into the twentieth century: Sigmund Freud and his theory of psychoanalysis, with its disguise-censorship theory of dreaming; and the Spanish neuroanatomist Santiago Ramón y Cajal and his neuron doctrine. While Ramón y Cajal's revolutionary work, indicating that each brain cell is discrete and physically discontinuous from all others, is the basis for contemporary knowledge and theories of the brain and hence of dreaming (see chapter 4), the most widely known dream theory of this psychoanalytic age is undoubtedly that developed by Sigmund Freud and published as *The Interpretation of Dreams* in 1900. In the decades since then, psychoanalytic dream theory has gained a strong hold upon both popular and professional thinking; and most laymen and many professionals assume that psychoanalysis is scientifically sound—or at least medically reputable. Furthermore, practically all modern psychological concepts are colored by Freudian doctrines. Hence, we must examine the theory at some length to understand its sources and evaluate its claims. As a way of highlighting its intrinsic scientific weakness and its deeply controversial nature, we will also examine the quite different dream theory of Freud's most famous psychoanalytic co-worker, Carl Jung.

From the beginning, psychoanalysis placed undue reliance upon speculative philosophy to develop its ideas and undue reliance upon a political organization to promote them. It is to Freud's distinctive leadership style that the current sterility of psychoanalysis must in large part be ascribed. And the related tendency to regard progress as coming through the vision of an enlightened and heroic genius has also contributed to the isolation of psychoanalysis from medical science. The quandary in which the field finds itself today is a function of these two features. On the one hand, there is the bland, humanistic, but untechnical and antibiological revision of the hermeneuticians—clarifying perhaps, but unscientific. On the other hand, there is a profusion of quasi-technical linguistic elaborations— obscurantist and pseudo-scientific.

Let me therefore say at once that, in giving Freud's and Jung's theories extensive and detailed treatment, I do not accept their claims as genuinely scientific. I suggest that they are not for two important reasons: First, I believe that psychoanalytic dream theory is not scientific because it is not empirically based. Freud derived the disguise-censorship postulate from his clinical observations of patients in whom repression of sexual drives and related ideas seemed to him to be pathogenic. The repression idea derived, in turn, from an erroneous picture of the nervous system. The idea did not come to an unbiased Freud after he had systematically collected dream reports from many subjects. Psychoanalytic dream theory is thus largely a speculative, *a priori* theory. And even as such it is based upon almost no evidence. All of the data in *The Interpretation of Dreams* is subjective: most of the dreams are Freud's own; otherwise, they are second-hand reports; and none is treated quantitatively.

Second, psychoanalytic theory is not logically constructed in such a way as to make it amenable to direct experimental test. In fact, psychoanalysts have never even defined the sort of evidence that could refute the theory. It is thus no surprise that, in almost ninety years, Freud's dream theory has given rise to no critical experimental tests.

FREUD'S DREAM THEORY: DISGUISE CENSORSHIP AND SYMBOLISM

Freud's dream theory can be defined as follows: The ego is the mediator between the demands of conscience and society (embodied in the super-ego), and the urgings of instinct (the id). As this is a tiring job, the ego wishes to sleep. It withdraws its cathexis from the outside world and simultaneously relaxes its vigil upon the previously repressed unconscious impulses in the id. These unconscious forces, or "wishes," threaten to escape from their unconscious jailhouse and beat upon the door of consciousness. But they are unwelcome. If they were to be admitted, they would, by their unruliness, disrupt consciousness and so terminate sleep. This uprising is often associated with the pairing of an unconscious wish with material still in consciousness from the day's previous experience—the so-called *day residue.* The motive force of dreaming is thus defined by Freud as the repressed energy constituting the unconscious impulse. One common formal aspect of dreams—the incorporation of recent wake-state experience into dream scenarios—is explained by the pairing of the unconscious wish with the day residue.

But the most distinctive—and interesting—formal aspect of dreaming is not the inclusion of recent experience, but bizarreness. By *bizarreness* Freud was alluding to odd and apparently nonsensical changes in time, place, and person, incongruities of dream plot, character, and action, and uncertainties of thought (all of which our laboratory has recently quantified) and ascribed them to the dynamic transformation of the information contained within the unconscious impulse or wish. Thus the *latent content,* the true instigator and meaning of the dream, is denied access to consciousness by the censor. The censor does not need (or wish) to sleep; the censor is tireless and, if it is to protect sleep, can never sleep.

The latent dream content is *disguised* by the censor through a variety of functions that later were to become incorporated into Freud's theory of psychological defense. The defensive transformations include displacement, condensation, symbolization, and pictorialization. Thus, the bizarreness of dreams—their most distinctive cognitive features—are only *apparently* meaningless. And this very disorder was, for Freud, evidence of the efficacy of the censor's effort to disguise a dream's true meaning.

As for the amnesia for dreams, Freud postulated that even the transformed and muted manifest content of a dream might still be psychonoxious. It is therefore subject to repression, an active replacement in the unconscious from which it originally has sprung. He also postulated a further, *secondary* elaboration of even the manifest dream which further detoxified or transformed the unacceptable wishes in the remembering and retelling of the dream during conscious waking life.

Dream Symbolism

Most of the scientific reports on dreams appearing between the publication of *The Interpretation of Dreams* in 1900 and Freud's *Revision of the Theory of Dreams* in 1932 were concerned with the symbolic aspects of dreams. Freud noted that some physicians at an unnamed American university had already denied to psychoanalysis the properties of science because it could furnish no experimental proof of its postulates (1932). His rejoinder drew a parallel between psychoanalysis and astronomy. Since no one criticized astronomers for being unscientific because they had difficulty doing practical experiments on the heavenly bodies, it was unfair—in Freud's eyes—to criticize psychoanalysis for not doing experiments on the unconscious mind and its ideas.

While Freud was correct in observing that, in psychoanalysis just as in astronomy, one is limited to observation from afar, his analogy overlooked two crucial criteria of science: quantitative observations and accurate predictions. While astronomy has achieved both, psychoanalysis has done neither. The astronomers' accounting for movements of the spheres—on the basis of precise observational data—made possible increasingly accurate predictions about what is to occur in the future. The predictive accuracy of astronomy—based upon quantitative observations at a distance—has yet to characterize psychoanalysis. Accurate observations and accurate predictions about dreaming have come, rather, from physiology. It may thus be more appropriate to compare psychoanalysis to astrology than to astronomy. Both have captured the human imagination but neither has yet given its divinations of character and behavior a firm scientific base.

A few psychoanalysts had attempted to do experimental work on the symbolism of dreams. In 1912, Klaus Schrötter reported that when hypnotized subjects were given a suggestion to dream of sexual material, the subsequent dreams contained convex objects (which are phallic) and concave objects (which are vaginal). A problem here is that if *all* dreams are highly charged with symbolic representations, and if most objects are concave or convex (presumably, only completely flat objects being devoid of sexual symbolism), then Schrötter's finding may be trivial or misleading, or both.

Freud also recounted a study by Bruno Bettelheim and Heinz Hartmann, published in 1924, which reported the effect of telling grossly sexual stories to patients with a severe defect in recent memory (Korsakoff's syndrome), and then observing the deformations these patients' minds produced when asked to repeat the stories. The authors concluded—correctly, according to Freud—that the occurrence in the accounts of symbols of sexual organs and of sexual contact (such as a stairway) could be produced only by an unconscious sexual desire that has been deformed. An alternative explanation, not considered by the authors or by Freud, is that the narrative structure of consciousness cannot be maintained by either the dreamer or the Korsakoff patient because of the fundamental change in the memory and orientation functions of the individual's brain-mind. The successive associative changes in material introduced into consciousness could thus be a simple result of this cognitive failure rather than an effort to disguise unacceptable mental content. The two explanations are not mutually exclusive, but it is significant that Freud considered no other interpretation than disguise-censorship in accounting for mental content, *even for subjects with known organic deficits.* This example is of particular interest since the dream state is formally similar to that seen in the organic mental syndromes: both have amnesia, disorientation, visual hallucinations, and confabulation.

Freud then reconsidered "dream-work's" supposed transformation of ideas into images in respect to Herbert Silberer's description of the degradation of his thoughts when tired and the subsequent elaboration of mental imagery from them (1909). Although Freud identified this process as identical to that occurring in dreams, there are important differences.

Having earlier expressed dismay and surprise at critical reactions to his theory of dream symbols as being overly schematic and overly sexual, Freud approvingly cited a 1920 paper by Theodore Reik. In support of the contention that, in the dreams of women, the appearance of a coat signifies a man, Reik pointed out that, in Bedouin marriage rituals, a husband dresses his wife in a special coat (called the *abba*) and says, "May no other than I cover you ever." The use of the word *cover* thus has a sexual connotation obvious to psychoanalysts. In a similar vein, Freud quoted Karl Abraham (1922) who claimed that spiders symbolize the mother in dreams and, specifically, a phallic mother whom one fears; Abraham alluded to the head of Medusa and the fear of castration. Sándor Ferenczi (1921, 1922) pointed out that bridges symbolize the penis, which during sexual intercourse unites the parental couple; in accord with this interpretation, the woman who has not succeeded in repressing her desire to be a man often dreams of bridges that are too short and do not allow one to reach the opposite bank.

Freud saw the interpretation of dreams as similar to the interpretation of myths; moreover, the psychoanalytic interpretation of dreams enhanced the credibility of the psychoanalytic interpretation of myths, and vice versa. As an example, he cited B. J. Eisler (1919) who—inspired by the dream of one of his patients—was able to explain analytically the deep meaning of the statue of Hermes by Praxiteles. While Freud did not give the analysis in full, he saw significance in Hermes playing with a garconnet (a slingshot), and then added that the fable of the labyrinth may represent an anal birth—the torturous pathways representing the intestines, and the thread of Adriadne, the umbilical cord.

In the space of a few pages, Freud has moved a long way from his contention that psychoanalysis has as great a right to the claim of science as does astronomy. These anecdotes do not qualify even as observations; and their interpretation more closely resembles speculative literary criticism than it does scientific reasoning.

Freud never considered the possibility that the symbolic function of the brain-mind is open-ended, allowing a multiplicity of meanings to be suggested by a single object. Nor did he seem to realize that the occurrence of symbols can neither prove nor disprove anything about the mechanism or function of mental process in the elaboration either of dreams or of myths—except that when meanings are unclear and imprecise, symbols are the best vehicle to carry ambiguity and hence to support a multiplicity of possible interpretations.

Freud makes the limitations of his theory clear when he offers this most telling dream interpretation: a young woman dreams of entering a large room and sees one person sitting on a chair; then she sees six or eight identical people, all bearing the image of her father. Freud explained this dream by assuming the large room to be her mother's abdomen and the repetition of the father's image to be a disguised rehearsal of his coital comings and goings during the young woman's interuterine life. This is an example, according to Freud, of the translation of frequency into accumulation: the dream process transforms temporal and spatial relations and makes them appear as accumulation rather than as repetition. The father is thus present simultaneously in the room eight times (accumulation), whereas the thought that gave rise to this memory is his coming and going eight times in sexual union with the mother (frequency). Again, however rich and literary Freud's imagination, we cannot give scientific credence to this kind of reasoning.

According to Freud all the dreams of one night deal with a single theme. In support of this notion, he cited Franz Alexander's 1925 study showing that pairs of dreams may sequentially elaborate the same theme. If, for example, one wants to do something with someone, in the first dream the someone may appear but the something is unclear; whereas in the second dream, the something is clear but the someone is unclear. The logic of this explanation is elusive.

Are all dreams the fulfillment of wishes, especially since many dreams contain anxiety, scenes of punishment, and other unpleasant feelings? In any dream of punishment it was easy for Freud to detect the unconscious wish for which the dreamer was consciously being punished. Making an analogy between the inversion of wishes in punishment dreams and in neurotic processes, he cited the intervention of the superego (which translates a wish into its opposite, a fear) and equated the function of the censor of dreams to the operation of the superego in the waking psyche.

Freud then admitted that there are two serious problems with equating the realization of wishes with the inverted fulfillment of wishes. The first is the well-known fact that individuals who have undergone severe trauma often find themselves precisely reliving the traumatic situation in their dreams. A reciprocal problem concerns the appearance in dreams of overtly sexual themes when, according to Freud, the amnesia that normally covers the first years of life should make it difficult for one to remember early sexual experiences. In addition, these early sexual memories are associated with painful impressions: fear, the sense of the forbidden, deception, and punishment. Thus, Freud could readily account for the repression of these memories but not for their reappearance in dream fantasies.

Undaunted by these contradictions, Freud stepped onto his theoretical tightrope and slipped gracefully across the void of reason: the extraordinary plasticity of the dream explains how it can *both* repeat the painful experience *and* translate that experience into a pleasurable one. He concluded his discussion of trauma and infantile wishes by stating that these exceptions actually prove his rule. But, not wanting to give too much weight to this explanation, he says that the dream is not simply the fulfillment of a wish but is the *attempt* to fulfill the wish, and that this attempt sometimes fails. In the repetitive dream of the traumatic experience, it is the *failure* of repression that allows the event to recur in dreams. Here Freud was having his cake and eating it, too.

Thus, while not all dreams *succeed* in fulfilling wishes, they all try to do so. Regardless of its nature, the literature that Freud reviewed confirmed his theory: he simply explained away any puzzling or contradictory data. By 1936, his thinking was characterized by arbitrariness, authoritarianism, and a failure to specify rules or imagine data that could contradict his theory.

Freud's Revision of His Dream Theory

Psychoanalysts have objected to my critique of Freud's *The Interpretation of Dreams* on the grounds that he substantially revised his ideas, and corrected many of his early errors, in the many books he wrote in the nearly forty years after its publication in 1900, when he was forty-four. I contend, however, that Freud did not, in subsequent work, substantially change his original position.

One "revisionist" text to which psychoanalysts have often referred me is included in Freud's *New Introductory Lectures on Psychoanalysis,* whose title suggests that it was conceived as a sequel to the first series of lectures on psychoanalysis held in 1915 and 1916 and published in the subsequent year. The date line under the introduction to the later book is Vienna, 1932, when Freud was seventy-six and internationally well known. Since this work thus constitutes his last words on the subject of dreams, I have examined the first conference, entitled "Revision of the Theory of Dreams," page by page, in search of substantiation for Freud's claimed revisions.

In the three decades since 1900, Freud observed, the dream theory, like psychoanalysis in general, had changed but little. I argue that it had not changed at all.

Freud emphasized the importance of the theory of dreams to the history of psychoanalysis: it marked a turning point at which, thanks to the dream theory, psychoanalysis passed from being only an empirical psychotherapeutic method to becoming a depth psychology. The young science has not furnished another more impressive principle, another more original theory than that of dreams, said Freud. The dream theory is a "stretch of new country" reclaimed from the mysticism of the past. It has such originality as to play the role of a shibboleth, a test used to judge the capacity of psychoanalysis. With these strong claims, Freud clearly implied that if the dream theory does not hold, the rest of psychoanalysis is also in some doubt.

Since 1913, the *International Review of Psychoanalysis* contained all the important works of "Our Science," said Freud. In the first volumes, in a section called "The Interpretation of Dreams," several papers on the subject appeared; but then this section was dropped. It was as if, Freud noted, the analysts had nothing more to teach us, as if the science of dreams had said its last word. On the other hand, many psychiatrists and psychothera-

pists had come "to cook their little stews in our fire without even recognizing our hospitality" (1932), some, for example, believing that all dreams
are sexual—a claim never made by psychoanalysis.

Freud enumerated four misunderstandings: First, many psychiatrists
and psychotherapists had ignored the fundamental distinction that must
be made between the manifest content of dreams and the latent dream
thoughts. A second point of persistent misunderstanding was the apparent
contradiction between the occurrence of nightmares and the theory of
dreams as realization of a wish. A third was the impossibility of interpreting dreams when the dreamer does not give associations. The fourth and
final point was that, above all, the essence of a dream is the process of its
elaboration.

From the outset, it is clear that Freud was more strongly motivated to
reiterate the fundamental points of his theory than to revise them. He
justified this reiteration by pointing to the misunderstandings evident in
the letters of the many people who had written to him claiming to have
read the science of dreams. In 1932, he was in a didactic, theory-promul-
gating frame of mind.

FREUD'S THEORY OF THE BRAIN: THE PROJECT FOR A
SCIENTIFIC PSYCHOLOGY

In the early 1890s, Freud (figure 2.1), then in his middle thirties, turned from
a promising academic career in experimental and clinical neurology to
attempt to develop a psychology based upon what was then known about
the action of the nervous system.* Based entirely upon principles that could
be developed from the physical sciences, this psychology was to be "per-
spicacious and free from doubt"—as Freud wrote in *Project for a Scientific
Psychology* (1895), a germinal and controversial work (see figure 2.2). The
Project is germinal because it clearly shows that the seeds of almost all of
Freud's important psychological ideas grew from the soil of the neurobiology of 1890; and it is controversial because he recognized the inadequacy
of his integrative effort and decided against publishing it. While many
contemporary psychoanalysts therefore absolve Freud and his dream the-

---

*While it is well known that Freud was once a neurologist, it is not so widely ap-
preciated that he actually worked in cellular neurobiology. The fresh-water crab, on which
he performed detailed neuroanatomical investigation, has become a popular preparation in
the development of detailed knowledge of neuronal function at the cellular level.

FIGURE 2.1

Sigmund Freud

When Freud was thirty-nine and had just left the university to embark on a career in clinical neurology, he began to conceive his "Project for a Scientific Psychology." A direct intellectual descendant of Helmholtz (see figure 1.1) and the anti-vitalists, Freud was initially committed to a materialist psychology constrained by physical science. Fascinated by the clinical phenomena of hypnosis and hysteria and dissatisfied with the model of the mind then supportable by neuroscience, Freud officially renounced his project; but the same ideas resurfaced—in psychological guise—in his first major psychoanalytical work, *The Interpretation of Dreams,* in 1900. *Source:* Rare Books and Print Department, Francis A. Countway Library of Medicine, Harvard Medical School. Dick Wolfe, Director.

ory from any criticism derived from analysis of the *Project,* its pivotal role in his intellectual development has been clearly enunciated even by such loyal psychoanalytic allies as James Strachey and Ernst Kris who, in the introduction to *The Interpretation of Dreams,* state, "The ghost of Freud's project haunts all of his subsequent work." I, too, believe that, despite his own disclaimers to the contrary, the neurobiological ideas he set forth in the *Project* did not die with the unpublished manuscript but resurfaced in *The Interpretation of*

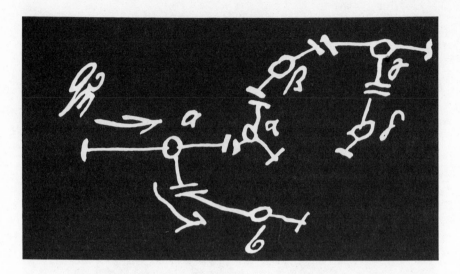

FIGURE 2.2
Freud's neurons

In his "Project for a Scientific Psychology," Freud depicted a neuronal circuit that conducted imposed stimulus-energy along one of two paths. Path *alpha* (α) to *gamma* (γ) led to discharge of the imposed energy as motion, while the "side-path" (*a* to *b*) stored the energy for later discharge—for example, in dreaming or in a psychological symptom. Most of the neurophysiological assumptions of this model proved to be incorrect (see pages 63–64), as did the psychological constructs that derived from them. We now know that the brain creates and cancels its own energy, such states as REM sleep and dreaming occurring automatically, spontaneously, and independent of stimulus energy. *Source:* Sigmund Freud, "Project for a Scientific Psychology," 1895, in *The Origins of Psychoanalysis: Letters to Wilhelm Fliess, Drafts and Notes: 1887–1902,* ed. Marie Bonaparte, Anna Freud, and Ernst Kris, trans. Eric Mosbacher and James Strachey (New York: Basic Books, 1954), pp. 347–445.

Dreams, there clearly translated into "psychological" concepts. Freud's mind theory is thus Freud's brain theory. Further, *The Interpretation of Dreams* arose primarily from neither his dissatisfaction with previous dream theories, as its chapter 7 would suggest, nor from the careful study of dream reports, but rather from a set of *a priori* assumptions based upon his efforts to develop a psychology from the neurobiology of the 1890s.

Freud assumed, above all, that the nervous system was devoid of either synaptic contact or inhibition; that *it was incapable of losing, discarding, or canceling information;* that it was, in fact, a passive receptacle of both energy and information; able to create neither and to get rid of either one only via some motor action. We now know that none of these ideas is correct. The nervous system has the metabolic means of producing its own energy (though it is dependent upon external fuels) and the genetically derived means of creating its own information (though it is dependent upon external input for specific information about the outside world). It is further capable of canceling both endogenous and externally provided energy and information.

Although most modern psychoanalysts agree that Freud's energy concepts are completely outmoded and must be discarded, few seem to appreciate how extensively these tenets impugn informational aspects of his theory. An important aspect of his reasoning was the tight interconnection of its component parts, so that when any one is changed, others are affected—a characteristic of rationalistic thought generally.

The following three concepts, drawn from Freud's antique neurobiology, determined his dream theory:

Energy Source. For Freud, all of the energy within the nervous system comes from the outside; there is no internal source—a view equivalent to seeing the nervous system only in terms of reflex action, as a system operating only when driven by externally provided forces, and not creating its own action. The erroneous notions that Freud maintained about energy sources in the nervous system made it impossible for him to recognize that the system might have intrinsic rhythms and sequential phases of activity, and that both might be internally programmed and internally regulated. This is a surprising oversight, especially in view of his familiarity with the theories of his colleague Wilhelm Fliess, who ascribed many psychic phenomena to the operation of biological rhythms.

Energy Flow. Not only was it impossible for Freud's nervous system to create its own energy, but even when external energy had entered the system, it could only be dissipated by motoric discharge. There was no intrinsic mechanism for the cancellation of energy. This oversight is related to Freud's failure to take account of the emerging concept of inhibition.

Energy Transmissions. Freud's nervous system receives from the outside world energy that is unchanged in quality or quantity; there is no transduction of external energy (or of information) at the peripheral portals of the nervous system.

These three interrelated concepts show that Freud's nervous system and the mental activity that it supports are completely dependent upon external energy and information. Such a system is as vulnerable as it is dependent, being subject both to invasion by large sources of energy from the outside world and to the constant threat of disruption by internally stored energy that can be discharged only in motoric action. These ideas became crystallized in the concept of the dynamically repressed unconscious and were carried into the dream theory as the tendency for unconscious wishes to erupt during sleep when the repressive forces of the ego are relaxed. Freud's nervous system is in constant need of checks and balances to deal with the threat of disruption from within and without, and his whole concept of psychic defense is related to this erroneous view of how the nervous system actually operates. I am not saying that the concept of defense is in itself erroneous, but both its theoretical justification, and the weight placed upon it are excessive. If the system has its own means of producing energy, it is likely to have its own means of regulating energy. If it has its own means of creating information, it is likely to have its own means of regulating information. And if it is protected at every sensory-input gateway by transduction mechanisms, it is *intrinsically* immune to overload from the outside world. This property is particularly evident in newborn human infants who simply "tune out" when they are either overloaded or not ready to process external inputs.

In addition to his own good and proper reasons for rejecting the *Project for a Scientific Psychology* on intellectual grounds, Freud had other important historical strategic and even economic reasons for wishing to hide the influence of this work. These reasons include the wish to give a new look to *The Interpretation of Dreams*—and to all subsequent psychoanalytic thought. Furthermore, the new look was to be purely psychological and categorically independent of neurobiology. Only thus could the dream theory be both resistant to the critique of reductionism and immune to overthrow by the findings of neurobiology. At the same time, Freud constantly reiterated his hope that some day the neurobiological basis of the phenomena that he had "discovered" would be found.

It is now well established that Freud took great pains to hide the fact that his psychology was derived from neurobiology. These track-covering maneuvers of Freud's regarding the transitional period of his life have been detailed by the historian Frank Sulloway in his important *Freud, Biologist of the Mind* (1979).* According to Sulloway, it was Freud's propensity to myth making, even about himself, that led him to adopt a quasi-heroic position, appearing to develop his theories completely independently—and without the support of contemporary thinkers. There is thus an analogy between Freud's desire that his theory not be seen as derived from neurobiology and that it not be seen as borrowed from Fliess. As long as psychoanalysis could be viewed as an independent psychological theory, it could not be tested by any other means. This intellectual isolation is one of the key reasons the theory has changed so little over the decades—in contrast to

---

*Although Sulloway was at Harvard working on his book at the same time that McCarley and I were developing the ideas published in "The Neurobiological Origins of Psychoanalytic Dream Theory" (1977), we did not know each other then, and each of us was completely unaware of the other's work.

the radical developments in neurobiology over the same time span. In pondering the static nature of psychoanalytic theory compared with the extraordinarily dynamic one of neurobiology, I feel that psychoanalytic dream theory has languished (like Sleeping Beauty awaiting the kiss of her prince) owing to the loss of neurobiology (which put the sleep charm on the dream theory in the first place).

THE TRANSPARENCY HYPOTHESIS OF CARL JUNG

The tension that arose between Carl Jung and Sigmund Freud about the source and meaning of dreams increasingly differentiated their schools of psychology as time passed. Jung's dream theory emphasizes transparency and creativity, in contrast to Freud's emphasis on obscurity and psychopathology. While Freud admitted that some dreams do not display disguise and censorship, he thought that the most unique dream features reflect the operation of these concealing processes. Jung saw dreams as no less symbolic but viewed the symbols as more directly expressive of universal human concerns and as not necessarily serving the purpose of disguise.

For Jung, dream interpretation was more clearly related to the literary exposition of texts than to scientific reductionism. With a view of dream symbols more literary than that of Freud, Jung tended to link the dream process to the mythopoetic propensities of the human mind, which he took to be derived from archaic concerns residing in the so-called *collective unconscious.* Because the Swiss psychoanalyst's approach to dreaming and other related mental processes was rather more positive than Freud's, the former has appealed as a psychologist to artists, mystics, and religious thinkers but has not commanded the respect or interest of scientists or psychiatrists, as has Freud. Activation synthesis may help to redress this imbalance (see chapter 9).

The backgrounds of Freud and Jung give some insight into the importance of the difference of their positions with special reference to dreams. Both were medically and neurologically trained, and both found medicine somehow inadequate to meet the demands of their interest in psychology.

Sigmund Freud (1856–1939), educated in the Vienna school with its strong physicochemical orientation, was committed to this approach until his unsuccessful effort to create his scientific psychology in the early 1890s. After this time, he became increasingly disenchanted with science and could gain neither a position in the physiological institute nor academic support.

Carl Gustav Jung (1875–1961), who was educated in Zurich and strongly influenced by his mentor, Eugen Bleuler (1857–1939), was trained in a tradition of descriptive psychiatry stemming directly from the great German psychiatrist Emil Kraepelin (1856–1926). These scientists favored experimental psychological approaches that, in Jung's early scientific career, were in associationist psychology,* a school strongly relevant to the interests of both Freud and Jung as they developed their theories of the unconscious.

While Freud was trained in rigorous laboratory research, he had little experience in systematic clinical research; when his own break from medical science occurred, he seemed to leave behind any semblance of critical scientific thinking. Jung, on the other hand, was less deeply biological in orientation but had actually performed clinical experiments. His efforts to describe and understand the loosening of associations in schizophrenia, the clinical problem to which Bleuler made significant contributions, were thus less deep—but more scientific—than were those of Freud.

Another significant contrast between the two men is in their ethnic and religious backgrounds. Whereas Jung, the son of a Swiss Protestant minister, was steeped in fundamentalist and transcendental Protestantism, Freud found his cultural orientation in the Hebraic tradition but had little commitment to religious education or practice. He was determined to leave religion behind, if not do away with it altogether. Jung was considerably more accommodating, and even positively constructive, with respect to the possibility that his psychology might enrich the visionary traditions of religion.

Jung was an enthusiastic early disciple of Freud and became his official representative among the Swiss. It was Freud's goal to win the allegiance of Bleuler through their common disciple. Jung's mentor was a well-established scholar, famous for his revolutionary conceptual developments in the field of schizophrenia which moved from a solid base in the descriptive Kraepelinian approach to dynamic psychopathology. For Bleuler, schizophrenia was not a single organic disease but a syndrome that could also be the expression of psychological conflict (1950). But while sympathetic to Freud, Bleuler remained skeptical and aloof with respect to certain key

*The associationists held that information was stored—and retrieved—according to the common properties shared by diverse items. For example, a bat and an umbrella might be associated by blackness and/or by their winglike silhouettes. Leading proponents of associationism were Scottish psychologist Alexander Bain (1818–1903) and English philosopher John Stuart Mill (1806–73), who in turn took their inspiration from John Locke and David Hume.

aspects of psychoanalytic theory. And Jung himself underwent a progressive personal disenchantment with Freud and an intellectual alienation from his early enthusiastic alliance.*

On some substantive issues, Freud, ostensibly the more scientific, was paradoxically the more religious; while Jung, ostensibly the more mystically religious, was the more scientific. For example, the latter was initially and immediately skeptical about the heavy emphasis Freud placed upon the sexual instincts, and tried hard to get him to moderate this position. Freud viewed this and other efforts to influence his theory as resistance and strongly rejected this collegial criticism. Jung's reserve extended to the general theory of instincts and to the theory of dreams in which he found Freud overly rigid and overly pathological in emphasis. Jung's independence on these points rankled Freud, who was creating a movement that demanded adherence, not dissent. Freud's monolithic and monotheistic orientation was also clearly evident in the authoritarian style with which he led the psychoanalytic group.

The famous example of the moving cabinet which occurred at Freud's house in Vienna is emblematic of the difference in their positions. Jung was open to the possibility that a noise that both had heard but could not identify was caused by a cabinet moving mysteriously, perhaps even prophetically. Freud, rigidly mechanistic in his psychological thinking as well as in his physiological orientation, was appalled that Jung could admit to the possibility of extraphysical causes. As the tension between the two men grew, Freud used Jung's credulity as grounds for rejecting even his intellectually sound suggestions, and ultimately extruded Jung from his inner circle.

The view of Jung as gullible and credulous, which Freud promoted, is an oversimplification. Jung was admittedly more spiritually inclined and, like the great American psychologist William James (1842–1910), more cognizant of the spiritual dimension of human conscious experience. For both Jung and James, the reality was in the experience, and its cause was not easily reducible to instinctual forces, as Freud asserted. Jung and James were both curious about poltergeists, precognition, and extrasensory perception. But while both wondered whether there might be causes behind or beyond the physical, both were rigorous with respect to the methods of answering their questions. Pragmatic and experimental, they refused to accept any hypothesis that was not scientifically justified. Meanwhile, phenomena that could not be so explained were not to be denied existen-

*The history of this traumatic relationship is given in vivid and splendid detail in the Freud/Jung Letters (1974).

tial status, *ex cathedra.* Thus the apparent religiosity of James and Jung can obscure their fundamental scientific rigor. In contrast, Freud was consciously, openly, and superficially antireligious and evinced behavior that was unscientific and even antiscientific in an essentially religious defense of his own ideas.

The splintering of psychoanalysis that began with the Freud-Jung schism has continued to our day. For the modern dream scientist, this poses the problem of knowing *which* psychoanalytic dream theory is under experimental scrutiny. By criticizing Freud, this book aims to persuade all theorists who retain the assumption of a disguise-censorship in dream formation to consider the alternative of activation-synthesis. As will be made clear later, this theory does not entail giving up examination of dreams as revelatory of the dreamer's drives, fears, and associations. On the contrary, activation-synthesis acknowledges these processes as highly relevant but finds them, as Jung did, transparently and directly evident in the dream, and thus makes no distinction between manifest and latent content. Emphasis on the dream report itself as the scientific data of interest was shared by the early-twentieth-century investigators, to be discussed in chapter 3, who thought that as much could be learned by direct observation of sleep and dreaming (at the bedside and at night) as by eliciting recollections on the couch the next day.

3

Dream Investigation in the
Early Twentieth Century

Although, I suppose, we all spend a considerable proportion of our life in dreaming, it is curious to find how
many people, when they are asked such a question,
cannot answer it, or recall with clearness anything
about these aspects of their dream life.

—Mary Arnold-Forster
Studies in Dreams (1921)

For some must watch, while some must sleep
So runs the world away

—William Shakespeare
Hamlet (1601)

Freud's *Interpretation of Dreams* did not immediately inhibit the scientific investigation of dreaming. Thus, at the turn of the century, a few investigators were continuing the experimental tradition of Maury and Hervey de Saint-Denis and making interesting observations on the sleep of humans and even of animals. As the psychoanalytic movement gained momentum, it overshadowed the work of both of these investigators and of many of their predecessors, so that they have been largely lost to modern knowledge.

Sleep as an Instinct: Nicholas Vaschide

In 1914, the French physician Nicholas Vaschide (1873–1907) published his extensive observations on sleep and dreaming in *Le sommeil et les*

FIGURE 3.1
Nicholas Vaschide

This French sleep scientist was one of the first to make all-night observations of sleeping humans and to note periodic motor activation in association with dreaming. Based upon his correct inference of an active brain process, Vaschide hypothesized that sleep is a vital instinctual process in its own right and not just the absence of waking, as many previous philosophers had supposed. The Darwinian concept of adaptation was easily fitted to Vaschide's views, bringing the study of sleep into the mainstream of modern dynamic biology. *Source:* Rare Books and Print Department, Francis A. Countway Library of Medicine, Harvard Medical School. Dick Wolfe, Director.

rêves (see figure 3.1). Vaschide was aware of Freud's theoretical work and complimented it for its systematic character. He was impressed with Freud's capacity to deal with the subjective aspects of hypnagogic hallucinations and with the psychology of both dream amnesia and dream bizarreness. But he was not convinced that dreams should be interpreted as wish fulfillments because he was bothered, as was Freud, by the problem of unpleasant dreams. And Vaschide felt that the weakest point of Freud's theory was the necessity of distinguishing between manifest and latent content.

Vaschide was also inspired by the French psychiatrist Jean-Etienne-Dominique Esquirol (1772–1840), who championed the method of direct observation because he felt that only data can convince skeptics.

Esquirol sat by the bedside of sleeping mental patients and studied their facial expressions and movements in an attempt to predict the content of their dreams. He concluded, from the state of pulse and respiration, and from body movements and spoken words, that he could almost always decide whether an individual was dreaming. He further claimed that he could often predict the major themes of the content of a dream.

Vaschide decided to use the direct-observation method and repeat Esquirol's experiments in normal subjects. Using four young adults, Vaschide kept himself awake all night and manually recorded his observations of their behavior, heart rate, and respiration (1911). Periods of vasoconstriction and vasodilation alternated throughout the night. Although the duration of this vascular cycle is not mentioned by Vaschide, it may well have been the 90-minute non-REM–REM interval (see chapter 6). At times Vaschide interrupted his subjects' sleep to elicit reports of mental activity. He noticed that at sleep onset there were lapses of attention associated with a loss of synergy of the eye movements; hallucinations then began and were immediately vivid. These hypnagogic hallucinations became increasingly vague until, with true sleep onset, they disappeared altogether. Vaschide thus objectively confirmed what Maury had reported in his self-observation experiments.

Of his observations, Vaschide made the following poetic and prophetic summary: "The muscles have their own grammar, the contractions and tremulousness of the eyelids give you messages as do the contraction of the masseters, obicularis oris, and the temporal facial muscles, the nasal dilatation, the color of the face: all the physiology sketches an alphabet for you" (1914). Today it still remains for someone to follow up on these observations by making a systematic film or video record of facial expressions in sleep.

Monsieur Rousseau, one of Vaschide's subjects, had dreams occurring during two periods of the night while two other periods were dreamless. From sleep onset at 11:00 P.M. to 2:00 A.M., there were no dreams; from 2:00 to 4:30, there were abundant dreams; from 4:30 to 6:00, sleep was deep and dreamless; from 6:00 to 7:30, dreams again occurred. It seems possible that here, again, Vaschide was on the brink of discovering the periodic occurrence that is the non-REM–REM sleep cycle. He confirmed the tendency for the first three hours of sleep to be dreamless (a correlation we now know to be due to the predominance of non-REM sleep stage IV in those cycles) by studying two brothers with direct observation for two weeks. John, age thirteen, had deep dreamless sleep from 11:00 P.M. to 2:00 A.M.; from 2:00 to 5:00, dreams were easily elicited; while from 5:00 to 7:00, light dreamless sleep was observed. Henri, age ten, had deep sleep from sleep onset at 9:30 P.M. to 2:30 A.M.; from 2:30 to 6:00, dreams could be elicited; and light sleep followed from 6:00 to 8:00. Vaschide was impressed by the logic and the continuity of the dream content of both subjects. When interviews were conducted immediately following those awakenings (occasioned by the observation of facial movements), the dream content corresponded to the previously observed motor behavior of the sleeping subject. Unfortunately this important claim was neither quantitatively documented nor even anecdotally illustrated, and Vaschide was apparently not aware of possible bias or suggestion in these experiments.

He was interested in the failure of memory during sleep, and thought the amnesia for dreaming was far more impressive than had been previously assumed. The increased mnemonic capacity and the distortions of memory within the dream were also phenomena that he underlined. Most spontaneously recalled dreams were those that occurred either in the early morning or at sleep onset. But since his experimental results suggested that as much—if not more—dreaming actually occurred in the middle of the night, Vaschide correctly insisted upon the importance of direct observation and upon experimental awakening to gain an accurate notion of how much dreaming actually occurred. When they were not awakened, 87.5 percent of his subjects recalled nothing at all!

Vaschide also criticized existing dream theories because the dream content of spontaneously recalled dreams was contaminated by the confusion that typically occurs during awakening. He claimed that this confusion could be eliminated by using trained subjects.

Like his countrymen Maury and Hervey de Saint-Denis, Vaschide was interested in the incorporation of external stimuli into ongoing dreams. He played music to his subjects and then, having awakened them with a bright light, was able to obtain reports of music and dancing in the dreams. Noting an amnesia that occurred immediately on awakening and lasted from 1 second to 3 minutes before clearing, Vaschide thought of the awakening process as an organically determined analogue of aphasia.

Although Vaschide presented no systematic data in his book of over three hundred pages, he was obviously on the right track in emphasizing the importance of direct observation. His book is also valuable because of its tolerant, careful, and appreciative summaries of the state of the art of dream research in 1914, a period now effectively obliterated by the combined impact of psychoanalysis and modern dream research.

Vaschide thought that sleep had a positive function, with its own mechanisms, and was thus more than a cessation of brain activity, as most contemporary theorists believed. He believed sleep to be an instinctual function of the brain, and thus a preprogrammed process and not either a response to exhaustion or the result of brain depression by some substance built up during the waking period. Sleep might well serve the purpose of recovery from fatigue—and even of elimination of toxic substances built up during fatigue—but was not itself the result of such processes. Rather, sleep was an evolutionarily determined and active protection against such threats. These ideas of Vaschide's reflect the first impact of Darwin's thinking upon theories of sleep.

Since Vaschide's work reached the behavioral level of analysis, it may be worth considering his distinction between a *reflex* and an *instinct.* The reflex was the most advanced level of functional organization supported by the neurobiology of the 1890s; Freud relied heavily upon the instinct concept without carefully defining it and without distinguishing it from reflex behavior (see pages 54–55). For Vaschide, in contrast to reflex behavior, instinctual behavior was global as opposed to partial; it was plastic as against fixed; and instincts showed mutual dependence upon one another rather than evincing the mutual independence of the reflexes. For Vaschide, the internal state of the organism was relatively unimportant in determining whether a reflex would occur, but internal state was highly significant in determining the probability of instinctual behavior. Reflexes were neither plastic nor mental, whereas instincts were both. Reflexive behavior was limited to response to stimulation, whereas instincts were spontaneous. Reflexes were specific to the stimuli that evoked them, whereas instincts might be evoked by secondary or displaced stimuli.

In these terms, sleep qualified as an instinct: it was a complex global behavior; it was characterized by anticipatory investigation of a place suitable for its occurrence; it was preceded by a transitional phase of relaxation and/or falling asleep; it was associated with the psychological occurrence of dreams; it was reversible with the possibility of arousal.

A Dream Accountant: Mary Calkins

Mary Calkins (1863–1930) was an American psychologist who performed empirical studies of the character of human dreaming at Wellesley College. She analyzed samples of 335 and 298 dream reports of normal subjects sleeping at home (1893). In a precise replication of Vaschide's findings, most dreams appeared to occur in the morning; only about 11 percent of them could be vividly recalled, and another 34 percent exactly recalled; 30 percent were only fairly recalled, while 19 percent were poorly recalled. Calkins itemized the sensory modalities and found only two instances of gustatory imagery. This formal characterization of dreams, with notation of overrepresented and underrepresented sensations, is of direct relevance to the isomorphism agenda of modern dream science (see chapter 10). Calkins also pioneered intensive studies of individual subjects: a thirty-two-year-old male whom she studied for forty-six nights; and a twenty-eight-year-old female whom she studied for fifty-five nights (1893).

The Brain Activation Theory of Henri Beaunis

Another turn-of-the-century scientist who anticipated the methods and findings of the modern era was Henri Beaunis (1830–1921), pictured in figure 3.2. He published the results of an observational study in the *American Journal of Psychology* in 1903. Like Vaschide, Beaunis noted that dream recall was considerably better if another person awakened the sleeping subject. Beaunis concluded that he himself dreamed every night, though not continuously. He too noted that deep sleep of the early part of the night was dreamless, and that dreams were more easily and abundantly recalled from the second half of the night. With respect to the quality of his dream hallucinations, he established an order of clarity in which the visual modality was at the top of the list, followed by auditory and tactile sensations. Olfactory illusions never occurred, and gustatory illusions occurred only once.

That the auditory mode was considerably more uncommon than the visual mode impressed Beaunis because he spent so many of his waking hours listening to music. From this he concluded that dream content was determined as much by intrinsic factors as by the nature and quantity of previous experience. He also emphasized the predominance of what he called "motor images," which he thought must be fundamental to dream generation. In contrast to the diminution of audition during dreaming, he noticed that his dreams were characterized by considerably *more* motor activity than was his normally inert waking state. In his dreams, Beaunis had *many* more experiences walking, running, and climbing than he ever did awake. There were frightening falls and endless floating descents from precipices. There was even the wonderful experience of flying when he would rise above the ground with a sense of lightness and speed covering 15 to 20 meters at a stride, like an astronaut on the moon.

Beaunis was impressed that he never dreamed of writing though he spent a great deal of time writing when awake. Similarly, he never drew or modeled in his dreams despite his engaging abundantly in these activi-

FIGURE 3.2
Henri Beaunis

A member of the famous Nancy School of psychiatry, Henri Beaunis was imbued with Charcot's neurological orientation and shared his fascination with hypnotic states (which the French called *somnambulismes*). Believing that all mental states must reflect brain physiology, Beaunis made careful and astute observations of his own dreams and compared their formal qualities to his waking thoughts. By day quite sedentary, Beaunis the dreamer was athletically energized, a mental state change that he correctly surmised to derive from motoric brain activation that we now know to be integral to REM sleep. *Source:* Rare Books and Print Department, Francis A. Countway Library of Medicine, Harvard Medical School. Dick Wolfe, Director.

ties by day. In his dreams, he usually played an active role, as implied by his emphasis on increased motility. Objects and people were not as easily identified in dreams as they were in real life; they were nonetheless named, and often he attributed the names of famous people to the imaginary characters of his dreams. For Beaunis, the emotions of dreams were generally weaker than in the waking state, although pleasant feelings could be unusually intense. Beaunis even observed his own dreams long enough to notice changes in dream content associated with age. Between the ages of thirty and thirty-five, he had a great preponderence of what he called visual motor content, including flying; whereas after the age of fifty, he no longer experienced these magical movements. Likewise, at fifty, "grotesque" content stopped, and he more commonly experienced what he called intellectual dreams, with subjects more directly linked to his professional activity.

Beaunis summarized his astute observations as follows:

1. By taking the necessary precautions, one can be confident in the memories of dreams available upon awakening.
2. There must be three phases of the dream generation process:
   The *first phase* is a primary excitation which can be either external or internal; this leads to the secondary elicitation of a memory as the excitation spreads to the "cerebral centers."
   The *second phase,* the excitation of memory, can sometimes occur without any primary sensation due to a simple change in the pressure or chemistry of the blood, which may act directly on a cerebral center so as to trigger the occurrence of a memory as the starting point of a dream.
   In *phase three,* the activity then spreads to other centers of the brain: the sensory, the motor, and the association centers, where the full dream experience is elaborated.
3. Dream memories can be recent or remote or both mixed together.
4. In general, dream content corresponds to current wake-state activity, but there are remarkable exceptions to both the sensory and the motor representations of these.

Beaunis's view of dreaming as the result of activation of the brain, and its synthesis of information, is rationalistic. In postulating an excitatory event that may be both spontaneous and of central origin, he was, in 1903, as close as any writer since Wundt to escaping from the die-hard premise of a predominantly peripheral source of dream stimulation. Unfortunately, brain anatomy and physiology were then inadequate to give more precise form to this early version of the activation-synthesis hypothesis.

The Role of Motor Stimuli: J. Mourly Vold

In 1896, J. Mourly Vold (1850–1907), a Norwegian scientist at the University of Christiania, published a sixteen-page brochure describing his own dream theories and experiments. Like Beaunis, Vold was particularly interested in the motor elements of dreams and thought that the visual hallucinations of dreams might arise from nonvisual sources. Vold saw the visual hallucinations as resulting from the interaction of "cutaneo-motor stimuli" with prior visual experience. He studied forty subjects, both males and females, who slept with their fists clenched in specially designed gloves. After awakening them, Vold noted the descriptions of body position in the dream content and correlated these with the observed positions of the subjects' bodies. He found that motor input was potent in 50 percent to 80 percent of the cases, especially in good dreamers. Such subjects tended to be gregarious and were often theater goers.

In Vold's theory, cutaneous input led to the incorporation of the stimulated part into the dream, while motor input led to incorporation of the movement itself. For example, forced flexion of the feet led to dreams of running, climbing stairs, and walking on tiptoe. Vold also noted that the experimental setting was frequently directly incorporated into the dreams of his subjects.

Vold concluded his writing with intelligent speculation about the mechanism of dreams. As in epilepsy and hysteria, he supposed that the movements imagined by dreamers could reflect the central states of the brain. He believed that in sleep an abnormal muscle state could excite the motor cortex, thus causing a central motor command. This might subsequently excite Broca's center,* leading to the elaboration of a verbal model of the movement. Finally, a visual model of the movement could arise from spread of the excitation to visual centers. In seeking the origin of dream stimuli, Vold oscillated between favoring the periphery (the skin) and the center (the motor cortex).

Vold acknowledged that his theory was inspired in part by the sympathetic partial movements of subjects when observing the movements of others during waking. In sleep, the weak muscle tone allows the central representation of movement to act unopposed; likewise, the visual cortex is free of external input and hence freer to respond to internal stimuli. Echoing Hehmholtz (see chapter 1), Vold stated: "The nervous signals produced by the motor stages go not only to the motor cortex but also to the visual centers to produce an image" (1896).

Animal Models of Dreaming: Sante de Sanctis

In 1899, the Italian scientist Sante de Sanctis (1862–1935) published his book on dreams (I Sogni, Studi Psicologici e Chimici). (See figure 3.3.) His observations of the sleep of dogs led him to conclude that they dreamed. During their sleep, his canine subjects made distinctive movements of the muzzle and even barked. De Sanctis also observed the sleep of horses and

---

*Paul Broca (1824–1880) localized articulate speech to the left frontotemporal region of the brain in 1861.

FIGURE 3.3
Sante de Sanctis

Following in the footsteps of his fellow Roman, the poet-naturalist Lucretius, the psychiatrist Sante de Sanctis was the first modern scientist to make detailed observations of sleeping animals and to compare his findings with those made on humans. De Sanctis was convinced that in order to succeed, human psychophysiology needed animal models so that the brain processes underlying dreaming could be investigated. It is embarrassing to admit that, like Lucretius and de Sanctis, any one of us could have discovered REM sleep simply by watching the twitching paws and eyes of our pet dogs and cats. *Source:* Courtesy of Fabrizio D'Orrichi.

speculated that the episodes of muscular twitching seen in the sleep of that species were correlated with dreaming. Similar observations had been made, and an identical conclusion reached, by two other Italian predecessors not cited by de Sanctis. One was the Roman poet Lucretius who, in *De Rerum Natura* (44 B.C.), described the twitching feet of a dog as it lay asleep upon the hearth and concluded that it was chasing an imaginary rabbit. In the seventeenth century, Lucia Fontana also specifically noted the movement of the eyes during periods of animal sleep, and concluded that these were associated with dreaming.

De Sanctis's methods of record keeping and quantitative data analysis were primitive, and automatic recording techniques nonexistent. As a result, while the Italian scientist was correct in emphasizing the importance of direct observation, the detailed and credible description of sleeping and dreaming that was necessary to produce a viable alternative to Freud's speculative theories did not fully materialize.

Dream Control via Systematic Autosuggestion: Mary Arnold-Forster

Working in the tradition established by Hervey de Saint-Denis was Mary Arnold-Forster, an English gentlewoman of uncommon originality (1861–1951). For English language readers, her *Studies in Dreams* (1921) is a magnificent sequel to Hervey's less easily accessible work. The foreword was written by Morton Prince, an early exponent of Freud's work in the United States. Arnold-Forster describes the technique of systematic dream autosuggestion and dream content control. Before falling asleep, she just told herself to notice her subsequent dreams. And she did! She was particularly fond of flying dreams, and her book includes some vivid and amusing descriptions of her use of flying to achieve unusual social goals.

> The actual process by which I fly in my dreams has always been the same since the earliest days when I first fluttered down the nursery staircase. From what others have told me, there seems to be a good deal of variety in the manner in which different people fly. By giving a slight push or spring with my feet I leave the ground and fly without further effort, by a simple act of volition. A slight paddling motion by my hands increases the pace of the flight, and is used either to enable me to reach a greater height, or else for the purpose of steering, especially through any narrow place, such as through a doorway or window. If I am at all fatigued by a long flight, this motion of the hands is of great assistance and gives confidence and increased power. [1921, p. 39]

By teaching herself to wake up during dreams, Mary Arnold-Forster also anticipated Stephen LaBerge's current laboratory studies of dream lucidity (see chapter 14). She conditioned her intended arousal to an awareness of the bizarreness of a dream, and would tell herself that if crazy things were happening it must be a dream, and therefore she would wake herself up. In this way, she was able greatly to increase her access to dream content and also to gain control over the course of dream events. She found, as have all those who have attempted to replicate Hervey's methods, that, following self-arousal, it is possible to return to the same dream on going back to sleep. (See figure 3.4.)

FIGURE 3.4

Mary Arnold-Forster

Unaware of the earlier work of Alfred Maury and Hervey de Saint-Denis in France, the English psychologist Mary Arnold-Forster duplicated their self-observation and autosuggestion experiments on dreams. By means of diligent and attentive self-study, she was able not only to increase her dream recall but to develop an awareness of dreaming while in that state. From this base in trained dream consciousness, Arnold-Forster achieved dream control and her own personal goal of flying in dreams. Interpreting her findings with sound common sense, Arnold-Forster recognized that dreams are a natural concomitant of sleep and can be studied and understood without recourse to complex psychological theories. *Source:* From Mary Arnold-Forster, *Basset Down: An Old Country House* (London: Country Life Limited).

Mary Arnold-Forster recognized that dreams tend to occur periodically—a hypothesis she tested by alarm-clock self-awakenings. She also correctly inferred that dreams are of substantial duration, and not the instantaneous events that Freud and others had taken them to be. And, critical of the disguise-censorship hypothesis, Arnold-Forster believed dreams to be the psychological concomitant of a distinctive physiological state, and thought that Freud's emphasis on the psychopathological aspects of dream formation was exaggerated, if not completely erroneous.

Perhaps most important of all, she viewed dreaming as a unique state of mind which could be actively appreciated and even actively controlled—a position that the new activation-synthesis hypothesis affirms most comfortably and even enthusiastically, especially in the work of the contemporary sleep scientist Rosalind Cartwright, who views dreams as rehearsals for behavior. As such, dreams can be programmed so as to change attitudes and feelings. In viewing the dream as the subject's own active anticipation of the future rather than as a prophecy sent from a god, we have come full circle from animistic theism—to scientific humanism.

With the relevance of their work to so many currents of modern dream science, it is puzzling that the work of these pioneers is so seldom cited in the contemporary literature. There are two complementary reasons for this neglect: one is the commanding attention that psychoanalytic dream theory received as the Freudian movement grew and spread during the early decades of the century; the other is that it was not until the late 1930s that the techniques for making the study of human sleep and dreaming instrumental and objective were developed. And it was not until the middle of this century that definitive findings began to be made. In Part II, I will review these epochal discoveries and show how they led in the 1970s to the specification of a brain-based theory of dreaming that supports many hypotheses of the turn-of-the-century dream scientists.

PART II

DREAMING AND NEUROBIOLOGY

4

A Spark of Nature's Fire:
The Electrical Brain

Gie me ae spark o' Nature's fire,
That's a' the learning I desire
      —ROBERT BURNS
        "First Epistle to J. Lapraik" (1786)

If I do not greatly deceive myself, I have succeeded in
realizing . . . the hundred year dream of physicists and
physiologists, to wit, the identity of the nervous principle with electricity.
      —EMIL DU BOIS-REYMOND
        Researches on Animal Electricity (1849)

THE PROBLEM that forced Freud to abandon his *Project for a Scientific Psychology* was the inadequacy of knowledge about the brain. Perhaps more clearly than his experimentally minded contemporaries, Freud recognized two important aspects of this problem. First, he knew that a psychology that waited for brain science to supply the missing pieces might for a long time be impoverished. And, second, he was convinced that the information necessary to test and to complete any psychology, including psychoanalysis, would ultimately come from brain science. Just how quickly and abundantly this information has accrued, and how far it now allows us to go in developing a scientific psychology of dreaming, will be the subject of Part II.

EARLY NEUROSCIENCE

Since the classical period in Greece, debate on the location of mind (or soul, or spirit) alternated between the heart and the brain. While Aristotle (384–22 B.C.) speculated that the mind resides in the heart, it was Galen (A.D. 129–99) who first advanced experimental evidence for localizing the mind in the brain. Galen was born and educated in Pergamon in Asia Minor, the site of a shrine to the healing god, Asclepius. Distinguished personalities from the Roman empire made the pilgrimage to Pergamon to have their physical ailments diagnosed in accordance with their dreams.

In Galen's experiments on Barbary apes, squeezing the brain of an animal caused unconsciousness while squeezing the heart allowed the animal to remain conscious. By tying off the nerve from the brain to the vocal cords, he was able to demonstrate that brain controls the voice. He therefore concluded that the brain is the organic seat of consciousness, and further localized the soul to the ventricles within the brain by assuming that "psychic cells" make these ventricular spaces their home.

Galen's formulations, which integrated Platonism, Aristotelianism, Stoicism, and Epicureanism, and articulated the theory of the four humours,* became the dominant theoretical framework for medicine in the Middle Ages. With his humoral theory, Galen anticipated the modern specification of hormones as determinants of physical and mental states.

During the Renaissance, the Galenic theory of brain as the locus of mind was strengthened. The anatomical details of brain structure began to be described in detail as Leonardo da Vinci (1452–1519) and Vesalius (1514–64) began careful dissections of the human brain itself. (Galen's observations had been limited to experimental animals.) Thus began the modern era of empirical neuroscience. (See figure 4.1.) In 1614, the British anatomist Thomas Willis (1621–75) localized consciousness to the tissue of the brain and again emphasized the cerebral ventricles. That the ventricles so long remained the leading candidate for the substrate of soul was owing possibly to their wing-shaped form and their fluidity. We now know that the brain ventricles do contain a functionally significant liquid. This *cerebrospinal fluid* not only serves to cushion the brain against mechanical shock but may also serve as an internal bath through which important chemicals can percolate slowly from one part of the brain to another.

---

*Galen posited that health required an equilibrium among phlegm, black bile, yellow bile, and blood. In addition, a blood-bone material called *pneuma* guided many bodily processes.

The most famous historical statement of the relationship of brain to mind is that of René Descartes (1596–1650). On 10 November 1619, the French philosopher had a dream in which was revealed to him the outlines of a universal science that would link all human knowledge into an all-embracing wisdom. In making a firm distinction between the mechanics of body and of soul, Descartes became the father of modern mind-body dualism. His specification of the anatomical basis of the soul was nonetheless as precise as one could desire: the soul, for him, resided in the *pineal body,* a small nubbin of tissue above the brain stem and known as the "third eye."

In primitive animals, the pineal was a sort of light meter: like the retina, it was sensitive to light; but instead of faithfully copying visual objects (with the purpose of aiding navigation through visual space), the function of the pineal seemed to be to detect major changes in the level of external light so as to regulate major metabolic functions such as body-heat generation and skin color. We now know that even in higher mammals the pineal retains some of these functions. And although most mammals have lost the capacity to detect light levels (because of the thickness of the skull and overlying scalp), the pineal controls such hormones as melatonin, which contributes to the determination of skin color and to the regulation of energy levels and mood.

The history of neurology is a graveyard of well-intentioned efforts to clearly establish the cerebral basis of consciousness. Perhaps the best example is the flowering of phrenology in the late eighteenth and early nineteenth centuries. This pseudoscience ascribes specific aspects of the human personality to specific parts of the brain's surface (or cortex) whose relative size, it was thought, could be estimated by measuring bumps on the surface of the scalp. This technique, by which personality traits were assessed, was called *cranioscopy;* it led to a lucrative business and even to successful academic careers for such proponents as Franz Joseph Gall (1758–1828) and the Viennese Johann Kaspar Spurzheim (1776–1832).*

Only the perspective of time helps us recognize the fatuity of the phrenological effort. And yet there is no doubt that Gall, at least, was on the right track. He correctly assumed that in the brain the gray matter is composed of neurons and the white matter of fibers. His localizationist strategy was powerfully vindicated by the French neurologist Paul Broca's

---

*Spurzheim was invited to come to Harvard and was regarded as a great savant throughout his lifetime. He was buried, with full academic honors, in the Mount Auburn Cemetery in Cambridge, where his grave can be visited by anyone seeking relief from the hustle and bustle of Harvard Square.

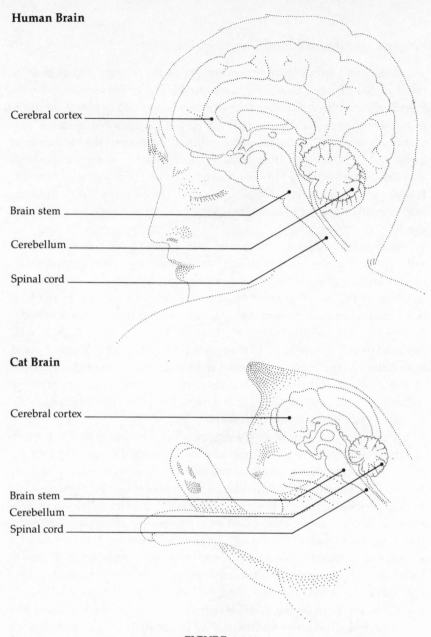

Human Brain

Cerebral cortex

Brain stem

Cerebellum

Spinal cord

Cat Brain

Cerebral cortex

Brain stem
Cerebellum
Spinal cord

FIGURE 4.1
Brains of man and cat

All mammals share several common brain structures. Between the spinal cord and the cerebral cortex lie the brain stem, a region specialized in the control of sleep, and the cerebellum, a large structure controlling posture and movement. By coordinating the activity of the cortex and spinal cord, the brain stem provides unifying control of our behavioral, physiological, and mental states. Whether we are awake, asleep, or dreaming depends upon the condition of nerve cells in the brain stem. In dreaming, for example, the brain stem activates the cortex (arousing the mind), shuts off the spinal cord (blocking body movement), and sends signals to the eyes (causing REMs), to the cerebellum, and to the visual brain (stimulating imagery). *Drawing by Barbara Haines.*

1861 definition of a speech center in the left hemisphere. The problem was with the bumps.

It seems possible that many of our contemporary theories about the mind may be equally pseudo-scientific. The substitution of invisible psychodynamic forces for the then only static neurologic structures may ultimately prove to have even less substance than phrenology for scientific understanding of human behavior and personality. Thus we must be constantly cautious lest we make unjustified and overly ambitious leaps from the still inadequate information that we have about brain function to the domain of psychology. Caution is especially important today because the pendulum is now swinging back to the position which favored the birth of phrenology and away from that favoring the growth of psychoanalysis. The end of the twentieth century will undoubtedly see the promulgation of many more neurobiologically based theories of mind. Let us hope that the data is rich enough to sustain their healthy growth and that modesty will protect us from ambitious excess.

The discovery of the electrical activity of nerves and of the brain itself was crucial to establishing the dynamic physical basis of consciousness and to explaining the distinctive differences between its waking and dreaming states.

This long line of investigation has its origins in the work of the English anatomist Charles Bell (1774–1842) and the French electrophysiologist François Magendie (1783–1855). Bell and Magendie were both concerned with conduction of the nervous impulse and with the electrical properties of peripheral nerves, those tiny wire-like structures that conduct signals to the muscles (producing movement) and from the sense organs and skin into the central nervous system (producing sensation). Together these two paths constitute the basis of reflex activity.

Bell's *New Idea of Anatomy of the Brain,* published in 1811, correctly differentiated the sensory and the motor roots of the spinal cord and thus established the structural basis of the reflex concept. This work, which has been called the Magna Carta of neurology, was expanded in 1830 as *The Nervous System of the Human Body.* In 1822, Magendie was able to demonstrate the essential irritability of nerves—first, by mechanically stimulating nerves and, later, by applying electricity to the nerves and causing the muscles to twitch. Magendie worked mostly with frogs whose spinal cord or peripheral nerves are easily exposed. He not only demonstrated the functional veracity of the reflex concept but showed that its excitability could be influenced by such drugs as strychnine and morphine.

The impact of Bell and Magendie's discoveries upon mind theorists was immediate and strong. For over a century, the controversy engendered by two philosophers, the German Gottfried Leibnitz (1646–1716) and the Englishman John Locke (1632–1704), had raged over the issues of whether consciousness depends upon sensation, and whether it is suspended or continuous during sleep. Continuing Leibnitz's postulate of innate ideas, Locke insisted upon the dependence of consciousness upon sensations and asserted that they continue to influence the mind in sleep though at a lower and sometimes even imperceptible level. Isaac Newton (1643–1727) had further proposed that sensation is mediated by the vibrations of a "very subtle spirit" through the nerves. Following Bell and Magendie, the spirit could be identified as electricity and later further analyzed as the flux of ions across the nerve membrane. By the early nineteenth century, the reduction of mind to brain had begun in earnest.

BRAIN STRUCTURE: THE NEURON

I now turn to a contemporary of Freud's whose work in neurobiology is well known but whose interests in psychological phenomena have been almost completely ignored: the Spanish neuroanatomist Santiago Ramón y Cajal (1852–1934), whose studies of nerve cells led him to develop the neuron doctrine for which, in 1906, he was awarded a Nobel Prize in physiology and medicine (see figure 4.2). Ramón y Cajal is also the father of modern neurobiology, a field of science that has flourished as the study of individual nerve cells and their dynamic interactions; and most of the scientific information presented in this book derives in some direct way from his epochal contributions.

Hypnosis and Sleep

Ramón y Cajal and Freud had reciprocal careers: the latter, with his early interest in neurobiology and, later, psychology; and the former, who put aside his early interest in psychology to devote himself exclusively to neurobiology. The psychological phenomenon of central interest to both men was hypnosis. Long recognized as a quasi-experimental method for inducing an altered state of consciousness in human subjects, hypnosis clearly demonstrated the extraordinary degree of plasticity of the human mind. It suggested, to Ramón y Cajal and to Freud, an equally dynamic organic substrate of these impressive behavioral and psychological mani-

FIGURE 4.2
Santiago Ramón y Cajal

The Spanish neuroanatomist is known as the father of modern neurobiology because his description of the neuron as a discrete functional unit allowed the brain
to be understood in cellular terms. A versatile and energetic man, Ramón y Cajal
also practiced hypnosis and was both an avid amateur photographer and a fancier
of paella, which he sought out on his long Sunday walks in the country. While
excited by the prospect that his view of the brain as a colony of neurons might one
day help resolve the mystery of consciousness, Ramón y Cajal was skeptical and
remained a dualist. *Source:* Rare Books and Print Department, Francis A. Countway
Library of Medicine, Harvard Medical School. Dick Wolfe, Director.

festations. At the end of the nineteenth century, it was through the study of hypnosis that both neurology and psychiatry saw the opportunity to change from relatively static descriptive disciplines to truly dynamic ones. And now that after nearly a hundred years each field has achieved a certain dynamism, it is appropriate to assess the ways in which the dynamic formulations of each are formally similar. Formally similar dynamics of mind and brain could suggest a common set of rules to explain the phenomena of interest to both neurology and psychiatry. I aim not for an eliminative reduction but for an integration in the tradition of Freud's abandoned *Project for a Scientific Psychology.*

The man who inspired Freud, and led him first to consider a shift in his own career, was the Parisian neurologist Jean-Martin Charcot (1825– 93), who demonstrated—and attempted to explain—the phenomenon of hypnosis in his famous clinic at the Salpêtrière Hospital. Freud spent several months visiting Charcot's clinic in 1885. While Charcot did not, of course, discover hypnosis, he brought it into the orbit of academic medicine.* The very fact that the hypnotic state was called *somnambulism,* and those in the state *somnambulists,* indicates the close relationship of concepts of hypnotic phenomena to sleep states.

It is thus in a comparative spirit that I view the shared interest of Freud and Ramón y Cajal and connect it to my own perspective on hypnotic phenomena. Hypnosis is an artificially altered state of consciousness. Sleep is a naturally altered state of consciousness. Can similar rules govern the transition of state change in both the experimental and the natural conditions? The fact that induction of both hypnotic and sleep states involves rhythmic stimulation and eye fixation may not be a coincidence. Both procedures may help to gain access to and control over the brain-stem centers that appear to be fundamental to conscious-state regulation.

Hypnotic-trance induction, like sleep induction, involves abandonment of volitional control with the implicit relative abeyance of cortically mediated cognitive processes. In hypnosis, another individual's will and idea is substituted or transplanted into the now susceptible and plastic brain-mind of the recipient. In the natural state changes of sleep, cortical processes relent as other parts of the brain-mind become active. In both sleep and hypnosis, the emerging states are characterized by a relatively high ratio of unconscious to conscious mental processes.

Freud was particularly impressed with the release from conscious control of what he took to be sexual impulses during both the hypnotic

---

*A fascinating and well-documented account of the development of hypnosis and related phenomena leading to the modern concept of the unconscious mind is given in Henry Ellenberger's monumental *The Discovery of the Unconscious* (1970).

and the dreaming states. The fact that most of Charcot's subjects—like most of the famous somnambulists throughout history—were women may be a historical and cultural accident. Or it may be a historical-cultural exaggeration of a biological propensity. Women may be either biologically and/or culturally more in touch with their internal states, more plastic, and hence more easily able to regulate their internal states (especially in response to external suggestion). Feminists might well view this trait as representing either the constitutional superiority of women with respect to intuition and sensitivity or women's socially defined role as passive instruments of the male will.

Hysteria and hypnosis were both in the air and women were susceptible to both states in the 1890s, the decade during which Ramón y Cajal was formulating his neuron doctrine while Freud was developing his psychoanalytic theory of the unconscious. Ramón y Cajal actually practiced hypnosis at the same time that he was beginning his work in fundamental neurobiology. With respect to the early period of his work, the Spanish neuroanatomist made the following amusing observation:

My time during my residence in the Valencian capital (the years 1884 to 1887) was not devoted entirely to hard and feverish labor in the laboratory. The artistic and philosophic furrows of my brain were also employed. It was necessary to allot to each cell its rations and to each reasonable instinct a convenient opportunity for exercise. In the guise of relaxing agents for neurons in danger of hardening from disease, I developed 2 kinds of amusements: picture taking excursions and the experimental study of hypnotism, a budding science which at that time was attracting the curiosity of and inspiring a passionate interest in the minds of the public. [1937, pp. 310–11]

With other young colleagues, Ramón y Cajal formed the Committee for Psychological Investigation and confirmed the experimental observations of Charcot, Ambroise-Auguste Liébeault, Hippolyte Bernheim, and Beaunis (all members of the Nancy school of psychiatry) regarding hypnosis, acquiring what he humorously referred to as his "naturalization papers in science" (1937, p. 312).

For those of us who work in well-equipped institutions today, it is humbling to find that Ramón y Cajal did not only his anatomical work but also his psychological studies at home: "Through my house, converted for the purposes into a clubhouse, there streamed the most remarkable kinds of hysterics, neurasthenics, maniacs, and even accredited spiritualistic mediums" (p. 313). He became accomplished at establishing hypnotic trance in normals and in successfully communicating hypnotic suggestions to patients:

The fame of certain wonderful cures accomplished in cases of hysteria and neuras-
thenia spread rapidly through the city. Crowds of unbalanced people, even those
completely mad, flocked to consult me. That would have been a fine opportunity
to create for myself a lucrative practice if my dispositions and tastes had been
suitable. However, having satisfied my curiosity I dismissed my patients to whom
naturally I did not choose to send any bills. I was sufficiently recompensed if they
lent themselves docilely to my experiments. [p. 314]

Ramón y Cajal's Neuron Doctrine

Ramón y Cajal's own institutional opportunities for a research career
were scarcely more favorable than Freud's in Vienna. In 1880, at the age
of twenty-six and following the model of the great anatomist Louis-An-
toine Ranvier (1835–1922), Ramón y Cajal set up a histology lab in the attic
of his house in Zaragoza, Spain. He made most of his original preparations
using the Golgi silver-impregnation method* and inexpensive technical
equipment. His great strengths were persistence and self-reliance; and he
worked from nine in the morning until midnight with intense concentration and a remarkable combination of observational and analytic skill.
Ramón y Cajal was one of those rare individuals who combine an aesthetic,
almost artistic response to the forms of nature with a rigorously scientific
intellectuality about its structure and function. Since he was capable of
thinking physiologically at the same time that he made his anatomical
observations, he was at once structural and dynamic in orientation.

Ramón y Cajal's effervescent enthusiasm applied to all things that he
saw and did. He referred to the nervous system as the "masterpiece of life"
and described a successful experiment in histology thus: "What a delight
it was, when by dint of much patience, we succeeded in isolating completely a neuroglia element, with its typical spider like form, or a colossal
motor neuron from the spinal cord. Its robust dendrites and axis cylinder
free and well-separated!" (1937, p. 305).

The phrase "free and well-separated" indicates that Ramón y Cajal
was working within a framework of thought that assumed all of the
elements were continuously connected as a syncytium; and further, that
the physical continuity between the elements was established by protoplasmic bridges. Since early measurements of nerve-impulse conduction
had indicated that there were considerable delays not easily attributable
to a physically continuous system, Ramón y Cajal pointed out, "Nobody

---

*Camillo Golgi (1844–1926) discovered that—in contrast to other stains then in use—
silver salts stained individual neurons selectively but completely. Thus, while only a few cells
imbibed the silver salts, they drank their fill and could be observed in their entirety: the cell
bodies, the dendrites, and the axons were all visible, so that the processes between the
neurons could be traced.

could answer this simple question: How is the nervous impulse transmitted from a sensory fiber to a motor one?" (1937, p. 305).

In enunciating the neuron doctrine, Ramón y Cajal made four essential points: (1) that the nerves end as *free arborizations,* not as an interconnected network; (2) that the ramifications are *applied closely* to dendrites and cell bodies, but are not continuous with them; (3) that the cell body and the axon must participate actively in the *conduction of the impulse* and not play just a nutritive role; and—the key conclusion— (4) that the nervous impulse is *somehow ferried across the contact points* between cells and does not pass from cell to cell by direct and continuous conduction.

At the time that Ramón y Cajal issued this set of statements, they constituted virtual heresy. In suggesting that each individual nervous element or cell is a discrete structure and (as we now know) completely bounded by a continuous membrane setting each individual element off as a functional unit, he was basing his conclusions mainly on the sorts of anatomical preparation that he was able to make and carefully draw. He correctly concluded that the impulse proceeds from the *dendrites* (the receptive or sensory elements of the cell) to the cell body and is then propagated down the *axon* (the effective or motor side of the cell). The idea that each cell is discrete logically forced his conclusion that the nerve impulse must somehow be transmitted across the contact junction. The concepts of the synapse and of synaptic transmission were crucial to the emerging reflex paradigm, successfully exploited by the English physiologist Charles Sherrington, as I shall discuss in the next section. Both Ramón y Cajal (in 1906) and Sherrington (in 1932) were awarded Nobel Prizes for their fundamental contributions to modern cellular biology.

Ramón y Cajal's observational skills were related to his aesthetic response to nervous structure; indeed, he insisted that all of his students take lessons in watercolor painting (see figure 4.3) so as to refine their capacity to represent their observations:

If our study is concerned with an object related to anatomy or natural history, etc., observation will be accompanied by sketching, for, aside from other advantages, the act of depicting something disciplines and strengthens the attention, obliging us to cover the whole of the phenomenon studied and preventing, therefore, details from escaping our attention which are frequently unnoticed in ordinary observation. In the natural sciences we can only satisfy ourselves with knowing form or structure when we are able to delineate them easily and in detail. This is all the more true because many morphological studies are incomprehensible without drawings. The great Cuvier* had reason to affirm that without the art of drawing,

*Georges Cuvier (1769–1832) was a French zoologist and statesman who established the sciences of comparative anatomy and paleontology.

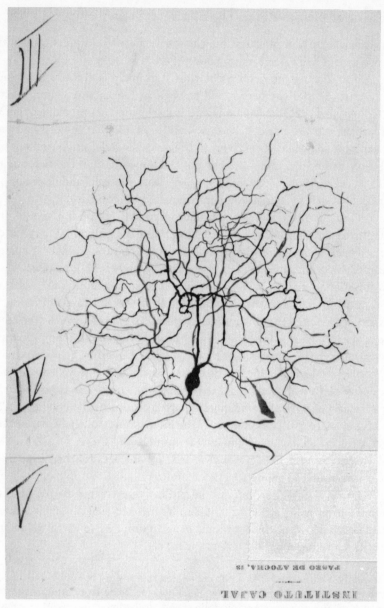

FIGURE 4.3
Neuron drawing

Rafael Lorente de Nò made this India ink drawing of an individual neuron on Cajal Institute (Madrid) notepaper. The silver stain introduced by Camillo Golgi enabled anatomists to visualize the spiderlike array of processes emanating from the neuronal cell body (or soma) and collecting information (as dendrites) or conveying information (as axons). Ramón y Cajal preferred an active, analytic mode of visual representation to the more accurate but passive and neutral technique of photography, and thus trained Lorente de Nò and his other students in the technique of pen-and-ink and watercolor illustrations. The Roman numerals refer to various layers of the cerebral cortex. *Source:* Courtesy of Rafael Lorente de Nò, Department of Otolaryngology, UCLA School of Medicine.

natural history and anatomy would have been impossible. It is not without reason that all great observers are skillful in sketching. [1937, pp. 134–35]

In this context, it is interesting to note that Freud's *Interpretation of Dreams* (which in the paperback edition runs over seven hundred pages) is devoid of either detailed descriptions or illustrations of actual data. There are no verbatim dream reports; and the idea of illustrating dreams apparently never occurred to Freud. Although dream drawing was a technique already extensively used by Hervey de Saint-Denis, the French amateur student of dreams (see pages 34–42), Freud did not mention it either in his account of his own dream recording techniques or in his review of the approaches of others.

Ramón y Cajal went on to point out other advantages of visual illustration:

If our studies pertain to either microscopic or macroscopic morphology it will be essential to illustrate the descriptions with figures copied in exact detail. No matter how exact and minute the verbal description may be, it will always be inferior in clarity to a good illustration. This is true because a graphic representation of the object observed guarantees the exactness of the observation itself and sets up a precedent of inestimable value for the one who attempts to confirm our assertions. [1937, p. 159]

Freud, as I have said, saw the nervous system as a syncytium of cells connected to each other by protoplasmic bridges—a concept that solved the problem of continuity since, in it, the flow of information was unimpeded. Then Ramón y Cajal's neuron doctrine interrupted this bridge—at the membrane boundary of every cell. Swept out with the syncytium were all of the physiological notions of energy and information associated with it.* Ramón y Cajal made it clear that the nervous system is a collection of independent but interdependent neurons, each of which is functionally discrete (see figure 4.4). Each has its own energy source and its own capacity for handling information.

It is not unfair, I believe, to contrast the approaches of Ramón y Cajal and Freud with respect to the weight that each placed upon detailed observation as against interpretive speculation—a basic distinction underlying the subsequent credibility of their contributions. The Spanish neuroanatomist's work was recognized to be classical in its time and has, with the succeeding nearly one hundred years, assumed an almost monu-

---

*In the early 1890s, Ramón y Cajal's theory was controversial. The German anatomists His and Kolliker opposed it. By the time it was accepted, Freud had already written his *Project for a Scientific Psychology*.

mental character; but it is still, I daresay, practically unknown to the literate public. The initial professional skepticism that greeted Freud's work was, by contrast, successfully converted into uncritical world acclaim so that his name is now a household word.

Ramón y Cajal shared with Freud the goal of a scientific psychology, and saw his neuron doctrine as an important step forward in its foundation:

Can it be that within our organic edifice there dwell innumerable inhabitants which palpitate feverishly with impulses of spontaneous activity without our taking any notice of them? And our much talked of psychological unity? What has become of thought and consciousness in this audacious transformation of man into a colony of polyps? It is certain that millions of autonomous organisms populate our bodies, the eternal and faithful companions of glories and of toils, of which the joys and sorrows are our own; and certain also that the existence of entities so close to us passes unperceived by the ego; but this phenomenon has an easy and obvious explanation if we consider that man feels and thinks by means of his nerve cells and the *not I,* the true external world begins for him at the frontiers of the cerebral convolutions. [1937, p. 296]

While Ramón y Cajal's phrase "unperceived by the ego" resembles Freud's notions of the unconscious, the former's "impulses of spontaneous activity" indicate that he saw the "unconscious" as an *intrinsic* aspect of the brain-mind system, whereas Freud's unconscious depended upon the external world for its energy and its information.

There is a tone to Ramón y Cajal's writing that is both reductionistic and dualistic. On the one hand, the human being has been transformed into a colony of polyps. For Ramón y Cajal, consciousness somehow arises out of the activity of this myriad of neural elements which, as an ensemble, possess spontaneous activity and information-producing capabilities. The idea that humans feel and think by means of nerve cells might be reduced to the idea that thinking and feeling are a complex activity of nerve cells. The subtle notion that the "not I" begins "at the frontiers of the cerebral convolutions" could be said to be an equation of the I, or ego, with the cerebral cortex itself. Updating Descartes, Ramón y Cajal would say: "I am (among other things) my cortex. I have a cortex; therefore, I think I am." He, nonetheless, did conclude that the wall between the subjective and the objective would always remain impenetrable. But, in laying the foundation for modern cellular biology, Ramón y Cajal himself effectively pierced that wall (see chapter 5).

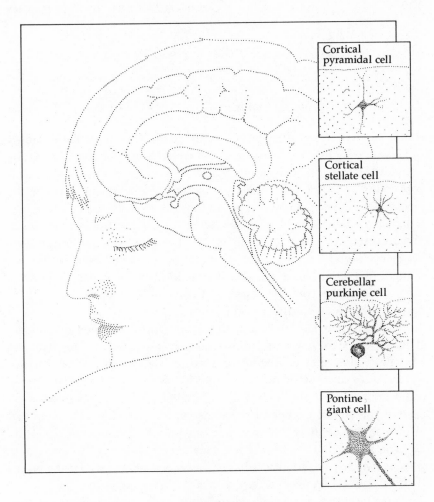

FIGURE 4.4

Neuronal types

While all nerve cells have the same general form, the size, shape, and disposition of their cell bodies and processes vary according to their specialized functional roles. Distantly projecting neurons, the cortical pyramidal and the pontine giant cells shown have large cell bodies and long, thick axons that conduct signals rapidly to the muscles. The locally projecting cortical stellate cell is much smaller, while the treelike branching of the cerebellar Purkinje cell dendrite is adapted to receive information about posture and movement from thousands of incoming neurons. *Drawing by Barbara Haines.*

Brain Function: The Action Potential

The Role of the Action Potential

In the late nineteenth century, at about the same time that Ramón y Cajal was establishing clearly that the *structural* unit of the brain is the individual nerve cell or neuron, the work of several physiologists was converging to indicate that the *functional* unit of the system might be the electrically propagated impulse—or *action potential.* While the action-potential concept has a long history, extending back to the fundamental work in basic electricity of Luigi Galvani (1737–98) and Alessandro Volta (1745–1827), even longer has been the search for an elemental agent of life and motion: this quest began at least with the Ionic philosophers of the sixth century B.C. and is commemorated by the name *ion,* given to the charged particles whose flux is the action potential.

The physiological application of basic electrical knowledge to understanding the excitability of animal tissues was pioneered by Bell and Magendie. They showed that nervous tissue does indeed conduct electricity and does so in a functionally significant way: when the sciatic nerve of a frog was electrically excited, muscle twitches could be observed in the limb of the animal supplied by that nerve. By 1875, Richard Caton had already shown not only that the nerves are wire-like conductors of electrical energy, but that the brain itself generates that energy. By applying a voltmeter to the surface of the brain, Caton was able to record the waves that we now call *electroencephalogram,* or EEG (see chapter 5).

This information was immediately integrated by Ramón y Cajal into his neuron doctrine. He recognized that the neuron might be at once a transducer, a conductor, and a transmitter of electrical impulses. Stimulus energy impinging upon the organism from the outside world could be converted into electrical signals: the *transducer function.* The transduced electrical signals are then propagated to the cell body and then down the axon: the *conductor function.* One cell influences another by converting these conducted electrical signals into chemical messages: the *transmitter function.* Furthermore, he correctly deduced that the flow of information might be from the dendrites to the cell body and then along the axon to the next cell.

In deducing that the flow of information is from the dendrites to the cell body, Ramón y Cajal set the stage for a cellular analysis of the reflex arc by Charles Sherrington (1861–1952), who worked out its details in the spinal cord of mammals (see figure 4.5). The English physiologist showed that *effector neurons* (those cells that send their fibers and impulses directly to the muscles of the limb) can be influenced to fire (by excitation) or not to fire (by inhibition). External influences are conveyed *to* the effector neurons by nerves from the same or opposite limbs. Sherrington summarized this interplay of excitation and inhibition, increasing or decreasing the excitability of final common-path motoneurons, in his classic work, *The Integrative Action of the Nervous System,* published in 1906.

Although Sherrington could elicit reflexes and correctly inferred their electrical basis, the measurement of the small and extremely rapid signals by which neurons communicate with each other depended upon technical developments in electronics. Just as the neurons are microscopically small in size, so their signals are infinitesimally small in energy. Axons have diameters on the order of thousandths or ten-thousandths of a meter *(microns)*—as small as a strand of hair split into one hundred filaments. Action potentials have voltages in the range of thousandths of volts *(microvolts)*—or so small that a pocket flashlight battery could easily energize five thousand such power sources.

To record the electrical activity of individual nerve cells, it was necessary either to increase the voltages sufficiently to drive a recording apparatus, or to design an ultra-lightweight recorder that could be driven by very low energy signals. Two important technical innovations made action-potential recordings possible. The first was the development, in 1903, of the string galvanometer by the Dutch physiologist William Einthoven (1860–1927) to record the activity of cardiac muscle, which is not only electrically excitable but generates its own rhythm. Since many cardiac cells discharge their action potentials in unison, it was possible, even with an electrode placed on the surface of the body, to pick up the signals and make what is now called an *electrocardiogram* (EKG). The string galvanometer was a voltmeter of extremely low mass that could be moved by the millivolt signals generated with each heartbeat. For his discovery, Einthoven was awarded the Nobel Prize in 1924.

The second breakthrough occurred in the early 1930s. Edgar Adrian and Brian Matthews, working in the physiological laboratories of Cambridge University, developed a prototype of the instrument that we now call the *oscilloscope,* a standard recording device for electrophysiology. Instead of having the nervous signal move a very fine string, the oscilloscope let the position of an essentially weightless electron beam be the indicator of voltages. The low-energy signals from nerves were applied to a magnetic field through which the beam was caused to move back and forth before falling on the back surface of a luminescent screen. This electron beam (or cathode ray) excited the phosphorescent material on the screen,

FIGURE 4.5
Charles Sherrington

By analyzing spinal reflexes in cellular detail, this English neurophysiologist provided the functional accompaniment for Ramón y Cajal's neuron doctrine and laid
the groundwork for an explosive growth of knowledge of the brain. But while the
reflex concept fostered an understanding of how one processes externally imposed
information, it did not account for the spontaneous activity of the brain-mind and
therefore led to inaccurate and even erroneous views of sleep and dreaming. Sherrington predicted, for example, that neuronal activity would be found to subside
or even cease in the absence of stimulation during sleep. Quite the opposite is the
case in REM sleep, when brain cells buzz and dreams are created. *Source:* Rare Books
and Print Department, Francis A. Countway Library of Medicine, Harvard Medical
School. Dick Wolfe, Director.

making it visible. When small voltages were applied to the magnets, the
beam was deflected vertically.

The development of the oscilloscope led to an explosion of neurobiological studies. The action potential of whole nerves was recorded and
found to be compounded of several discrete waves, with each component
related to the diameter of the underlying nerve fiber. Smaller fibers were

found to conduct impulses slowly, with action potentials smaller in size and of greater width than the larger fibers, which conduct rapidly and have larger amplitudes. Adrian and Matthews were also interested in knowing whether the voltages that Caton had recorded from the brain were the envelope of individual action potentials.

The Ionic Hypothesis of Action-Potential Generation

Although Adrian was able to record individual action potentials using fine-tipped electrodes called *microelectrodes* (actually fine-sharpened insect pins insulated to their tips with lacquer), a complete understanding of the action potential awaited the development of special preparations and special techniques for recording voltages between the inside and the outside of the cells. The technique of *intracellular recording* has enabled scientists such as Alan Hodgkin, T. H. Huxley, and Bernard Katz to demonstrate that the action potential is caused by the rapid influx and efflux of elemental ions across a semipermeable cell membrane. The award of the 1963 Nobel Prize in physiology and medicine honored the techniques of the three Englishmen as well as the philosophical intuitions of the Ionian Greeks.

The energy source and the signal source of the structural unit of the nervous system—the elements that Freud lacked in his *Scientific Psychology*—were thus found to be intrinsic to each and every neuron. Sodium, an important elemental constituent of blood plasma, is a derivative of salt water. The neuron contains an active pump capable of excluding the sodium ion across its membrane, which is punctured by tiny holes. This active pumping process results in an increased concentration of sodium ions outside, and of potassium ions inside, the cell. The chloride ion, the other half of the salt molecule, is also involved in this mechanism, which takes advantage of the membrane's impermeability to protein whose molecules are too large to squeeze through its holes. By constantly pumping the ions in one direction, the nerve cell creates a concentration gradient; and since the ions are charged particles, this concentration gradient also constitutes an electrical potential.

A constant energy tension is thus developed by each cell. This tension, called the *membrane potential,* is on the order of one tenth of a volt (90 millivolts). The inside of the cell is negative with respect to the outside of the cell. If the permeability of the membrane of the cell is changed, the membrane potential changes rapidly. When the cell is subjected to an excitatory electrical signal, sodium ions rush in and potassium ions rush out of the cell. This rapid change of ionic balance is the basis of the action potential. It spreads, as Ramón y Cajal correctly inferred, from the dendrites to the cell body and then down the axon. In this way an excited cell produces a unitary message that can be transmitted to other cells. And thus is animal motion engendered: not by air, as the Ionians supposed; and not by an immaterial psyche, as the idealists thought; but by ionic flux.

If a neuron receives an inhibitory message from a neighboring cell, the concentration gradient between the inside and the outside is rendered more electrically negative. More sodium is pumped out and more potassium is pumped in. This process of inhibition (or *hyperpolarization*) makes the cell less likely to fire an action potential. By this means the system can become less receptive to external information.

These discoveries and their detailed documentation were made by Alan Hodgkin and T. H. Huxley just before the Second World War. A key innovation was the use of very large nerve cells, the giant axon of the squid which—in one fell swoop—converts a sensory stimulus into an escape reaction. The squid's nerve cells are so large that an experimentor can actually squeeze the protoplasm out of the inside of the tubular membrane like a roll of toothpaste. The gutted membrane retains its capacity to concentrate ions. Electrodes can be inserted inside the cell, and the voltages across the cell membrane can be measured while the cell is electrically stimulated. By means of special electrodes, it was possible to measure the ionic concentration of sodium, potassium, and chloride inside and outside the cell, and to show that when the action potential is conducted, the ions move across the membrane. The precise quantitative description of these ionic fluxes in 1947 constitutes one of the landmarks of modern biology.

The mathematical description of the dynamics of action-potential generation depended upon another critical technical innovation in modern sleep and dream research—the digital computer. In order to solve the differential equations that resulted in the mathematical description of action-potential generation, extremely time-consuming calculations were required. Without the computer, developed during the research lull forced by the Second World War, these mathematical formulae would have taken at that time about twenty years to solve by hand.

The second great cornerstone of modern neurobiology was thus put into place at roughly the same time that dream theory was beginning to rediscover its moorings in neurobiology. During the subsequent decades, it was discovered that neurons use action potentials to produce excitation and inhibition, and thus conspire to bring the brain into a state of functional activity necessarily associated with dreaming.

NEURONAL COMMUNICATION: THE SYNAPSE

The development of knowledge of the action potential provided a physical basis for signal generation by the individual elements: when a given cell is sufficiently excited, it discharges an action potential, and this signal spreads over the cell's surface; when light falls on the retina, it causes the retinal ganglion cells to depolarize and to generate action potentials. But how these local electrical events are able to affect the neighboring cells then became a problem for research. Does the cell transmit its electrical energy directly across the gap between cells? Or is this information transferred in some other way? (See figure 4.6.)

Expanding anatomical knowledge suggested that the cell-to-cell junctions (or "contact barriers," as Freud called them) were specialized. These gaps became known as *synapses* from the Greek *synapsis,* meaning "contact." Ramón y Cajal had already indicated that the flow of information within the cell might be from the fine sensory terminals of the cell (the *dendrites*) to the cell body, or *soma,* and then down the fiber (or *axon*) to its terminals. And now we know that communication across the synaptic gaps occurs as an electrical signal, which arrives at axonal terminal endings, is converted into a chemical message, which then diffuses across into the synaptic gap or cleft. When these messenger molecules, called *neurotransmitters,* reach the postsynaptic cell membrane, they cause a change in the nature of that membrane such that the neighbor cell is either made more likely to fire *(excited)* or less likely to fire *(inhibited).*

The specialization of the synapse includes vesicles found in the terminals of the pre-synaptic cell, which are actually the storage spaces for the chemical substances that transmit the neuronal messages. The pre-synaptic cell synthesizes its own chemical messengers (either in the cell body or in its terminals) and then stores them in tiny packets (called *vesicles*) so that they are ready for release when the appropriate electrical signal arrives. Release involves a movement of the vesicle to the membrane edge and then a dissolution of a small portion of the membrane with release of the chemical into the synaptic cleft. This process, called *exocytosis,* is a key cellular event in the liberation of the neurotransmitters.

All of these complex events proceed effortlessly and instantaneously. They are the truly unconscious brain functions that we somehow experience as mind. As I have said, the electrical signal travels over the surface of the cell membrane at speeds of up to 100 meters per second, but is slowed at the synaptic gap. The transmission of information across the

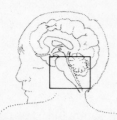

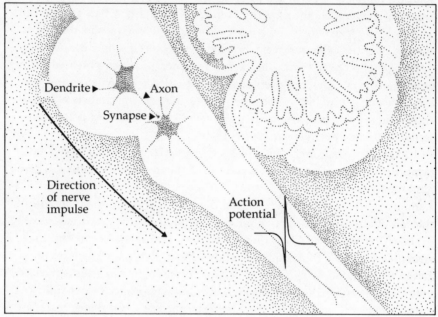

Dendrite ▶

Axon ◀

Synapse ▶ ▶

Direction
of nerve
impulse

Action
potential

Excitation

 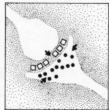  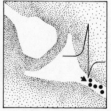

Inhibition

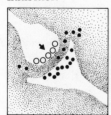 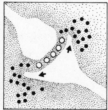

synapse may take 5 ten-thousandths of a second (or 0.5 milliseconds), an appreciable delay in the flow of information within the nervous system. These synaptic slowdowns contribute mightily to determining the speed of such vital functions as reaction time—for example, the startle response. (Evolution must already be considering a faster process if we moderns are to survive the motor vehicle!)

When the pre-synaptic cell has released its neurotransmitter into the synaptic cleft, it has not quite finished its job: it goes on to reabsorb any of the material that is available to it for re-use. But the main point of release is to effect the postsynaptic cell, and this is done by means of a clever matching device: the molecules released as neurotransmitters fit into specific modifications of the postsynaptic membrane called *receptors*. These receptors are actually proteins in the cell membrane which attract and hold the transmitter; they thus form a chemical complex of transmitter and receptor protein, which then has the capacity to alter the postsynaptic membrane so as to open small pores (called *ionophores*), thus allowing one or another species of ion to cross the membrane. In some cases, the pores close up, making the membrane *less* permeable to these ions.

For example, the chloride ion may be excluded by closing its ionophore. The cell will then become less permeable to chloride and less easily excited. This is one basis of the process of inhibition which actively prevents information flow across the contact junctions. When the organism is ready to sleep, for example, it would be possible to reduce the flow of information from the outside world and to exclude actively those stimuli that were normally arousing. The concept of the synapse and of neurotransmission is vital to an understanding not only of how sleep occurs, but also of how dreams are generated once sleep has been established. It is by virtue of dynamic changes in the neurotransmission systems of the brain that these behavioral and psychological states are mediated.

FIGURE 4.6

Action potential

Nerve cells communicate with one another by means of chemicals (called *neurotransmitters*) that are released from the endings of their axons by electrical signals (called *action potentials*). Each action potential is a reversal of voltage that spreads over the surface of the cell with lightning speed as minute particles (called *ions*) flow in and out of pores in the cell membrane. Whether an action potential will turn on *(excite)* or turn off *(inhibit)* a neighboring neuron depends upon the kind of neurotransmitter released; neurotransmitters excite or inhibit by opening or closing specific ion channels. Release of excitatory transmitter (open squares) causes ions (black dots) to rush into the cell, and an action potential is generated; inhibitory transmitter (open circles) causes ions to flow out of the cell, and action potentials are not generated. *Drawing by Barbara Haines.*

Conclusion

The modern era is distinguished from earlier times in possessing physical concepts that are dynamic, as against the merely static ones available to the phrenologists. Thanks to the experiments of such pioneers as Magendie and Helmholtz, we now understand that brain function is electrically mediated. Each nerve cell is a sophisticated electrical element capable of generating a resting potential and of rapidly changing that potential through a reversal of its intrinsic membrane charges. These action potentials constitute a continuous stream of signals flowing through the vast system of neurons that is our brain. Somehow the stream of electrical signals is related to the stream of what we call consciousness. It is the action potentials that transmit information from the outside world to the brain; that encode the integration performed by the brain on all its externally generated information; and that, finally, then retransmit the integrated information to the periphery for the action that is human behavior.

As I have emphasized earlier, brain activity is not simply reflex. It neither depends upon, nor is it exclusively concerned with, externally generated signals. It generates its own signals. Hence, its activity is, to some extent, independent of the outside world. Our ideas and our consciousness are, to the same extent, influenced by the level and pattern of the spontaneously generated action potentials of our brain cells. By recognizing the role of both spontaneity and chance in mental life, the emerging view of human beings may, at first glance, be somewhat frightening. But in so modifying the deterministic notion of reflex action, we get freedom in exchange for security and acknowledge creativity as much as we admit chaos.

5

The Regulation of Consciousness by the Brain Stem

When I say, My bed shall comfort me, my couch shall
ease my complaint, then thou scarest me with dreams,
and terrifiest me through visions; so that my soul
chooseth strangely, and death rather than life.
— BOOK OF JOB

I maintain even that something goes on in the soul
which corresponds to the circulation of the blood to all
the internal movements of the viscera, of which we are
never conscious, however, just as those who live near
a water mill do not perceive the noise it makes.
— GOTTFRIED WILHELM LEIBNITZ
New Essays Concerning Human Understanding (1896)

ECSTATIC AT THE exquisite organization of the cortex (which he took
to be the seat of consciousness), Ramón y Cajal was dismayed at the
apparent disorganization of the brain stem (which we now know controls
the state of the cortex). He called the medulla and the pons, situated far
below the cortex and containing those chemically differentiated polyps
that tell us when to wake, when to sleep, and when to dream, a "wearisome
labyrinth." Then he added, with his characteristic optimism, "Neverthe-

less there is no more land, however bleak it be, which does not offer to the botanist some flower that is unassuming but of exquisite fragrance" (1937, p. 432).

The brain stem is intermediate, both structurally and functionally, between the cerebral cortex (that vastly expanded area of brain which is related somehow to the uniquely human states of consciousness) and the spinal cord (which is the locus of the kind of reflex activity shared by us with other vertebrates.

The cortex is involved primarily with parallel processing, and the spinal cord with serial processing. Reflex action, which must be both prompt and automatic, is served by the serial-processing mode for which the spinal cord is admirably designed: external-stimulus information is rapidly conducted to a chainlike array of neurons which performs sequential integrations and produces a motor-output signal. Consciousness, which is continuous and deliberate, is served by the parallel-processing mode for which the cortex is architecturally ideal: by virtue of its huge, convoluted surface, its greatly expanded numbers of neurons, and its fanlike system of fibers, external- and internal-stimulus formation is conducted in parallel pathways to disparate regions, each of which may simultaneously perform a specialized analysis of the data, resulting in perception, memory, and thoughtful consideration before action is commanded.

The difference between spinally mediated reflex action (where external inputs are essential) and cortically mediated spontaneous action (where external inputs are not essential) is also significant. The intermediate brain stem serves not only as a way station for reflex information from spinal cord to cortex (and vice versa) but as a mode selector for both structures determining the ratio of stimulated to spontaneous neuronal information processing. During waking, when there are many stimuli, the brain-mind is extroverted. During dreaming, when there are few stimuli, the brain-mind is correspondingly introverted—but no less active.

In evolution, the brain stem was one of the first structures to be added to the purely segmental spinal cord. In many primitive animals, the brain stem was all the brain there was. It enabled organisms to achieve control of such special sense organs as eyes and to coordinate the increasing number of motor acts that developed as animals became more specialized with respect to limb functions. Thus, the brain stem contains within it neurons that move the eyes and neurons capable of coordinating those eye movements with the position of the head and the body (see figure 5.1). The complex orchestration of head, eye, and body positions is conducted by the oculomotor, reticular, and vestibular systems of the brain stem.

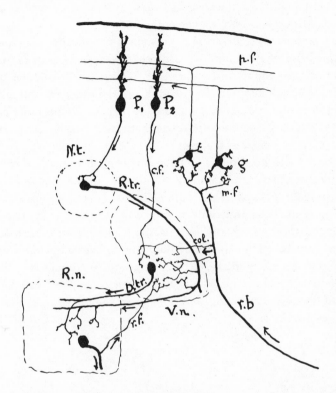

FIGURE 5.1

Brain-stem circuitry for eye-head-body reflexes

Attention and arousal demand precise control of eye and head position so that one can monitor the visual world quickly and accurately. Some of the brain-stem neurons involved in this task are shown in this pen-and-ink drawing made by Rafael Lorente de Nò to illustrate his classic 1933 paper on the vestibulo-ocular reflex. Lorente de Nò showed that every change in head position is immediately and accurately translated by the vestibular system into an appropriate change in eye position. Also participating in this neuronal calculation are the cerebellum and reticular formation. We now know that Lorente de Nò's circuit is spontaneously activated in REM sleep so that head, eye, and body position signals are internally generated. Thus, when one is lying immobile in bed, one has dream sensations of running, turning, and even flying. *Source:* Courtesy of Rafael Lorente de Nò, Department of Otolaryngology, UCLA School of Medicine.

The term *oculomotor* defines itself: eye movement is commanded by brain-stem neurons that send their axons directly to the eye muscles. The latter's highly complex activity, which we call *gaze,* is coordinated via interactions between three paired nuclei: the *oculomotor nucleus* (or third cranial nerve), which commands primarily vertical eye movements; the *trochlear nucleus* (or fourth cranial nerve), which commands primarily oblique movements; and the *abducens nucleus* (or sixth cranial nerve), which commands primarily lateral movements.

The vestibular system of the brain stem is specifically concerned with the complexities of head and eye control. Ask anyone with dizziness or vertigo about the important functions of this system. Vestibular neurons receive information about head position from the inner ear and relay that information to the oculomotor neurons. When the connections between the vestibular and the oculomotor systems are cut, as may occur in multiple sclerosis, paralysis of gaze will result.

Head and eye position are related, in turn, to the spinal control of posture by the reticular formation. Without the constant and precise operation of these three systems, we could neither walk and see nor sit still and read. None of the three functions described is exclusive to any one neuronal group, all three systems being in some way concerned with all three functions. Together with the cerebellum, the integrated activity of these brain-stem systems is responsible for giving sighted animals complex control of their acts. Think of the uncanny prowess of the Boston Celtics' Larry Bird for a vivid example. Such well-practiced motor control is almost entirely unconscious.

BEHAVIORAL STATES

Now a host of questions arises. How do all these systems know when to act? Should a certain posture be maintained at all times? Should eyes be consistently open? Should external signals always be processed? To these questions, and many more, the brain stem appears to have the answers. In addition to gaining control by allowing simultaneous synchronization of multiple reflex activities, animals with brain stems can also regulate whether these control systems will be active (awake) or not (asleep). In other words, the brain stem removes global aspects of behavior from the reflex level of control. We call the products of these global aspects of control the *behavioral states:* sleeping, waking, and dreaming.

Let me consider the implications of this concept. The reflex animal is wholly at the mercy of the environment; such an animal is impressively reliable but also impressively limited. By contrast, the state-controlled animal is able to predict when it will be favorable to respond and when it need not—a useful capability, especially if the time of no response can be used to maintain and restore functional efficiency of the brain.

As part of evolutionary specialization, an animal's ability to see allows it to respond strategically when light is available, and thus to make biological choices. Most sighted animals find it advantageous to limit activity to those periods when light is available, and distinctly disadvantageous to try to navigate in its absence. An animal may nonetheless have to retain the capability of doing so in the case of severe threat.

Now it could be argued that the turning on of behavior (during light periods) and the turning off of behavior (during dark periods) is also a reflex since it depends in part upon an external signal—namely, light. But we know that this function is independent of the light signals that normally regulate it. The reason is that the brain contains a "clock" capable of successfully predicting the time of occurrence and the duration of the light periods. This clock needs only slight daily resetting perfectly to synchronize bodily and behavioral activity with the availability of light.

Thus, the brain stem can be understood in terms of two important conceptual advances: the coordination of reflex activity; and the timing of the now highly sophisticated symphony of reflexes to those epochs in which the organism's biological aims are more likely to be achieved than that of others.

To achieve its control of sleep-wake state functions, the brain stem uses chemically specialized cells. By means of their long-acting chemical signals, they determine when and how the reflex circuits will process external information.

Some of the brain-stem cells that control human brain-mind states are found in the *locus ceruleus* (the "blue place"), where the neurons contain a colored pigment which is directly observable in unstained sections of the brain. The cells of the locus ceruleus contain norepinephrine. Chemically specific cells are also found in the raphe nuclei. The raphe itself is a white seam running down the middle of the brain stem. To the naked eye, the raphe is white because of the abundance of fibers crossing the midline. But under the microscope, and with special fluorescent stains, its cells can be shown to contain serotonin.

These two classes of biogenic-amine-containing cell appear to confer upon the brain stem the unique capability to regulate the state of the segmental nervous system (so that it will or will not process information) and the state of the higher cortical regions of the brain (so that they will or will not remember the processing of such information). It is in such terms as these that I will attempt to sketch a theory of both how the significant and distinctive features of waking, sleeping, and dreaming are caused, and of how these states are programmed so as to alternate reliably with one another.

THE MEASUREMENT OF BRAIN STATES: THE EEG

The explosive growth of the physics of electricity provided measurement devices, or polygraphs, to scientists interested in the dynamic properties of the nervous system. They soon learned that nerves not only can be stimulated and made to conduct imposed electrical signals but actually produce voltages themselves. Nerves thus act as batteries as well as wires. The first measurement of the voltages generated by the brain itself was made in 1875 by Richard Caton (1842–1926), a Scottish physiologist who connected a voltmeter to the surface of the rabbit brain. The tiny brain voltages Caton measured were also measurable across the human scalp once sufficiently powerful amplifiers became available. This discovery was made in 1928 by the German psychiatrist Hans Berger (1873–1941) and led to the *electroencephalogram* (or EEG) we know today.

As continuous records of voltage, the electrocardiogram and the electroencephalogram are essentially the same sorts of measurement. Applied to the head, a voltmeter will preferentially pick up brain waves. Applied to the trunk, it will preferentially pick up electrical activity that emanates from the heart. In both locations, such a voltmeter will also be sensitive to the electrical activity of muscle, the *electromyogram* (or EMG). (I discuss the EEG and the EMG as applied to the dreaming brain in chapter 6.)

For the neurophysiologist of behavior, the heart is an interesting tissue, because of the reliability of its rhythmic activity. It is an object lesson in how biological tissue can produce reliable rhythms. The autorhythmicity of the heart is a property of specialized cells in the heart called *pacemakers.* They were discovered by Jan Evangelista Purkinje (1787–1869), a Czechoslovakian anatomist and physiologist who interested himself in many things, including consciousness and sleep. With the strong support of the poet Goethe, Purkinje was able to establish the world's first department (1839) and laboratory (1842) of physiology. (It is as difficult as it is important to recognize how recent is the establishment of intellectual disciplines we now take to be classical.) The Purkinje cells of the heart (1839) are known to be autorhythmic: they fire action potentials in an automatic manner at fixed intervals. This "pacemaker" mechanism actually depends upon a leaky membrane. Leakiness was probably one of nature's design errors that turned out to be useful. Purkinje also did experiments that contributed in an important way to the localization of many state-regulatory systems to the brain stem.

The discovery of the spontaneous rhythmicity of nervous activity helped the theorist of mind answer two vexing questions: How can consciousness persist in the absence of strong sensory input (as it clearly does in dreams), and how can conscious states be rhythmically regulated (as they are over the course of the day)? Locke's assumption of the mind as a *tabula rasa* (or blank slate), to be written on by sensation, was thus shown to be incomplete in that it ignores the autonomous activity of the brain. Whether such autonomy could support Leibnitz's concept of innate ideas is another question.

We know that the action potential is carried down the nerve by a set of changes in the ionic permeability of the membrane. The nerve membrane is a porous sieve, pierced by microscopic holes. Once stimulated, these pores open in sequence allowing sodium ions to rush in (they are normally pumped out) and potassium ions to rush out (they are normally pumped in). But the leaky Purkinje cells of the heart have a built-in tendency to allow sodium to leak in and potassium to leak out until threshold is reached and the cell fires an action potential. This process occurs without any external stimulation. When we say that the rhythmicity of the heart is *autocthonous,* we mean that it is spontaneously generated. For the ancient Greeks, the *chtonic* forces of nature emanated from the depths of the earth and hence were revered in caves like the Grotto of Paradise in Siracusa on the island of Sicily. We moderns stand no less in awe of the neural forces constantly welling up—autonomously—from the cavelike depths of our brain stems.

Many nerve cells in the brains of simple animals depend upon pacemaker neurons, and true pacemaker activity has recently been discovered in the central nervous system of higher animals. Thus, while the heart is not a brain (in the sense of supporting consciousness), the brain may be a heart (in the sense of spontaneously generating rhythmic functions in a pumplike way). As we will see, dreaming is one psychic function rhythmically controlled by nerve cells with pacemaker activity.

Hans Berger used Einthoven's string galvanometer to record the electrical activity of the brain in human subjects. Berger's first reports of a successful recording of rhythmic electrical activity spontaneously generated by the human brain were greeted with incredulity. His critics felt that the wave forms he had recorded were an artifact, for many other electrical signals (some biological and some not) can interfere with anyone's attempt to record the low-level brain voltages.*

In order to convince himself (and the world) that he was recording electrical activity of brain origin, Berger resorted to a crucial test: Does a change in the recorded electrical activity of the brain parallel a change of conscious state? When he instructed his subjects to close their eyes as a prelude to falling asleep, Berger noticed an increase in the rhythmicity of their EEG. This rhythm, which has received mystic reverence as *alpha,* is a sinusoidal wave form of 8 to 12 cycles per second. When Berger's subjects' eyes were reopened, this alpha rhythm was blocked. The fact that a change in sensory input could so dramatically influence the EEG wave forms showed that they were unlikely to be artifacts. When subjects kept their eyes closed and began to fall asleep, their brain waves underwent an even more dramatic change: to the high-voltage slow pattern that we now know to be characteristic of *slow-wave* or non-REM sleep. This intrinsic change in the electrical activity of the brain, correlated with a change in conscious state of Berger's subjects, really clinched the argument, at least for him.

The rest of the world began to fall into line after 1933 when two English physiologists, Edgar Adrian and Brian Matthews, were able to confirm Berger's observation by recording their own brain waves using their cathode-ray oscilloscope. This instrument substituted an electron beam for the lightweight string in Einthoven's galvanometer. Adrian and Matthews took advantage of the virtually weightless state of electrons. When a beam of electrons was moved back and forth across a phosphorescent screen, the external voltages were visualized as deviations of the beam's path. These distinguished English investigators gained for Berger's discovery the scientific support it needed.

---

*In my own lab I have been entertained by the Children's Hospital page system, by commercial radio shows, and even by Boston Police cruiser intercoms, all picked up by brain electrodes acting as antennae. John Nicolls made a comic film to spoof the elaborate efforts of his British team to foil these electronic parasites. When the microelectrode was finally placed in a nerve cell, the audio amplifier played "God Save the Queen," and all the physiologists leaped to respectful attention!

CHEMICAL ASPECTS OF STATE REGULATION

At the turn of the century, although the concept of physiological inhibition had been clearly stated by Charles Sherrington, it was not known that the changes across cells were chemically mediated. This concept was developed and given unequivocal specificity through the work of the English physiologist Sir Henry Dale (1875–1968) and the Austrian pharmacologist Otto Loewi (1873–1961), who shared the 1936 Nobel Prize in physiology and medicine for their discoveries of the chemical transmission of nerve impulses. At the very time that Freud was promulgating his dream theory, Otto Loewi was struggling to understand the slowing of heart action when a nerve to the heart (the vagus) was stimulated electrically. This was a clear example of inhibition, not within the nervous system itself but between a nerve cell and the heart muscle fiber. The nerve from the brain to the heart that Loewi stimulated is called *vagus* because it wanders—like a vagabond—through the body, delivering its impulses to many organs, including stomach, bowel, and lungs. It is part of the autonomic nervous system, so-called because it regulates—automatically—vegetative functions that operate behind our awareness. The *autonomic nervous system* is thus distinguished from the *voluntary nervous system* of whose workings we are relatively conscious.

The vagus nerve exerts a braking action on the automatic rhythm of the heart. When stimulated, it slows heart action; whereas other nerve fibers, called sympathetic, speed the heart up. Heart rate is the net effect of excitation (on the sympathetic side) and inhibition on the vagal (or parasympathetic side). Like many other vegetative functions including sleep, the balanced operation of the heart depends upon the competition between the sympathetic and the parasympathetic systems.

It seemed possible that the vagus nerve exerted its braking effect upon the heart by liberating a chemical from its endings which then influenced the excitability of the cardiac muscle cells. But because these events occur almost instantaneously, Loewi was stumped in his efforts to find out whether this idea was correct. And because it was impossible to measure directly the presence of minute amounts of material in the blood by the then-existing chemical techniques, he had no idea what the postulated chemical substance might be. He simply called it the *vagustoff*. (See figure 5.2.)

After Loewi had been puzzling over his experimental problem for some time, he awakened from a dream in which the experimental solution had occurred to him. But he could not recall his dream! The next night, he

FIGURE 5.2
Otto Loewi

At the Twelfth International Physiological Congress in 1926, Otto Loewi demonstrated his crossed-heart perfusion experiment. The idea, which occurred to him in a dream, was to stimulate the vagus nerve of the frog, and then to transfer its blood to a second animal. If—as proved to be the case—the heart rate of the recipient frog was slowed, then the effect must be mediated by a chemical liberated by the stimulated vagus nerve. Loewi called his heart-slowing chemical the *vagustoff*, later shown to be acetylcholine, the very neurotransmitter now known to mediate REM sleep and dreaming. *Source:* Rare Books and Print Department, Francis A. Countway Library of Medicine, Harvard Medical School. Dick Wolfe, Director.

went to bed intent on redreaming his crucial experiment. When he woke up, he rushed to the laboratory and prepared two frogs. The vagus nerve of one frog was electrically stimulated, causing slowing of its heart action. He collected the blood from the heart of that frog; and after he had transferred it to the heart of a second frog, its heart action also slowed. In this simple way, Loewi was able to deduce that electrical stimulation of the first frog's heart had caused to be released in the blood a chemical capable of slowing the heart of the second frog whose vagus nerve had not been stimulated. Chemists were later able to show that Loewi's *vagustoff* was the chemical acetylcholine, which Sir Henry Dale had isolated in 1914.

Acetylcholine is the substance that is released by the motor nerves and that is excitatory to skeletal muscle. Every time we command a voluntary movement, that movement is effected via the release of acetylcholine. It is also the chemical mediator at most of the synapses in the involuntary (or autonomic) nervous system which controls, in addition to the pulse, respiration and the movement of the intestinal system.

At collections of excitatory synapses in the autonomic nervous system (called *ganglia*), at the neuromuscular junctions, and probably at synapses within the central nervous system itself, action potentials arriving at terminals cause depolarization of these terminals and release of acetylcholine from the vesicles in the terminals. The acetylcholine molecules travel across the synaptic cleft and find the appropriate receptor in the post-synaptic membrane, causing a conformational change in the membrane, and thus altering the conductance of that membrane to ions. Acetylcholine increases the permeability to extracellular sodium and intracellular potassium, leading to rapid flux of those ions across the membrane and to exciting or inhibiting the generation of an action potential.

To be efficient, synaptic action needs to be terminated as promptly as it is initiated. The acetylcholine molecules in the synaptic cleft are rapidly rendered incapable of further excitation by the operation of a second chemical substance which breaks them down. This substance is the enzyme *acetylcholinesterase.* As we will see in chapter 8, it has recently become possible to manipulate the acetylcholine system experimentally—so as to produce REM sleep and dreaming—owing to the discovery of still a third kind of molecule, which blocks the enzyme so that spontaneously released acetylcholine can continue to act. The substances that thus enhance the action of acetylcholine are called *acetylcholinesterase inhibitors;* and two examples are *neostigmine* and *physostigmine.*

Using drugs that enhance acetylcholine's action, scientists have thus been able to show that REM sleep and dreaming may be mediated by this neurotransmitter. The actions of acetylcholine can be enhanced not only by blockade of the enzyme that breaks it down; but the postsynaptic receptor can also be fooled by molecules that resemble acetylcholine. Because these molecules imitate the action of acetylcholine and cause the postsynaptic membrane to be hyperexcitable, they are called *cholinergic agonists.* When injected into the brain, these charlatan neurotransmitters (such as *carbachol* and *bethenechol*) increase REM sleep dramatically. The prolonged enhancement of REM sleep by these drugs is related to the fact that they are not broken down by the enzyme acetylcholinestrase. This immunity, while useful to sleep scientists, would be highly unwelcome to those sleepers who value their ability to wake up promptly and fully!

Insomniacs, needing a cholinergic booster to fall or remain asleep, might feel differently.

Opposite effects may also be obtained, depending upon the chemical nature of the drug. For example, an extract of the belladonna leaf contains a substance, called *atropine,* which blocks the postsynaptic receptor for acetylcholine. (*Belladonna,* Italian for "beautiful lady," was so named because it was used cosmetically to enhance feminine beauty by producing large limpid pupils.) After belladonna has been instilled into the eye, acetylcholine is unable to effect pupiliary constriction because the sympathetic nerve fibers in the pupil that cause dilatation act unopposed. Ophthalmologists now use atropine to dilate the pupils of their patients in order to examine the retina using Helmholtz's opthalmoscope. Atropine causes powerful effects at other cholinergic synapses—such as the salivary glands (dry mouth), the heart (palpitations), and the intestines (constipation)—where acetylcholine has an action. And every intern knows the effects of atropine overdosage: blind as a bat, red as a beet, dry as a bone, hot as a fire, and—most significantly for our subject of dreaming—mad as a hatter!

Both cholinergic and anticholinergic molecules are widespread in nature. Acetylcholine is used by animals to conduct their most essential neuronal transactions, and the molecule also exists in many plant forms. Related molecules, which affect acetylcholine transmission, have also been utilized in nature to accomplish specialized defensive or aggressive purposes of animals. Some snake and toad venoms contain molecules that block acetylcholine or compete with its degradative enzymes. The injection of such a molecule into the body of a biological enemy can be devastating. Humans have taken advantage of the naturally toxic effects of curare, a molecule of plant origin, and used it to coat the tips of arrows. Curare leads to motor paralysis because it blocks the action of acetylcholine at the neuromuscular junction. Respiratory failure may even occur after curare administration, since the molecule makes the muscles that move the chest wall in breathing unable to contract.

The availability of so many active molecules gives the scientist investigating cholinergic mechanisms a remarkably rich repertoire with which to manipulate the natural system. This is as true of the systems of the brain controlling dreaming sleep as it is of the autonomic ganglia and the skeletal muscular system. We can now either activate dreaming sleep mechanisms or "paralyze" them. By use of such molecules we may not only better understand how dreaming sleep is mediated by the brain, but we may also imitate or impede that mediation to achieve various clinical ends.

While many of the actions of acetylcholine are excitatory, some are inhibitory. Inhibitory effects are also caused by other molecules. GABA (or gamma amino butyric acid) effects the chloride ion channel leading to hyperpolarization of the postsynaptic membrane and making it less easily excitable. The inhibitory effects of GABA can be mimicked by the agonist bicuculline and antagonized by the well-known poison strychnine, which leads to unopposed excitation since an inhibitory braking mechanism has been disenabled. Animals given meat poisoned with strychnine may die of convulsive seizures.

The nervous system can be seen as an arena of constant competition; its excitability ebbs and flows as excitatory and inhibitory forces rise and fall. The fact that there are many synapses and many cells, each with such a constant gradation of probability of excitation, gives the whole system an extraordinary range of possible states. If we assume that each of the twenty billion cells (2×10 [to the tenth]) has ten thousand (10 [to the fourth]) communicative contacts, or synapses, then there are at least (2×10 [to the sixteenth] of them). The actual number looks something like this: 200,000,000,000,000. Now, if each synapse has a continuous probability of activity varying from -1 through 0 to $+1$, the modulatory range of the whole system is beyond imagining, making infinitely rich the multiplicity of mental states of which human beings are capable. Rich, too, is our capacity to modulate these states through behavioral and chemical means. Utilizing these facts, we can now begin to construct realistic models for understanding human emotional and conscious states and for their control by natural and artificial means.

The excitatory and inhibitory actions that I have discussed are, however, only a small part of the plastic range of the system. Neurotransmitters like gamma amino butyric acid (GABA) and glutamate act extremely rapidly and seem to be mainly involved in the immediate point-to-point transfer of information within the nervous system. In such reflex systems, fidelity depends on rapid release and rapid inactivation of the chemicals, for time is of the essence. Some of the actions of acetylcholine are of this rapid nature.

But the human nervous system is not switched on and off instantaneously. Instead, there is a gradation of states, which appears to be the result of slowly tuning the rapidly acting synapses. For this purpose, at least two other major classes of molecule play upon the synapses of the nervous system, increasing or decreasing their excitability over a much longer time than that of the rapidly acting neurotransmitters. One class, the biogenic amines, has already been mentioned with respect to the sympathetic nervous system, and the brain stem. It is sympathetic action that speeded Otto Loewi's frog's heart—and that causes the pupil of a *donna* to be *bella*. One sympathetic-nervous-system molecule is norepinephrine. Molecules that have long time-courses of action have been called *neuromodulators* because they seem to bias the excitatory and inhibitory synapses so as to make them more or less likely to be excitatory or inhibitory. These biasing effects can last many seconds instead of the few milliseconds characteristic of rapid synaptic action. This temporal extension enables the effect of a stimulus to give not only instantaneous reflex responses but to change the probability of future reflex responses—effects that we call *habituation* and *learning.*

To understand this process, one has only to think of the complicated sequence of effects following a near automobile accident. There is the immediate reflex adjustment which helps avert disaster—a prompt response that, measured in seconds as our reaction time, is too fast for conscious decision. There follows a flood of autonomic effects perceptible throughout the body as increased blood flow, increased heart action, and muscular tremulousness. These responses may last several minutes: they prepare the body to cope with injury and tell the mind, in no uncertain terms, that something important has occurred. This set of changes we experience as intense anxiety, sometimes even panic. And the events that trigger such feelings tend to be memorable. Many aspects of this complex response are mediated by the biogenic amines norepinephrine and serotonin.

Norepinephrine is called an *amine* because it contains hydrogenated nitrogen. All other modulatory molecules of the same class share this chemical signature. This important class of agent has been called *biogenic* because it mediates biological activity. The rate of human metabolism— whether one is active or passive, alert or sleepy, lethargic or dynamic, fat or thin—seems to be mediated in part by the play of these biogenic amines. One's mood and level of arousal also depend upon the interplay of these biogenic amines with the conventional neurotransmitters.

Another biogenic-amine molecule is serotonin, whose action was also first described in the heart. This heart was that of the common sea clam, called Venus, which lovers of cherrystones and little necks appreciate on the half-shell. Serotonin's chemical name is 5-hydroxytryptamine (5HT).

The social importance of the biogenic amines is all too clear from the fact that the drug culture has spent billions of dollars and countless hours in the development of molecules that can interact with these neuronal systems. The action of serotonin can be blocked by the well-known psychidelic substance LSD (lysergic acid diethyamide), causing hallucinations. The sympathetic action of norepinephrine is enhanced by the popular street "upper," amphetamine, and by cocaine, the drug that Freud promoted as a local anesthetic. Our states of consciousness are thus clearly susceptible—for better or worse—to manipulation by chemicals that inter-act with the biogenic-amine neuronal systems of our brain-minds.

A third class of chemical agent has recently emerged as important to the control of brain states. The peptide hormones are larger molecules with even longer and more widespread effects than those of the biogenic-amine neuromodulators. Peptides may be released from nerve cells to achieve precisely local economic adjustments but may also be circulated in the blood and/or in the spinal fluid like hormones, so as to effect huge popula-tions of cells over long periods of time. These agents seem ideally suited to mediate the control of states and mood over twenty-four-hour periods or even weeks; and there is already abundant evidence that rest-activity rhythms—and our non-REM sleep—are controlled by peptide hormones.

Otto Loewi dreamed of an experiment that would provide the key to a molecular study of the brain states at the same time that Freud was attempting to explain mind states by his radical psychological theory. The irony is that Otto Loewi's *vagustoff* was the very chemical key that Freud needed to unlock the biology of dreaming; and from it developed—on anatomical, physiological, pharmacological, and biochemical fronts—the neurobiological science upon which modern dream theory is based. Thus Freud's *Project for a Scientific Psychology*, which he abandoned in 1895, may now, nearly a century later, be seriously reconsidered. While some of its goals will remain elusive, many of the speculative errors of philosophy that were introduced into the psychological theory can now be corrected. And many of the goals of a general scientific psychology can be achieved via the establishment of a biologically based theory of dream forms.

Two Approaches to Sleeping and Waking

Once investigators had settled on the brain as the most probable material base of conscious states, they tried to localize the brain system that con-trols the changes in consciousness that occur in sleep. Two fundamental approaches were followed by the pioneer investigators: one was to stimu-late parts of the brain electrically and observe changes in an animal's behavior; the other, to destroy some part of the brain and observe whether a particular behavioral state was affected. Focal brain damage is called a *lesion*, while more extensive intervention is an *ablation*.

Since experimental brain damage may alter a state, it is tempting to conclude that damaged structures control a normal state. But such experimental results may be misleading since, while apparently pointing to a control region, they may equally well indicate that the *connections* between two (or more) essential (and distinct) regions have been destroyed.

From an intellectual standpoint, the most satisfying results of this approach come when a brain structure has been totally ablated and the state under investigation remains intact. It can then be confidently concluded that the remaining structures are sufficient to generate the state. Such a finding does *not* mean, of course, that the ablated structure plays no role in generating the state; or even prove that the structure itself might not contain the capability of controlling the state. A converse logic applies to selective lesions that result in *loss* of function. From such results, one can conclude only that the damaged structure is necessary for the generation of the state, not that it *is* the state generator. It is only when the results of both ablation and selective-lesion experiments complement each other that one can begin to have confidence that a particular brain region may indeed be both necessary and sufficient for the generation of any state of consciousness. The stage is then set for physiological analysis.

So it was with REM sleep and waking. We wanted to locate in the brain the nerve cells responsible for coordinating the activity of the cortex, the eyes, and the muscles, since all of these functions are clearly involved in the state change. From an architectural point of view, it is most efficient to place a control system at a nodal point within a structure so as to be in touch with all necessary points in the periphery. This architectural principle holds for the brain: the control system is in the brain stem.

An Experiment of Nature

However prescient classical philosophers may have been in anticipating certain ideas of modern dream theory, none clearly and confidently anticipated the localization to the brain stem of the control of the states of waking, sleeping, and dreaming. Instead of occurring intuitively, this idea was stimulated by an "experiment" of nature, the influenza epidemic of 1918. Influenza virus marched around the world as it does practically every winter; but in that year, the form of the virus was particularly virulent. It entered the brain and devoured neurons. The neurological syndrome that often followed brain infection by influenza virus was called *encephalitis lethargica* because the afflicted subjects were unable to maintain alert waking states. This "sleeping sickness" was often irreversible.

The discovery, by Constantine Von Economo (1876–1931), that the killed cells were localized to the subcortical regions of the brain was a

turning point in the history of the attempt to understand the brain basis of consciousness. Von Economo suggested that nerve cells in the subcortical regions might normally support the waking state; when such neurons reduce their activity—either naturally or in disease—waking will give way to sleep. In other words, the ravages of the disease presented the observant Von Economo with a model completely novel in three respects: it suggested (1) that the cells underlying sleep-wake state control might be localized; (2) more specifically, that they might be concentrated in the brain stem; and (3) that the waking state might be actively maintained by the physiological activity of those cells. Today we take these ideas for granted, but they are only some sixty-five years old—less than one average human lifetime.

Implied by Von Economo's discovery, but not recognized by him, was a fourth important principle: chemical specificity. The cells destroyed by the influenza virus were in a region of the brain stem called the *substantia nigra*, or "black substance." This region of the brain actually appears dark even in unstained histological sections because of the melanin pigment within the cells. While Von Economo noticed signs of viral inhabitation within the pigmented cells, he did not appreciate that the presence of the pigment in the cells was related to their chemical specificity. The black pigment in the substantia-nigra cells reflected the concentration of the modulatory neurotransmitter DOPA in those neurons. This compound is now well known because of its relationship to motor control. Deficiencies in this system result in such human diseases as Parkinsonism, which was another of the aftermaths of encephalitis lethargica.

DOPA is not only a neurotransmitter in its own right but also a metabolic precursor of the neurotransmitter norepinephrine. Without DOPA, the brain can not make norepinephrine. Evidence is now abundant that those neurons that use norepinephrine as their neurotransmitter are crucial to the active maintenance of the waking state. Decreases in their activity determine, as Von Economo suggested, the difference between waking and sleeping. Thus, the modern idea that the activity of localized and chemically specific neurons is crucial to the control of the states of consciousness was a logical outgrowth of medical and scientific discoveries.

The lesion approach to localizing sleep-wake-state control functions was inspired by the teachings of the influenza virus in the encephalitis epidemic of 1918, and thus antedated the electrophysiological era ushered in by Berger's development of the electroencephalogram (see pages 114–16). In the 1920s, the English anatomist Legros Clark found, after surgically destroying the hypothalamus of experimental animals, that they were no longer able to maintain alertness. We now know that the hypothalamus, which is in the most anterior part of the brain stem, is the seat of neuronal systems that are critical for controlling the daily (or circadian) rhythm of rest, activity, and body temperature, and for linking the rest-activity cycle to the sleep-wake cycle.

Sleep and Waking as Passive Processes

Complementing these early results was the work of Frederic Bremer (1935) in the 1930s. With the EEG, Bremer was able to record the brain-wave activity of his experimental cats. Being tested was a notion that had dominated thinking for centuries past: that the wake-state activity of the brain is dependent upon the energy of the outside world, and that energy is derived from sensory stimulation. Thus the waking state would be itself a reflex, just like the motor acts occurring within it.

Bremer assumed that, as the brain is deprived of sensory input *(deafferented)*, it is unable to sustain the wake state. This view of sleep as a passive process had no effective opposition at the time, illustrating once again how long-lived were the psychological and biological ideas of the nineteenth century. This deafferentation theory ascribes the onset of sleep to the gradual decay in the level of stimulation that occurs over the course of a day. For example, in sighted animals the onset of darkness would be paralleled by a massive decrease in visual input. In this view, sleep is simply the absence of waking, and both states are conceived as externally regulated.

Bremer interpreted the results of his first experiments as favoring the deafferentation theory. Having created a complete transection of the upper brain stem, he observed that animals were thereafter perpetually drowsy. And their electroencephalograms showed the brain-wave patterns typical of sleep: there was an impressive intensification of EEG spindle activity in the cortex. When stimulated, the cortex could still be activated via the intact sensory pathways from the nose; in fact, smell was the only effective input channel to the otherwise sensorially isolated forebrain. Bremer concluded that the forebrain was asleep because it had been deprived of stimulation from the surface of the body, from the ears, and from the deep joint receptors. This experimental preparation was called the *isolated forebrain* (in French, *cerveau isolé*).

Bremer's initial conclusion was almost immediately upset by his own subsequent experiment. When he divided the brain stem at a lower level (between the medulla and the spinal cord), he observed (instead of the sleep he expected) behavioral and electrical signs of enhanced wakefulness. This experimental preparation, which Bremer called the *isolated fore-and hind-* brain (in French, *encephale isolé*), was surprisingly hypervigilant, in contrast to the hypersomnolent *cerveau isolé:* surprisingly, because the *encephale isolé* cats were abnormally wakeful despite the fact that the input from the skin and deep-joint receptors could not reach the brain. The only major difference in input between the two preparations was that sensory stimulation from the surface of the head and face could enter the brain stem of the *encephale isolé* cats via the intact fifth cranial (or trigeminal) nerve. This huge nerve carries our toothache pain and more quietly monitors touch in head, face, and eyes. Bremer realized that his experiments strongly implied an active control system within the brain stem itself, between the level of the two transections.

By the late 1930s, Loomis and Harvey had described the fluctuating levels of brain-wave activity occurring in human sleep; and experimental neurologists had begun to understand that these fluctuations might indeed be actively controlled by the brain stem. Thus a new idea was ready to be born, but its delivery was delayed by the outbreak of the Second World War.

Active Control of Waking

After the war, scientific activity resumed slowly, especially in Europe where interest in the neurophysiology of sleep and waking had always been most keen. Many Europeans came to the United States to regain scientific orientation and momentum. And as part of its reconstructive efforts, the United States tried to resuscitate indigenous European science. In the area of the biology of state control, the U.S. Air Force encouraged support of the activity of two laboratories of particular interest to my story: the Institute of Physiology at the University of Pisa, Italy, under the direction of Giuseppe Moruzzi; and the department of experimental pathology at the University of Lyon, France, led by Michel Jouvet.

Moruzzi had learned the analytic approach of Anglo-Saxon neurophysiology through his early experience with Edgar Adrian, the co-confirmer, with Brian Matthews, of Berger's EEG findings. In Adrian's laboratory at Cambridge, Moruzzi first witnessed the recording of action potentials from individual neurons in the motor cortex. He had also been trained in the science of vestibular mechanisms at the University of Parma. The vestibular system is essential to the control of the body's position in space and to the integration of eye, head, and body position.

In the late 1940s, Moruzzi went to the United States to work at

FIGURE 5.3
Giuseppe Moruzzi and Horace Magoun

Following their 1949 description of the arousing effects of electrical stimulation of the brain stem, Giuseppe Moruzzi *(left)* and Horace Magoun *(hand on forehead)* traveled to Moscow to present their findings. On their way home they stopped in Warsaw to give a seminar at the Nencki Institute of Experimental Biology. (The third person in the photo is the Polish neurophysiologist Liliana Lubinska.) Establishing that the brain stem contains neurons that actively govern the condition of the brain centers of awareness (the cortex) and posture (the spinal cord) gave the concept of conscious state control a unifying physical foundation, and paved the way for the later discovery that this system is active during waking (when external information is processed) as well as during dreaming (when internal information is processed). *Source:* Courtesy of Boguslav Zernicki.

Northwestern University in the laboratory of Steven Ranson, a physiologist with a long-standing interest in the hypothalamus and its relation to behavior. There Moruzzi teamed up with one of Ranson's co-workers, Horace Magoun (see figure 5.3). Together they set out to understand better the functions of the motor system, in particular the neuronal system linking the motor cortex, where voluntary commands are issued, and the spinal centers which execute movement. Moruzzi and Magoun placed electrodes in the pyramidal tract of the brain stem in order to stimulate those cells of the motor cortex whose axons passed through the brain stem. They also placed electrodes in the motor cortex. From these cortical electrodes they were able to record the EEG. When they varied the parameters of stimulation applied via brain-stem electrodes, Moruzzi and Magoun were surprised to notice that sleeplike (high voltage, slow) EEG wave activity of the motor cortex of their cats could be converted to a wakelike (low voltage, fast) EEG pattern. And, more impressive still, this EEG effect was accompanied by behavioral arousal. Both the behavioral arousal and the brain-wave activation outlasted the stimulation, indicating that there were structures in the brain stem whose activation might simultaneously produce long-lasting arousal and EEG activation.

Moruzzi and Magoun found that their stimulating electrodes were actually in the reticular formation of the brain stem. This region, a complex meshwork of cells and fibers, was thereafter known as the *reticular activating system* of the brain. It is significant that the location of Moruzzi and Magoun's original stimulation was between the two levels of transection described by Bremer. But activating effects could be obtained from the entire sweep of the brain-stem reticular formation, from the medulla to the hypothalamus.

Moruzzi and Magoun realized that their experiments did not critically decide the case between an active neural theory of arousal and the passive deafferentation theory: because, of course, their reticular-formation stimulation could be activating sensory pathways known to conduct sensory stimuli through the brain stem. It was necessary to go a step further and to show that the activating effects of stimulation were due to the reticular-formation neurons and not to the sensory pathways coursing through the region. This was done in two ways. First, lesions were made in the reticular formation, leaving the sensory pathways intact: the behavior and brain-wave pattern of the *cerveau isolé* cat was the result. Second, lesions of the sensory pathways alone did *not* produce somnolence and EEG slow waves. But even with this strong evidence (that the activity of the cells of the reticular formation itself normally underlie the waking state), it still remained possible that fibers could have carried the activating signals to the cortex. Only recently has the elegant work of Mircea Steriade provided conclusive evidence that reticular-formation neuronal activity correlates with the level of EEG activation in the cortex.

The revolutionary findings of Moruzzi and Magoun immediately tipped the balance away from the notion of sleep as a passive deafferentation process and favored a theory of active central neural control.

Active Control of Sleep

That sleep itself might be actively controlled had already been suggested by the work of the 1949 Nobel laureate in physiology or medicine, Walter Hess (1881–1973), of Zurich, Switzerland. Hess was among the first to explore the brain stem using electrical stimulation techniques to understand the control of such functions as blood pressure, respiration, and heart rate. He had also discovered that rhythmic stimulation of the thalamus, a relay station of the brain between the brain stem and the cortex, could produce EEG slow waves and behavioral sleep. A problem with Hess's studies was that the frequencies of his stimulation were similar to those of the spindle waves, indicating that the thalamus was the final common path for the neural process that initiates sleep in the cortex. The mechanism of this process remained obscure.

When the excitement caused by Moruzzi and Magoun's discoveries had begun to die down, Moruzzi took up some of the old questions still lingering from the work of Bremer. In the late 1950s, Moruzzi's group in Pisa studied the effects of transecting the brain stem between the levels of the *encephale isolé* and the *cerveau isolé*. The purpose of the placement of this cut was to isolate from the forebrain sensory stimulation of head and face (conducted by the trigeminal nerve). Animals so treated were called *mediopontine pretrigeminal preparations.*

Moruzzi and his group were surprised to find a high level of arousal and wakelike electrographic activity in the medio-pontine preparation. The results more closely resembled those seen in Bremer's *encephale isolé* than in the *cerveau isolé.* It now seemed clear—beyond a shadow of a doubt—that sensory stimulation is neither responsible, nor even necessary, for the activation of the brain; but that, on the contrary, neural structures between the mid-pontine and upper brain stem levels are both essential to and alone capable of mediating behavioral arousal and the electrical activation of the forebrain.

The lesion and stimulation experiments I have examined followed the discovery of the EEG in the late 1920s and led to the era of cellular studies in the early 1960s. In this thirty-year span the control of conscious states had clearly been established as a brain function and as an active process of specific neural structures within the brain stem. The period between 1935 and 1950 can thus be counted as a watershed in the conceptualization of the neural control of the states of the brain-mind. The findings of Aserinsky and Kleitman, of Dement, and of Jouvet, and the school of cellular physiology which has developed within the last twenty years, all stand heavily in debt to this important conceptual shift.

In 1930, when the oscilloscope was used to record individual action potentials for the first time, it was suggested that the action potential might be the signal unit of the central nervous system. It is now well established that this is the case, making increasingly concrete Ramón y Cajal's image of the brain as a colony of pulsating polyps. It was immediately apparent to Edgar Adrian and his Italian student Giuseppe Moruzzi that the action potentials could be recorded not only from the peripheral nerves but from the brain itself.

I discussed this insight with Professor Moruzzi in his study at the Physiological Institute in Pisa, on 12 July 1977. The high walls of Moruzzi's office were lined with books, which were barely visible because the shutters were drawn against the Tuscan summer sun; the room was illuminated only by the feeble bulb of a gooseneck reading light. Most dramatically visible against this dark backdrop was Moruzzi's leonine forehead which housed a rich treasure of personal memory. The scene reminded me of Durer's St. Anthony in his cell.

Moruzzi recounted how he had first met Edgar Adrian in Bologna at the second centenary celebration of Luigi Galvani's birth in 1937.* Adrian invited Moruzzi to visit his laboratory in Cambridge. When Moruzzi did so, in October 1938, Adrian was attempting to record the electrical signals of the brain cells that command movement. As a wire 30 micrometers in diameter was lowered by Adrian into an anesthetized animal's brain, Moruzzi heard a noise, "like that of a train in the distance." The "choo-choo" sounds of the audio-amplified action potentials were, in fact, the puffs of the neuronal engine. They ceased abruptly when the command center for movement, the motor cortex, was removed.

CONCLUSION: NEURONS AND CONSCIOUSNESS

We now know that our brains consist of billions of individual elements, each of which has the capacity to generate its own energy, and this energy is used to create the signals of the system—a much more sophisticated nervous system than the primitive model available to Freud. The late-twentieth-century brain is dependent upon neither external energy nor external information. It creates its own energy and its own information. Our brain-mind has a dynamic life of its own with which it interacts with the external world. Thus is our psyche *materialized,* and thus is our brain *animated.*

Not only is our nervous system able, by its very nature, to trigger, to maintain, and to end the activation process on which dreaming depends, but it may be obliged to do all three in order to maintain its functional

*Frederic Bremer, W. R. Hess, and Hans Berger were also present.

integrity. This is a vast maintenance task. There are at least twenty billion individual elements in each human brain; some estimates exceed fifty billion. Indeed, each and every human brain has more individual elements than there are people in the world. This "colony of polyps" is thus more populous than the extended human family. And each individual element is capable of producing its own signals: it communicates by means of action potentials with its neighbors. It has been estimated that—by means of tiny extensions of the nerve membrane, the axons and the dendrites— each individual neuron communicates with at least ten thousand other neurons. It is as if each person in the world were in constant and simultaneous telephonic communication with ten thousand other people!

Furthermore, each of the twenty billion elements generates messages at a rate varying between one hundred and two or three hundred signals per second: hence, each of the twenty billion citizens of our brain-mind is talking to at least ten thousand others *at least once,* and as often as one hundred times, per second. With a chatterbox of such proportions, it is to me just as incredible that such a system would *not* have awareness of itself as it is incredible that it does.

We know that the internal communication from nerve cell to nerve cell is a continuous process: night and day it goes on and on and on. And we know that this ongoing nervous activity is spontaneous: it changes in relation to signals from the external world, coding them in its own way into its own language. But it is not created by—nor is it dependent upon— external inputs. And we know that during sleep the ratio of external to internal signaling changes; during dreaming sleep, there is just as much activity going on within the system as there is during waking. In other words, during dreams the system is literally talking to itself.

Not only is the brain an enormously complex information-processing machine—the number of its elements greater than the population of the world and its communicative capabilities several orders of magnitude greater than anyone of us has as an individual among people; but the communication from cell to cell is virtually instantaneous. The large fibers of the nervous system conduct at a rate of about 100 meters per second— faster than 200 miles per hour. The reflex "reaction time" of a man 2 meters tall who sends a message from his brain to his toe is less than 2 seconds, and most of that time is devoted to synaptic delay.

Imagine that all the twenty billion cells, each communicating with at least ten thousand others, is also sending messages at that same rate of speed within the system itself. The noise, if possible to describe, would be not the faint "choo-choo" of Moruzzi's distant train but a deafening roar, more like the "buzzing confusion" of William James's metaphor for consciousness. But this incessant activity all proceeds silently, with only our relatively peaceful consciousness as its product. The music of these spheres from the galaxy within our head is our consciousness. Consciousness is the continuous, subjective awareness of the activity of billions of cells firing at many times a second, communicating instantaneously with tens of thousands of their neighbors. And the organization of this symphony of activity is such that it is sometimes externally oriented (during waking), sometimes oblivious to the outside world (during sleep), and sometimes so remarkably aware of itself (during dreams) that it recreates the external world in its own image.

6

The Discovery of REM
Sleep and Dreaming

The amputation of the feet is a bar
  to a contemplated journey.
The burning of the body indicates
  a very evil reputation.
> —ASTRAMPSYCHUS
> The Onirocriticon (A.D. 350)

Dreams are nothing but the imaginations, fancies, or
reveries, of a sleeping man; and that they are deducible
from the three following causes, viz. First, the impressions and ideas lately received, and particularly those
of the preceding day. Secondly, the state of the body,
particularly of the stomach and brain. And, thirdly,
association.
> —DAVID HARTLEY
> Observations on Man (1801)

TODAY, more than fifty years after Berger's discovery, the electroencephalogram has become an indispensable tool of scientific students of
human consciousness. The fluctuations in electrical activity that Berger
observed, and found to be correlated with the subjects' state of consciousness, immediately suggested a link between the dynamic states of brain
activity and of the mind.

Applying the EEG to Sleep and Dreams

If a change in mind state (from waking to sleep) could be reliably associated with a change in brain state (from fast to slow EEG), we might not only view the EEG as a useful tool but begin to take seriously the idea that brain and mind are inextricably linked, perhaps even unified. When one is awake, the electrical activity of the brain tends to be of low voltage and fast. The usual EEG records rhythms with frequencies of up to 30 per second and with amplitudes of 50 microvolts. With Adrian and Matthews's oscilloscope, frequencies up to 150 cycles per second can be detected. When one becomes drowsy and then falls more deeply asleep, this low-voltage fast activity becomes slower and of higher voltage. First a *theta* rhythm of about 4 to 8 cycles per second comes to replace the mix of 8 to 12 cycles per second (eyes closed, awake) *alpha* and the 12 to 18 cycles per second (eyes open, awake) *beta* rhythms. This theta rhythm is irregular as well as slow, and its voltage progressively increases.

When one first loses consciousness of the external world and drowsiness gives way to true sleep, there arises in the EEG a stereotyped wave form called the *sleep spindle,* which augments and decreases in amplitude at a frequency of 15 to 18 cycles per second. The sleep spindle is the most clear-cut index of sleep onset. You might be able to read this paragraph with theta in your EEG, but spindles would put a quick stop to your reading. As sleep further deepens, the EEG comes to be dominated by very high-voltage, slow-wave activity of the same sort as might be seen in a patient with brain pathology. The frequencies of these *delta* waves of deep sleep are 1 to 4 cycles per second; the voltage has increased to over 200 microvolts. Since frequency and voltage are reciprocal, the product of voltage and frequency tends to remain relatively constant.

While the EEG is a valuable empirical tool, it is theoretically problematic, because we still do not really know the origin of the voltages that are measured. Each electrode applied to the surface of the scalp is distant from the possible signal sources in the brain. And since the EEG receives the signals only after transmission through several layers of tissue, the EEG must be considered a relatively remote and probably pale copy of the underlying neural activity. Finally, despite the fact that each individual brain cell is a battery and capable of changing its voltage rapidly, it is not yet clear whether the EEG represents the summation of these action potentials or is sensitive to other more slowly conducted potentials. It seems likely that both of these sources, and possibly others as yet undiscovered within the brain, contribute to the EEG.

If sleep researchers had only the electroencephalogram to go by, they would have difficulty in distinguishing the brain state associated with waking from the brain state associated with dreaming, because both states may show the same low-voltage fast pattern (called Stage I), and both may contain alpha rhythms. If we were not able to observe that a subject is behaviorally awake in the first case and asleep in the second, the EEG alone would not be capable of indicating whether a subject is awake or dreaming. Two other measures, one of eye movement and the other of muscle tone, pick up signals that help make the diagnosis of REM sleep.

The eye, with its light-sensitive retinal lining, is the only window opening directly on the human brain. The retina is nervous tissue of embryonic brain origin which has migrated outward from the primitive neural tube. This sac-like protrusion of brain tissue then inverts so that its nerve cells come to live along the back of the inside of the eye. Thus it is that an ophthamologist is able to observe one's nervous system when peering deep into the eye with a lighted ophthalmoscope.

Like the brain proper, the retina is electrically active tissue. Its function is to convert luminous data about the world into the brain's own signal code, a sequence of action potentials. Slower electrical signals of retinal origin can be recorded as the *electroretinogram* (ERG) by placing electrodes on the surface of the skin near the eyes. These electrodes can record the potentials generated by the neurons when flashes of light fall on the retina—just as electrodes placed over the visual surface of the brain can record a somewhat later potential when the electrical signals first generated by the retina have been conducted to the brain.

The windowpane of the eye, the cornea, is electrically neutral, while the light-sensitive retinal film is strongly electronegative. Each eye therefore has a strong negativity at its posterior pole. Each eye is thus a charged dipole; and when the eyes move, spontaneous potentials are elaborated. Since almost all eye movements are *conjugate* (meaning that both eyes move in parallel alignment), a pair of electrodes—one beside the left eye and the other beside the right—will record large potentials when the electrically negative posterior poles of the two eyes move. These voltage signals are 250 microvolts in amplitude, as large as the largest brain waves. Since the electrodes are also close to the anterior part of the brain, they may also pick up EEG activity from frontal lobes.

One way to distinguish eye-movement potentials from frontal brain-wave activity is to refer each ocular electrode to some neutral point (like the ear lobes) and to record each eye separately. Since the eyes move conjugately, the movement-potential traces will then be in opposite directions while the potentials of brain-wave origin will move in the same direction. Even in slow-wave sleep, eye-movement activity can thus be distinguished from brain-wave activity. Since the states that really need differentiation using the eye channel are REM sleep and waking—the two activated brain states in which the EEG is low voltage and fast—the eye-movement record has no high-voltage activity of brain origin to obscure it.

Since eye movements, some of them quite rapid, occur in waking as well as REM sleep, the distinction between the two activated brain states cannot be made by simply adding the electro-oculogram to the brain wave channels and creating the polygraph. Because the muscles are actively inhibited in REM sleep, their electrical activity is specifically sensitive to the state changes occurring within sleep. During the wake state, the muscle system must be continuously responsive to motor commands, so such inhibition never occurs during normal waking. Contrastingly, in order to maintain sleep in the face of an activated brain, muscular activity must be quelled.

As with the heart, the muscles of the body are electrically excitable tissues. In fact, a movement command that arises in the brain is conducted directly to the spinal cord by the long axons of cortical neurons. There the signal crosses one synapse and excites the motor nerve directly supplying the muscle. At the junction between that motor nerve and the muscle, the signal is again converted into a chemical message and reconverted to an electrical signal, which spreads across the membrane around the muscle to initiate the muscle contraction electrically. It is these muscle-action potentials that generate the *electromyogram* (EMG). In the electromyogram, we can actually observe the action potentials of individual muscle fibers.

When electrodes are placed on the skin over the middle of a muscle, the electrical signals that arise during movement or in the active maintenance of an erect posture can be recorded. The EMG potentials of most muscles decrease when one lies down at sleep onset, but some persist until the beginning of the brain-activated state REM; then all are obliterated. In humans, the best muscles for recording this state-dependent suppression of EMG activity are in the upper neck, just underneath the chin.

Since waking and sleeping states are global, involving virtually all of the one hundred billion neurons of the brain, many physiological functions fluctuate with changes in the behavioral and the conscious states. In other words, as the brain goes, so go most functions of the body. The measurement of many kinds of physiological activity can thus be made to form a multichannel picture of the state of an organism. Vital signs such as blood pressure, heart rate, and respiratory rate all undergo synchronously orchestrated changes. Each of these measures can be recorded, with the appropriate transducers applied to the surface of the body.

Blood pressure can be monitored simply by automatically inflating and deflating the sort of cuff that the doctor uses to record a patient's blood pressure. A stethoscope is applied to the depression in the inside of the elbow of the arm. When the pressure in the cuff rises to a certain level, all audible signals transmitted through the stethoscope (and converted into the electrical signals on the polygraph) are suppressed. At this point, the systolic blood pressure can be read. As the cuff is deflated, the turbulence within it (caused by partial transmission of the pulse wave under the cuff) disappears at the point at which diastolic pressure can be recorded. Young adult humans sleep—apparently normally—while their blood pressure is being measured in this crude fashion once a minute.

Heart rate is recordable either from the transduced pulse waves or as the electrocardiogram. Because the air that is moved in and out of the lungs is turbulent, it is noisy; and respiratory rhythms may be recorded from a microphone placed over the trachea. And since first warm, then cool, air follows the movements of respiration across the nostrils, temperature changes within a nostril can be monitored as a measure of respiration.

Surface and deep body temperatures can be recorded by placing thermistors on the skin of the body or within its cavities. Rectal temperature probes, unpleasant in installation, are soon ignored, and subjects are able to sleep admirably well while their core temperature is continuously monitored.

Electrical potentials are everywhere. They are recordable across electrodes placed upon the skin, where they probably reflect neurally mediated changes in the diameter of blood vessels or electrical activation of sweat glands. The *galvanic skin potential* (or GSP) is sensitive to stimuli and can be recorded overnight.

One remarkable motor expression of the state changes constituting the sleep cycle occurs in the sexual organs. The penis of the male and the clitoris of the female are both periodically engorged through the night in concert with changes in the brain. When the blood vessels emptying the penis are closed, the volume of the penis increases—a change that can be recorded by means of a volume recorder (called a *plethysmograph*). Especially easy to record in males, because of the size and shape of the penis, the erections that occur in concert with each REM-sleep period can thus be recorded on the polygraph.

Thus, each system of the body, changing in tune with behavioral and conscious states, may convey particular sorts of information. For example, an individual with high blood pressure may show dramatic increases in that function during sleep. Similarly, an individual with organically determined impotence may show a failure of erection during sleep. Hence, not only is the multiplicity of channels witness to the orchestration of state variables, but each individual channel may have its own specific diagnostic value. This diagnostic use of the polygraph is of great importance to the new field of sleep disorders medicine.

Berger's discovery of the EEG thus inaugurated a new era in the science of human nature. The scientist now has at hand an embarrassment of recordable riches—in contrast to the previous absolute inability to objectify those states of behavior and physiology that are correlated with states of consciousness. Combined with the more penetrating neurophysiological approaches in animal models, the capability of recording puts us on the threshold of the first description of the music of those spheres that are the neurons within our head. For the student of consciousness, the development of the polygraph is no less portentous than was the discovery of the telescope for the student of the heavens. Numerous myths that we hold about ourselves may come to seem as outlandish as the Copernican idea that the sun moves around the earth. Already, for example, it is clear that dreaming comes not from angels, nor from incubi, nor even from wishes, but from the automatic activation of our brains in REM sleep.

The Breakthrough: Eugene Aserinsky and Nathaniel Kleitman

In 1953, Eugene Aserinsky, a graduate student working in the physiology laboratory of Nathaniel Kleitman at the University of Chicago, achieved the breakthrough that gave modern sleep research its current coherence. After studying with the French physiologist Henri Pieron in Paris, Kleitman had sought to provide a thorough physiological description of sleep. His 1939 book and its 1963 update constitute an encyclopedic compendium whose bibliographic thoroughness has never since been imitated.

It was probably the combination of innocence and ambition of the younger investigator, Aserinsky (see figure 6.1), and the wisdom of the experienced and older investigator, Kleitman (see figure 6.2), that led to the key observation—and its correct interpretation. In graduate school, Aserinsky was interested in studying attention in children. While making clinical observations of his young subjects' efforts to attend, he noticed that eye closure was associated with attentional lapses, and therefore decided to record these eyelid movements using the electrooculogram (EOG). In order to obtain a more complete picture of the attentional state of his subjects, he also recorded brain-wave activity. This combination of measures was propitious because, unlike adults, children often enter the REM phase immediately at sleep onset; and these sleep-onset REM periods are especially likely to occur during daytime naps. When Aserinsky's subjects lost attentional focus and fell asleep, their EEGs showed an activation pattern and their electrooculograms showed rapid eye movements. Kleitman quickly deduced that this brain-activated sleep state, with its rapid eye movements, might be associated with dreaming. The two investigators immediately applied the combined EEG and EOG measures to the sleep of adult humans and were able to observe the periodic alternation of REM and non-REM sleep throughout the night. And the awakenings that they performed during REM sleep yielded accounts of dreams.

In 1953, Aserinsky and Kleitman reported their findings in *Science*. Like many really important articles, this one was short and to the point. It even included the observation that other physiological functions change with the state of the brain-mind: respiratory frequency and heart rate had both been noted as increasing; and their rhythm became irregular. Aserinsky and Kleitman provided more systematic observations of this "Phase of Ocular Motility Occurring in Sleep" in the *Journal of Applied Physiology* in 1955.

William Dement confirmed Aserinsky and Kleitman's hypothesis that these periods of brain activation during sleep are highly correlated with dreaming. When normal subjects were aroused from REM sleep, they gave

---

FIGURE 6.1

Eugene Aserinsky

In 1952, Eugene Aserinsky was preparing his report (with Nathaniel Kleitman) for the journal *Science* on the discovery of REM sleep and its correlation with dreaming. Here is his own description of the origin and meaning of this photograph: "The entire family unit depicted in that photo was implicated in the development of the procedures leading to the REM discovery. The first inkling of the presence of REMs came about during recordings in the boy (Armond); his data were identified in my thesis by the initials, AA, and he was further identified as 10 years old. Since all my sleep subjects were young infants or adults, Armond represented all ages in between. Observations on the baby (Jill) when she was younger than in the photo confirmed my conclusion at that time that the fast eye movements in young babies did not meet my rigid criteria for classification as REMs." Below we see recordings of rapid eye movements as they appear on sleep lab polygraphs. *Source:* Photo courtesy of Eugene Aserinsky; polygraph from author's data.

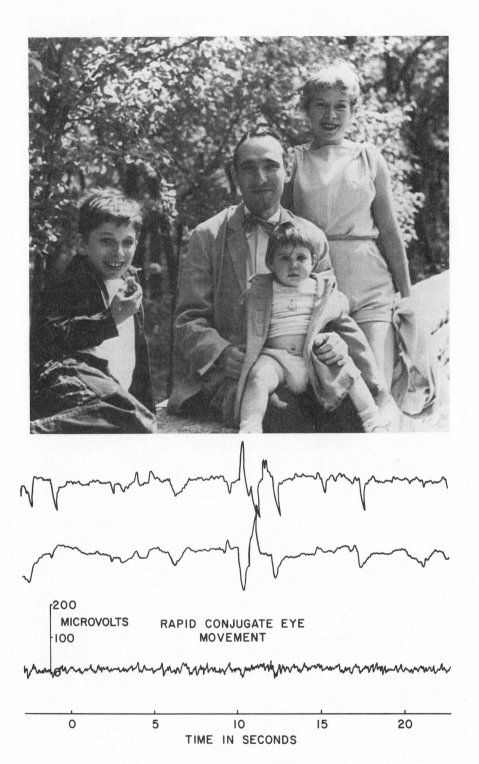

200
MICROVOLTS   RAPID CONJUGATE EYE
-100   MOVEMENT

        0   5   10   15   20

                    TIME IN SECONDS

detailed reports of dream activity. The capacity to recall dreams appeared to be related to the nature of the awakening process; subjects who learned to reach a fully aroused mental state without moving greatly increased their recall capacity. Within the REM period, dream intensity tended to parallel the intensity of phasic physiological events, especially the clusters of rapid eye movements; arousal during REM sleep with eye movement activity yielded reports fulfilling the definition of dreaming given here in 90 to 95 percent of the cases. When scored for vividness, emotionality, and imagined physical activity, these psychological measures also correlated positively with the quantitative intensity of the eye movement in the REM sleep just prior to awakening.

By contrast, awakening during REM sleep when the eyes were not moving rapidly yielded reports of lesser intensity and in a lower proportion of awakenings (70 percent). These figures dropped to 5 to 10 percent when awakenings were made during non-REM sleep. Awakenings from non-REM sleep yielded reports of antecedent mental activity in about 50 percent of the trials, but a large proportion of these reports described thought-like mentation. Reports qualitatively indistinguishable from dreaming were obtained from Stage 1 sleep at sleep onset, a phase of sleep without sustained eye movements; but these reports were quantitatively less impressive in duration and intensity than those obtained from emergent REM-sleep periods later in the night.

So great was the excitement caused by the Aserinsky-Kleitman discovery of the correlation of hallucinoid dreaming with REM sleep that interest in non-REM sleep was put in eclipse for a decade.*

Non-REM is an unfortunate term. To define any phenomenon by the absence of some feature present in another state says only what it is *not* but not what it *is*. Non-REM sleep is better called "slow-wave sleep" (describing the distinctive EEG), "deep sleep" (describing the high threshold to arousal), or "quiescent sleep" (describing its relative tranquillity). In respect to the EEG, some have referred to the non-REM phases as "synchronized" sleep and to the REM phase as "desynchronized" sleep. While both positive and nicely symmetrical, these terms are misnomers when used to imply coordinated firing of the underlying neurons in the case of synchrony, and disorganized firing of the neurons in the case of desynchrony. Since neither of these implications is strictly justified, it would be preferable to refer to these two stages in completely descriptive terms—

---

*In response to this negligence there arose a school of sleep scientists, led by Wilse B. Webb, a psychologist at the University of Florida, which calls itself the Society for the Prevention of Cruelty to non-REM Sleep. (See figure 6.4.)

sleep with high-voltage, slow-EEG activity; or sleep with low-voltage, fast-EEG activity; but such accuracy is cumbersome.

Since REM sleep occupies no more than 25 percent of the entire night in adult humans, the other three-quarters of our sleep is spent in the non-REM phase (sleep with high-voltage, slow-EEG activity). And it was immediately clear to Dement that dreaming is not entirely confined to the REM phase, especially if dreaming is defined as *any* mental activity occurring in sleep. Half of the arousals performed during non-REM sleep yielded reports: individuals might describe the presence of a persistent idea or imagining a waking experience. And some of the reports from non-REM sleep were indistinguishable by any criterion from those obtained from post-REM awakenings. Thus, depending upon the definition chosen for dreaming, the correlation with REM was high or low. And dreaming could not be conceived as confined to the REM state no matter what definition one applied.

Some people have gone so far as to call non-REM sleep nondreaming sleep, and REM sleep, dreaming sleep. A danger here is of confusing a subjective experience with its physiological sign. While the term *dreaming sleep* is not inaccurate of REM, there is evidence of mental activity during non-REM sleep; and while non-REM sleep mental activity is statistically less dreamlike, there are reports from non-REM sleep that are indistinguishable from those obtained during REM sleep. We thus need a nomenclature recognizing the statistical nature of both physiological and psychological states and that no *absolute* distinction can be made between them.

While recording the state of the brain—by means of brain wave, eye movement, and muscle tone—does not reveal the state of the mind, it can predict mental state with high statistical confidence. In upward of 80 percent of awakenings from REM sleep, reports of historically active, visually detailed dreams, with episodic stories and bizarre mental content, are elicited. This percentage is even higher, reaching 95 percent, when awakenings are made during the clusters of eye movement that punctuate each REM-sleep epoch. And all dream features in such reports are more pronounced.

Unfortunately, the thinking that occurs in non-REM sleep is nonprogressive. Humans do not appear to solve cognitive problems by sleep thinking. Rather the mind seems to be running in place. Ideas are mulled over without one's being able either to conclude them or to leave them behind. In non-REM sleep, the electroencephalogram undergoes a progressive set of changes from low voltage and fast waves to high voltage and slow waves. This progressive set of changes, called by A. L. Loomis stages A through E (Loomis et al. 1937), are now known as stages I through IV,

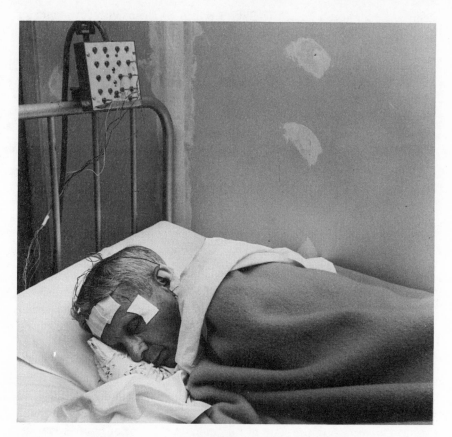

FIGURE 6.2
Nathaniel Kleitman

The objective and instrumental means of recording sleep is illustrated here and in figures 6.3, 6.4, and 6.6. The sleeping subject in this figure is the co-discoverer of REM sleep, Nathaniel Kleitman, then a senior member of the physiology department at the University of Chicago and a seasoned sleep scientist. Kleitman's brain activity was recorded via electrodes attached to his scalp (EEG), while his eye movement (REM) and muscle potentials (EMG) were recorded via electrodes taped near the eye and under the chin. The wires conducting Kleitman's electrical signs of sleep were connected to the electrode box on the bedstead and from there via a cable to a recording polygraph in the next room (see figure 6.4). The contributions of Kleitman's "Chicago School" to sleep and dream research continue to shape the field today. *Source: Scientific American* 203 (1960). Photo by William Vandivert.

in the nomenclature of Allan Rechtschaffen and Anthony Kales (1968). See figure 6.4.

In stage I, the EEG is dominated by low voltage and fast activity, and differs from that seen in waking in that there is an admixture of theta waves with more disorganization of rhythmicity and a slight slowing. This stage of sleep occurs during drowsiness and at nocturnal sleep onset. Subjects who are aroused from stage I sleep at sleep onset often report dream-like mental activity. There may be visual imagery, and one may imagine oneself to be engaged in an act. But there is not a well-sustained episodic story, and the degree of bizarreness associated with such mentation is considerably less impressive than what later develops in the emergent, or ascending, stage I-REM sleep phases. These descending stage-I epochs may last from a few seconds to 5 or 10 minutes following sleep onset, and give way to stage II as soon as the first spindles appear. Spindles are those 15- to 18-cycle-per-second stereotyped waveforms associated with such lapses of consciousness as may occur while reading or dozing off at a lecture. Stage III is defined by the admixture of spindling with higher voltage and slower waves than have previously been seen, but no more than 50 percent of the record may be occupied by slow waves. In stage IV, the 50 percent criterion is exceeded; in its deepest and fullest manifestation, slow-wave activity at a frequency of 1 to 3 cycles per second and with voltages exceeding 200 millivolts, occupies 100 percent of the record.

Subjects awakened from stages II, III, and IV are increasingly disoriented and have more difficulty in reaching full arousal and in recalling previous mental activity. Following many arousals from stage IV, subjects often seem to be actively confabulating. Many of us in the laboratory have had the experience of interviewing a subject after arousal from stage IV and hearing him or her describe mental experience that we knew would later be judged a dream report, and noticing that the subject's EEG was still in stage IV. This experimental sleep talking, with its completely disorganized brain activity, puts in grave doubt the validity of any reports obtained from stage IV awakenings; and subtracting such confabulatory reports may further reduce the amount of dreaming that is actually occurring in the non-REM phase of sleep.

The persistence of stage-IV EEG into the subsequent waking periods suggests that we may be actually dealing with subjects in an experimentally altered state of brain and mental activity—a state that strikingly resembles the organic mental syndromes also characterized by confusion, disorientation, and confabulation. Consider your own confused state when you attempt to answer a telephone early in a night of sleep: the difficulty in orienting yourself and in responding appropriately may be dramatic; and the motive to stay asleep or quickly to return to sleep may be compelling. This compelling force may add to the confusion of early night awakenings. Subjects who perceive that the experimenter wants a dream report may thus be encouraged to confabulate such a report so that they will be allowed to go back to sleep.

Problems abound in any experimental technique that relies on retrospective subjective reporting, especially when the psychological states of interest are known to be intrinsically disorganized and confused. One can never be completely confident that any report is a genuine reflection of what is now, or was just, going on in the mind. But when we rely on the amassing of reports from many subjects who are unaware of the states from which they are awakened, the correlations are surprisingly strong. And the correlation between mental state and brain state is in all likelihood much stronger than we now suppose.

AN ANIMAL MODEL FOR SLEEP AND DREAMING

Following Aserinsky and Kleitman's discovery of human REM sleep in 1953—and their immediate recognition of REM as the physiological basis of dreaming—William Dement established that an identical phase of sleep occurs in cats: in 1958 he published his findings in the *EEG Journal*. (See figure 6.3.)

At the same time (in Lyon, France), the young neurosurgeon Michel Jouvet was conducting experiments designed to study the brain basis of learning: when his cats became bored and entered REM sleep, he observed that they lost all of their muscle tone. This muscular atonia turned out to be caused by an active inhibition from the pontine brain stem which Jouvet identified as the brain's REM sleep center in 1962.

Jouvet set out to study the brain basis of learning but, like Pavlov before him, quickly appreciated its *state-dependent* nature: that is, that animals, including people, that have been placed under controlled experimental conditions and exposed to stimuli that they are expected to learn, rapidly become bored. They stop paying attention. They stop learning.

FIGURE 6.3
Sleep cycle of man and cat

During sleep, the brain alternates between the non-REM and REM states at regular intervals, and the length of each complete cycle varies in proportion to brain size (adult man, 90 minutes; cats, 30 minutes).

The REM stage in both humans and cats is characterized by an activated electroencephalogram (EEG) and by eye movement (EOG)—as is also true of waking; but muscle tone (EMG) is suppressed in REM sleep. Awakenings from REM sleep, especially during times of intense eye movement, typically yields dream reports.

Non-REM sleep in humans is divided into four stages (I–IV), according to the progressive change in the EEG to a high-voltage, slow-wave pattern. Awakenings from non-REM sleep, especially from stage IV, yield reports of thoughtlike mental activity, if any recall is present. *Drawing by Barbara Haines.*

Human Cycle

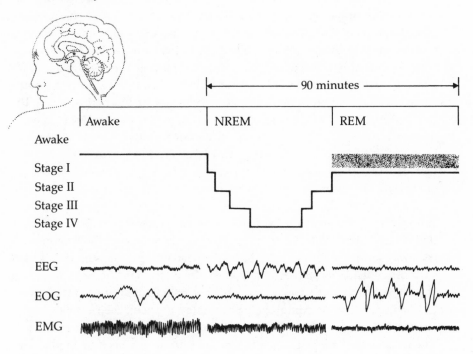

Cat Cycle

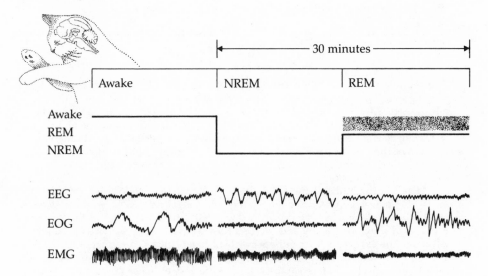

And they not only daydream but fall frankly asleep. In other words, unless the stimulus properties are constantly changed, the brain of the learner often becomes "habituated." Consider the emotional modulation of the voice or the introduction of humor and other attention-getting devices that are the stock of good lecturers. In other words, our brains tend quickly to become inattentive to familiar inputs but to be stimulated by novelty and change. To this tendency, Jouvet's cats, which he was attempting to condition by classical Pavlovian techniques, were no exception. As a consequence, his experimental efforts were frustrated by the animals' tendency to go to sleep instead of learning. In these conditioning studies, Jouvet recorded the electroencephalogram because he was interested in using evoked potentials as an index of learning.*

But how to cope with the problem of more precisely measuring the animals' level of arousal? Jouvet wanted to be certain that each conditioning stimulus was applied under constant background conditions, and the EEG was sensitive not to minor but to important lapses in attention. One suggestion, made by Jouvet's co-worker, the neurologist François Michel, was to record the electromyogram. Michel noticed that when cats began to lose interest in the stimuli being presented to them, their heads would start to fall, a sign often elicited by soporific lecturers or tedious books. Michel proposed that the posterior muscles of a cat's neck be implanted with electrodes sensitive to the muscle potentials; he reasoned that these signals might be more sensitive than the EEG to loss of attentional focus.

Evoked potentials are distinctive EEG waves caused by a stimulus.

FIGURE 6.4
Wilse Webb

The thorough documentation of the human sleep cycle—at all ages and under varying conditions—proceeded apace in the 1960s. One leader of this investigative effort was Wilse Webb, shown here with a sixteen-channel polygraph in his University of Florida laboratory in Gainesville. Literally thousands of nights of human sleep were recorded on millions of feet of EEG paper, and the data analyzed to produce the now classic sleep graphs shown. Typically, REM occupies about 25 percent of each night's sleep and occurs in three to four bouts lasting from a few minutes to over an hour.

Even in the midst of the REM sleep-dream excitement, Webb kept his eye on the biological significance of the earlier and longer non-REM phase of sleep, especially its deepest aspect (stage IV), which he showed to be related to the duration of previous waking and—like REM—to be precisely regulated in length. Although the exact functions of both non-REM and REM sleep remain unknown, Webb's behavioral theory constitutes a coherent framework for experimental work on this problem (see chapter 15). *Source:* Photo courtesy of Wilse Webb; sleep charts from author's data.

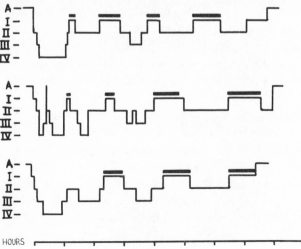

HOURS

Adding this second channel of measurement, the EMG, was as important in Jouvet and Michel's case as was the addition of the electrooculogram (EOG) to measure eye movement in Aserinsky and Kleitman's original studies of children; and remember that the Chicago workers were initially more interested in monitoring subtle changes in attention than they were in sleep. The American and French scientists were thus independently able to make the discovery that these motor channels are not only sensitive to fluctuating levels of arousal during the wake state but also capable of detecting the major periodic reorganizations of brain function that occur within sleep.

Although Jouvet and Michel had already observed REM sleep, they could not at first accept or correctly interpret this periodic activation of the EEG in their sleeping cats. So fixed was the notion that waking was indicated by an activated EEG that when Jouvet and Michel saw cats sleeping with activated EEGs, they were simply unable to infer the new, third state of brain-mind, REM sleep. The journals of the Lyon lab in the late 1950s contain words to the effect that the animal appears to be asleep but the EEG shows it to be awake—an example of what Alfred North Whitehead called the fallacy of misplaced concreteness. The sign of a state (EEG activation) had become the equivalent of the state itself (waking). As it turns out, two distinctly different states are associated with brain activation: one is arousal, when we process information from the outside world; and the other is dreaming, when our brains become predominantly concerned with internally generated information.

Upon reading Dement's 1958 article on REM sleep in cats, Jouvet was immediately able to appreciate what he and Michel had previously observed. In this classic example of a paradigm shift (a change in an investigator's way of looking at data), Jouvet was able to change his focus from the changes evoked by experimentally delivered stimuli (learning) to the endogenous cyclical changes in the animal's readiness to respond (states). In other words, he made a shift from the stimulus-response, or *reflex*, paradigm to the *state* paradigm.

Jouvet also immediately recognized that, in discovering muscle atonia, he and Michel had identified a third cardinal sign of the stage of sleep that Dement had dubbed REM. Jouvet used the term *paradoxical* sleep to emphasize his surprise that an apparently sleeping animal could have an activated brain. And the atonia that they observed was crucial to understanding the paradox: at the same time that the sleeping animal's brain was internally aroused, most of the body's muscles were actively inhibited. Through Jouvet's work, we now know that we would act out our dreams were it not for this inhibitory suppression of motor output.

The behavioral concomitant of this electromyographic silence is well known to cat lovers. When cats doze, they usually assume the sphinx position, the forepaws curled underneath the chest, the head held semi-erect. As the eyes close, the head may droop a bit, only to be raised again with each brief arousal. But if drowsiness gives way to sleep, the head will fall gently to the sleeping surface. At the same time, the postural tone melts and the sphinx position gradually dissolves. Now as it falls over on its side, all of the cat's muscles are manifestly relaxed.

For the amateur sleep naturalist, the observation of REM sleep behavior in cats is a continuous source of wonder—and the more so because one can also observe tiny paw movements that come and go in clusters, or "runs," together with the movements of the eyes. An additional paradox of this REM-sleep state in cats is that the threshold to arousal may actually increase; for this reason, it is possible to raise the eyelid of the sleeping cat (using the eraser end of a pencil) and to observe directly the dramatic flurries of rapid eye movement, the REMs themselves.

Thanks to Dement and Jouvet, we now know that the REM sleep syndrome of sensory unresponsiveness, totally relaxed muscles, and small movements of the eyes and extremities is a behavioral state characteristic of the sleep of all mammals. Since many opportunities exist to observe REM sleep directly, it is remarkable that its association with dreaming was never previously established. Clear anticipation of the correlation is found in the work of the Roman natural philosopher Lucretius who, writing in 44 B.C., described the twitching movements of dogs sleeping upon the hearth. In recent times, REM sleep was described by scientists who failed to appreciate either that the syndrome they discovered was physiologically important or its correlation with dreaming. This recognition and demonstration is properly credited to Aserinsky, Kleitman, and Dement, in their 1953, 1955, and 1957 papers. In 1959 Jouvet and Michel first published their observation on the inhibition of muscle tone in conjunction with the EEG activation of sleep in cats. The 1950s is thus the decade of the establishment of a third major brain-mind state: REM sleep-dreaming.

THE GENERATION OF REM SLEEP BY THE BRAIN STEM

Jouvet thereupon mapped out an experimental program that would help him to establish, in the 1960s, the brain localization of the structures controlling the periodic appearance of the REM sleep syndrome. Having

FIGURE 6.5
Michel Jouvet, William Dement, and Allan Rechtschaffen

In 1963, Michel Jouvet organized the International Symposium on Sleep in Lyon, France. Here he is shown *(left)* with William Dement *(center)* and Allan Recht-schaffen *(right)*, two students of Nathaniel Kleitman. During that year, Recht-schaffen had been working in Jouvet's laboratory on the neurophysiology of REM sleep, which Dement had described in the cat in 1958 and Jouvet had shown to be controlled by the pontine brain stem in 1962. The Lyon meeting, the first of its kind, was also attended by Raul Hernandez-Peon, who described the chemical triggering of REM sleep by acetylcholine; and by Edward Evarts, who showed that neurons of the motor cortex were dramatically active in REM sleep (see chapter 7). Thus the details of how brain-stem activity might control REM sleep and explain dream experience were already emerging in 1963, and debate was lively then as it is today regarding the correct interpretation of these exciting findings.

been at UCLA—where the brain stem had been shown to be important in the control of level of behavioral arousal—Jouvet knew that this brain region was also a strong candidate for controlling brain activation during sleep. (See figure 6.5.)

Because he was adventurous, and wanted to overcome the scientific isolation of Lyon, Jouvet had developed the habit of traveling abroad to discuss his results with other behavioral physiologists. Then, as now, there were surprisingly few in the world. During a visit to Baltimore in the late

1950s, he shared his observation of muscle-tone obliteration with the behavioral physiologist Philip Bard of Johns Hopkins University. Bard had worked with Walter Cannon at Harvard on the bodily changes during fear, hunger, and rage and had later pursued his studies of the brain's control of emotional behavior at Baltimore with the neuropsychiatrist David Rioch. Bard and Rioch had made brain transections in order to determine what parts of the brain are necessary and sufficient for triggering the rage reaction. One of their preparations had a transection of the brain stem just anterior to the pons. Bard recalled to Jouvet that those cats, which were normally spastic, showed a periodic obliteration of muscle tone.

When Jouvet returned to Lyon, he performed Bard and Rioch's prepontine transection experiment and found that the periodic and spontaneous obliteration of muscle tone occurred at exactly the same frequency as physiological REM sleep. It was also accompanied by two other signs of REM sleep: eye movements and a characteristic EEG pattern called the *ponto-geniculo-occipital* (or PGO) waves.

In his classic 1962 paper, Jouvet reported five major kinds of evidence suggesting that the neuronal control mechanism of the periodic occurrence of REM sleep resides in the pontine brain stem:

1. REM-sleep signs persist after prepontine transections. Even if the forebrain is removed, there is essentially no change in the periodic occurrence of REMs and atonia. Jouvet concluded that the forebrain is both incapable of generating REM and unnecessary for the generation of REM. Of course, this does not mean that the forebrain contributes nothing to the syndrome in the intact animal; it means only that it is neither necessary nor sufficient for triggering that state.

2. REM sleep is reduced by small lesions in the upper part of the pons. Jouvet's lesion experiments showed that bilateral damage to the upper pontine reticular formation resulted in marked decreases in the amount of REM sleep, lasting from five to ten days.

3. Electrical stimulation of the pontine brain-stem was occasionally capable of producing REM sleep, but only if the cat was already well into its non-REM sleep phase. Now that we recognize the competitive nature of different populations of brain-stem neurons, the failure to evoke REM sleep by electrical stimulation of this brain region is clearly understandable. Electric stimulation indifferently excites both the neurons that suppress REM and the neurons that trigger it, and thus produces a standoff.

Jouvet observed that pinching the foot or tail of the pontine cat often generated immediate and sustained REM-sleep episodes. Such behavior in the pontine cat could be evoked only periodically, indicating not only that the trigger but also the clock for timing REM sleep was within the pons.

4.   The triggering of REM sleep in the intact or pontine cat could be enhanced by drugs that mimic the action of acetylcholine. Contrastingly, REM sleep could be suppressed by atropine, a blocking agent of acetylcholine. In the pontine cat, REM-sleep episodes were more frequent and longer when the acetycholinesterase inhibitor, physostigmine, was administered. These results all suggested that an increase in endogenous release of acetylcholine was involved in the production of REM sleep.

5.   There was a difference in the mechanism of electrical activation of the brain in REM sleep and in waking—a difference Jouvet was at a loss to understand. Drawing upon the differences in subjective experience between dreaming and waking in humans, he inferred that more primitive brain structures are activated during REM sleep than in waking; and his early results suggested that lesions of the limbic midbrain circuit are more effective in disrupting the cortical activation of REM sleep than are other reticular lesions.

Conclusion

The discovery that REM sleep is regularly recurrent, and that dreaming is its concomitant state of consciousness, opened the doors to a truly objective and instrumental investigative approach to the mind-brain question. By means of information about the state of the brain, dreaming was, for the first time in history, physically diagnosable. The recognition of REM sleep as a predictable phase of brain activity in the sleep of all mammals further provided animal models for exploring the physical basis of dreaming in depth. As a consequence, we may now propose explicit theories of how REM sleep is generated, and account for many puzzling features of the dream state in physiological terms.

PART III

A NEW MODEL
OF THE
DREAMING BRAIN

7

A Window on the Brain:

Neural Activity

When, on the following night, much to his dismay,
[Caesar] had a dream of raping his own mother, the
soothsayers greatly encouraged him by their interpretation of it: namely that he was destined to conquer the
earth, our Universal Mother.
—SUETONIUS
The Twelve Caesars (A.D. 120)

As Shakespeare wrote in the Merchant of Venice:

"There's not the smallest orb which thou beholdest
But in its motion like an angel sings."

The poet thought of the stars and of the spheres, but
this verse applies even more aptly to the individual
cells of our nervous system. We know already how to
hear isolated cells among the millions of elements in
the system. I cannot imagine a more important task
than the reconstruction of their symphony.
—H. L. TEUBER
Perception, Voluntary Movement, and Memory (1967)

THE LABORATORY STUDY of human REM sleep and dreaming
promises a direct correlation between specific aspects of dream content and
specific aspects of brain physiology. This *top-down* approach to dreaming
begins with dream content and looks down to the level of the brain for its
correlate. Such an approach is fraught with conceptual, methodological,
and analytic problems. One is the difficulty of obtaining any detailed

physiological information from the brain of sleeping humans. Fortunately there is an alternative solution to the unknowns on the brain side of the equation: that is, the *bottoms-up* strategy, which focuses attention upon the details of brain physiology (of REM sleep) in animals and then makes inferences back up to the psychological level (of dreaming) in humans.

That the mind should be thought of as "on top" is probably a residue of classical dualism which regarded spirit as weightless. Even today the Pope says angels are weightless but possess free will; and flying as they do, they are certainly "on top." Heaven is full of them. For the more scientifically inclined, "information" or "meaning" is the rational equivalent of the Pope's weightless angel.

The main difference between the bottom-up and the top-down approach is that, in starting from physiology, especially in an animal model, one must begin by modeling far more general features of dreaming than is usual in the top-down approach. We thus seek formal correlates of dreaming instead of specific content correlates. Detailed examples of this formal approach are presented in Part IV of this book to support such bottom-up hypotheses as: if the brain's visual centers are active in REM sleep, then dreaming will be characterized by visual sensation; similarly, if the brain's motor centers are active in REM sleep, then dreams will be characterized by intense imaginings of movement. Corresponding top-down predictions are of specific eye-movement directions from dream reports of gaze direction; and of, say, respiratory movements from dream reports of speech.

The formal approach to brain-mind isomorphism was taken by such pre-Freudian nineteenth-century psychophysiologists as Wilhelm Wundt, but was abandoned following Freud's categorical pronouncements regarding the psychological meaning of dreams. His top-down program of interpretation was immediately appealing in being independent of physiology. But such an approach is a literary and not a scientific enterprise; and such interpretations are open-ended and cannot be conclusively proven, however interesting and even helpful they may be.

The scientific study of dreams can therefore now take up again where the nineteenth-century psychophysiologists left off almost a century ago. It is not that the meaning of dreams or the meaning-attribution power of the brain-mind will never be explained. On the contrary, it seems likely that the formal approach may quickly build from its solid foundation in brain-state to mind-state correlations, to details of cognitive and emotional processes that are also the formal correlates of REM-sleep physiology.

The Observation of Visual and Motor Neurons in REM Sleep

However useful the electroencephalogram has been, it cannot reflect precisely what goes on within the brain during waking and sleep, because it measures electrical activity only from the brain's surface; and the scalp electrodes are too far from the brain's constituent cells for the EEG to resolve the signals of these individual elements. An analogy with blood may help to make this limitation clear: knowing that blood is red is one thing; knowing that the redness is a function of the amount of oxygenated hemoglobin within the individual red corpuscles, another. Only the latter description conveys functional meaning. In the case of the brain, functional significance became clear only when it was possible to record the specialized activity of neurons and how it relates to the EEG.

Two leading twentieth-century physiologists had theories about sleep that predicted decreases in the electrical activity of the individual neurons of the brain. Because sleep is an objectively immobile and unresponsive behavior and subjectively both unconscious and restful, the English physiologist Charles Sherrington (1861–1952) assumed that neuronal activity would diminish—or even cease—during sleep. In his shuttle-loom analogy for consciousness, the twinkling lights that represent neuron activity during waking are progressively extinguished during sleep, until "the great knotted headpiece of the whole sleeping system lies for the most part dark. Occasionally at places in it lighted points flash or move but soon subside" (1955, p. 183).

In his studies of the conditioned reflex, the Russian physiologist Ivan Pavlov (1849–1936) explained the rapid development of inattention and the onset of sleep in his dog subjects when they were exposed to repetitive stimuli, in terms that specified an inhibitory mechanism for Sherrington's "lights out" metaphor:

Under the influence of our conditioned stimuli the cortical elements invariably enter sooner or later into an inhibitory state. With frequent repetitions of the stimuli this happens extremely quickly, and it may legitimately be regarded as an expression of the fact that the cortical elements which represent the highest point of development of the nervous system are extremely sensitive and functionally exhausted with relative ease. [1960, p. 250]

By introducing the notion of easy fatigability, Pavlov was adding an internal factor to the reflex view of sleep already well articulated in the deafferentation concept. With the development of the microelectrode, the evidence overthrew almost all the speculative hypotheses of these eminent scientists.

The Invention of the Microelectrode

The invention of the microelectrode was an important methodological advance because it enabled brain scientists to record the electrical activity of individual nerve cells. The giant squid's axon, part of a huge invertebrate neuron, had already been proved useful in demonstrating the ionic basis of action-potential generation. Successful recordings of individual mammalian nerve cells were reported in 1953, the same year that REM sleep was discovered. The pioneer neurophysiologists Ralph Gerard and Birdsey Renshaw wanted to record individual action potentials from the neurons of animals. To do this, they fashioned fine-tipped metal electrodes: first, a thin wire was sharpened, usually by electropolishing, and then was insulated with varnish or glass. The uninsulated tips of these electrodes could be made microscopically small. When placed in the vicinity of an individual nerve cell, the microscopic tips were capable of picking up the electrical signal of a single cell. This approach ultimately led to the production of glass capillary electrodes capable of penetrating neuronal membrane and recording potentials inside the living cells.

With this technique, scientists were able to communicate directly with the nerve cell, the functional unit of the nervous system. This is the neurobiological equivalent of the astronomer's ability to discern individual celestial bodies, and is analogous to the recognition, in physics, of the atom as an essential organizational element of matter. Neurobiology, and the study of the relation of brain to mind, had, for want of such an analytic technique, lagged far behind the other physical sciences. But now, after thirty years of experience, we can begin to understand how brain activity may be organized so as to account for the succession of states called sleep, waking, and dreaming. We perceive already how the reorganization of activity in neuronal populations may enable us to account for some of the peculiar features of each of those states. Why, for example, do the powers of reasoning and memory decline in our dreams? And how we are able so clearly to perceive visual images in our dreams? Although our present, preliminary answers will probably prove inadequate, the microelectrode has opened a veritable window onto the brain.

The Hubel-Evarts Microdrive System

Two scientists deserve credit for the initial application of the micro-electrode technique to the study of neural activity in sleep and waking: David Hubel and Edward Evarts. Hubel (figure 7.1), a Canadian who worked first at McGill Medical School and later at the Walter Reed Army Hospital in Washington, abandoned the study of sleep for his now famous studies of the visual system with Torsten Wiesel at Harvard University (1959, 1960). They shared the 1981 Nobel Prize with Roger Sperry, in recognition of their achievements.

Evarts, a Harvard educated physician-scientist, was early influenced by both Karl Lashley (who studied learning in the cortex) and Horace Magoun (who studied arousal and the reticular formation). Evarts's inno-vative work led to the first descriptions of individual neuronal activity in the motor system during natural sleep and during the performance of trained motor acts in waking monkeys.

From a technical point of view, the importance of both Hubel and Evarts's work lay in their development of a mechanical system that ena-bled them to bring microelectrodes sufficiently close to a nerve cell to record its electrical activity without damaging it—a particularly challeng-ing feat in an animal that has not been anesthetized and is sufficiently free of experimental influence to demonstrate the natural behavioral changes that occur in sleep and waking. Recall that the brain is composed of some twenty billion neurons, all densely packed together in a gelatinous mass, so that any movement of the animal, even breathing, is likely to impart small but definite changes in the position of the brain. To understand this problem, imagine carrying a bowlful of Jello across a room without causing a ripple. Likewise, each nerve cell moves with each movement of the animal. If the recording microelectrode is stationary, the amplitude of the cell's signal will tend to change and/or to be lost. There is also a definite possibility that the cell will be damaged by the electrode. If the membrane of the cell is suddenly penetrated, the cell may even be killed.

Hubel designed a simple piston-in-cylinder hydraulic drive system and attached a fine-tipped microelectrode to the shaft of the cylinder. The whole apparatus was fastened to the skull over an aperture through which the electrode could enter the brain. Oil was pumped into the upper part of the cylinder so that the piston could be hydraulically driven into the brain. With this system, an experimenter could lower and raise the elec-trode without disturbing the sleeping subject.

Evarts improved upon the Hubel system by making refinements in the

FIGURE 7.1
David Hubel

Convinced that the individual neuron's action potentials might tell us how the brain mediates sensation, movement, and conscious states, David Hubel built a miniature piston-in-cylinder device that could move a microelectrode through the brain of an unanesthetized animal. Hubel first looked at the activity of neurons in visual centers during sleep and was surprised to find that as many cells increased their firing rate as decreased it. Hubel's technique has since been used by Edward Evarts (figure 7.2) and Mircea Steriade (figure 7.3) to complete the picture of this surprising finding which upset the then-prevailing notion of sleep as a state of brain rest. Hubel himself used the technique to analyze visual processing by the brain. *Source:* Courtesy of David Hubel.

microdrive itself and by applying B. F. Skinner's operant conditioning techniques to control the behavior of the animal. Instead of pairing two stimuli, as Pavlov had done, Skinner provided rewards or punishments for the particular spontaneous behavior that he wished to increase or decrease. By supplying fruit juice rewards to his monkey subjects, Evarts was able to observe the firing patterns of individual neurons under a continuous series of spontaneously varying states—just as was needed to study sleep mechanisms. This approach also allowed the experimenter to change the behavior of the animal during the waking state, as was essential to study the motor system. Evarts was also the first to quantify the cellular activity that could now be recorded from microelectrodes when an animal was exhibiting a variety of forms of behavior.

The analysis of data in such experiments could not have been accomplished prior to the development of the digital computer. Because each of the twenty billion individual elements of the brain generates signals at rates of 1 to 300 signals per second, many thousands of signals may be emitted in a single minute. Even counting data at this rate necessitates an automatic system, while the analytic task of ordering and understanding the meaning of the data further depends upon computer technology. Evarts was the first to apply these techniques to the study of changes in rate or pattern of neural activity during natural states.

An Animal Model for Sleep

Cats are good experimental subjects because—as all pet lovers know—of their great propensity to sleep, which is probably related to their relatively high body temperature and their relatively low loss of heat during exercise. Cats are animals that live in the wild by stealth. They make quick movements that are fatal to their prey, but do not indulge in prolonged periods of dynamic motor activity: hence, we walk our dogs but not our cats.

These characteristics make cats a favorite subject of sleep physiologists. And even though cats are a mongrel species, they also have the attractive property of relative uniformity of size and shape of brain—in contrast, for example, with the widely varying head size of dogs. The cat brain can be easily contained within the human hand, and it is not difficult to fashion mechanical devices to be attached to fit any cat's head. Cats are extremely cooperative subjects; their well-known independence extends to the grace with which they adapt to the constraints and obligations of the experimental situation.

An ideal sleep subject should be able to ignore the experimenter; such indifference is not in the character of dogs and monkeys. Dogs are loved by their owners because they are affectionate, relate directly and personally to people, and appear dependent upon their owners, even whimpering when ignored. Monkeys have the charming but undesirable traits of active curiosity and manual dexterity. Their brain and their behavior thus approximate those of man. There is nothing more intrinsically comical than a tired sleep scientist staring at an alert, inquisitive monkey subject: who, one wonders, is studying whom?

Neuronal Activity During Sleep

"Does brain activity really cease during sleep?" was the question posed in 1957 by Herbert Jasper, Hubel's mentor at McGill University.

Does neuronal activity abate, as one might expect from one's own experience? Are the cessation of motor activity and the decrease in sensory threshold, which constitute the key criteria of sleep, paralleled by a cessation of firing in motor and sensory neurons? Jasper had been a pioneer among the scientists studying the brain stem's reticular-activating system in the 1950s. Having focused on reticular influences upon the thalamus, the relay station conveying sensory impulses to the cortex, he was therefore much interested in learning what the individual cortical cells do during sleep and waking and during the arousal produced by electrical stimulation. Jasper developed a system capable of recording from several individual cells at one time. It was immediately apparent that nervous activity certainly does not cease in sleep:

When the animal was drowsy or asleep, with large slow waves in the EEG, many cortical cells were found to be firing as actively as when the animal was alert. In fact many cells appeared to fire only during bursts of slow waves and would cease to fire when the EEG showed the activation or "arousal" pattern of low voltage, rapid waves. [Jasper et al. 1958, p. 280]

This unexpected finding was more amply documented by Hubel who developed his microelectrode and microdrive technique at Walter Reed after he had left McGill. To make recording easier, Hubel lightly anesthetized his experimental subjects, and by this means was the first to record from individual nerve cells as animals passed from waking to sleep (1960). To his surprise, many visual-cortex neurons actually increased their rate of discharge when the cats went to sleep. This finding, which has now been confirmed by other investigators, completely overthrew the notions of Pavlov and Sherrington: the latter's innocent expectation that the tiny lights of his shuttle-loom brain would go out at night; as well as the former's slightly more advanced, but equally erroneous, notion that the cortex would be actively inhibited, and its electrical activity thus extinguished.

Hubel's consternation in the face of his results was related in part to his recognition that the reorganization of neuronal activity during sleep would necessitate a quantitative statistical approach, and he was looking for simpler and more direct answers to his physiological questions. He therefore abandoned the statistical study of neurons and turned his attention to the changes in the activity of the visual cortical cells which could be induced by using light to stimulate the visual system of awake cats.

But many questions about sleep *had* to be answered statistically and quantitatively. Does net neuronal activity increase or decrease during sleep? Are there, with change of state, distinctive changes in the pattern of activity of the individual cells? How is the change in activity of the cells, whether increasing or decreasing in rate, orchestrated by the brain? How is the succession of states realized in the electrical activity of the brain's vast populations of neurons? Are special neurons in special locations responsible for changing the levels of activity through the brain? And what, after all, is the neuronal correlate of our sensation of refreshment after sleep?

It was the functional question that fascinated Evarts most deeply. If the net change in energy consumption of the brain is not significantly lower in sleep, then why do we feel so much more alert in the morning than at night? And why do we feel rested by sleep? Does the action-potential–generating mechanism of some cells decrease so that they rest? This was the central idea that drove Evarts to develop elaborate computerized bookkeeping techniques. The millions of neuronal signals that he collected from his individually recorded cells were used to create the first realistic pictures of what might be going on in the brain during sleep.

Visual Perception and REM Sleep

The study of REM sleep involves the study of visual perception, which is defined by the capability of the brain-mind to create elaborate imagery, as it does in dreaming. The study of visual-system activity during sleep is thus of value to scientists interested in the operation of the perceptual brain in the absence of external stimuli. In REM sleep, the spontaneous activity of the visual system can be studied when it is "seeing," or perhaps I should say "visualizing." While scientists have yet to compare the response of a single cell to a visual input from the external world during the wake state with the activity of that same cell in REM sleep when the visual system is internally stimulated, activation synthesis predicts that the patterns of response to both internally generated and externally generated stimuli will be remarkably similar. A scientist who has only the cell's electrical response pattern to judge may even find it impossible to predict whether an animal is processing external or internal visual information.

Here we see the necessity for a shift from the stimulus-response paradigm of reflex physiology (the paradigm used by Hubel when he stimulated the visual system and recorded the activity of cells) to that paradigm necessitated by the recognition that the system activates and stimulates itself. In REM sleep/dreaming, spontaneous activity is as fully capable of generating formed visual imagery as is activity from the outside world. In waking, the form of the outside world dominates the form of visual imagery; while in dreaming, the form of the system itself, including its recent and remote history, determines the visual imagery.

The study of visual activity during REM sleep is thus not only the study of dreaming but is also, fundamentally and deeply, the study of the brain's autochthonous visual capabilities—as well, as a result, of imagery and imagination. According to the activation-synthesis theory, the form of visual imagery during dreams is in part related to the activation of an internal signal system within the brain, a system that operates during the wake state to keep track of the position of the eyes, and informs the visual centers of eye movement. And it is the specific signal properties of this internal bookkeeping system of the brain which may account for some of the distinctive aspects of visual experience during dreams.

In studying neuronal activity in the visual cortex of the cat, Evarts quantitatively documented Hubel's finding that, in the transition from waking to slow-wave sleep, slowly discharging cortical cells increase rate while rapidly discharging cortical cells decrease rate. When Evarts also recorded cells through the subsequent periods of REM sleep, they all increased rate of discharge to levels at least as high as those seen during waking with visual activity.

Evarts added the important observation that cell activity not only increased in REM but increased in a particular way: clusters of activity were observed at the same time that the eye movements were being generated. One obvious implication of this finding is that the activation of visual cortex neurons during REM sleep is linked to the generation of the rapid eye movements. This observation also hinted at the possibility that the activity in the visual sensory neurons was somehow a response to eye movement commands in the visual motor system. They certainly could not have been responding to external stimuli, because the eyes were closed and the lights were out. In REM sleep, a motor event could thus become the stimulus of a sensory response. Under these conditions, what is normally construed as an effect could become a cause!

Intrigued by the change in the *pattern* of discharge that distinguished REM-sleep neuronal activity from that of the wake state, Evarts was led to conceive of the sleep-wake state change as neuronal (or brain) reorganization, rather than a change in net energy level. He thus transcended the commonsense hypothesis of sleep as rest which had bound both Pavlov and Sherrington, and was the first to enunciate this shift in interpretive focus from energy to information. Evarts said, in essence, that the function of sleep may not be so much to rest the brain as to reorganize its information. In subsequent chapters of this book, I shall present variations of this important idea.

The Motor Cortex and a Theory of Neuronal Rest

Another significant contribution made by Evarts was to select a uniform group of cells for study. If the brain is complicated with respect to the absolute number of its elements, this complication is increased by the fact that, in any particular brain region, there are numerous functionally distinct species of cell. In a social research analogy, we need to distinguish between the responses of men and women, city dwellers and country folk, black and white, rich and poor. While neurons may be created equal, like human beings, they quickly differentiate according to their heredity and environment. In the cortex, some cells send their messages, via axons to points at great distance from the cell body: these are the *Golgi Type I*, or long-axoned, cells. Other cells appear to influence only neighboring neurons in a given locale: these are the so-called *Golgi Type II*, or short-axon, neurons. There are many different kinds of such short-axon cells in the cortex. (See figure 4.4, page 99.)

Evarts performed the first study of an identified cell population: the pyramidal cells of the motor cortex which send their axons to the spinal cord when they make contact with the neurons that will convey movement commands to the appropriate muscles. Voluntary movements always involve at least a two-neuron arc: one in the motor cortex, and the other in the spinal cord. All of the axons carrying the impulses from the motor cortex to the spinal cord travel in a discrete pathway called the *pyramidal tract*, which descends through the brain to the brain stem. There it emerges on the ventral surface before crossing to the other side and continuing its route to the appropriate level of the spinal cord. (See figure 7.2.)

By placing a stimulating electrode in the pyramidal tract of the brain stem, Evarts was able to excite the axons of the cortical motor neurons and to cause them to backfire in response to this stimulation. This abnormal but experimentally useful mode of stimulation is called *antidromic activation* because the impulse propagates back up the axon, instead of down as is the case under physiological conditions. This mode is useful because one can say unequivocally that the cell under study sends its axon into the pyramidal tract, and thus positively identify the cell *and* distinguish it from all of the local circuit neurons.

By studying a physiologically distinct population of neurons, Evarts was able to show that much of the heterogeneous change in activity pattern was related to heterogeneity of cortical cell type. In a social analogy, the variation in response to a sexual questionnaire would decrease if one interviewed only men or only women, and would decrease further still

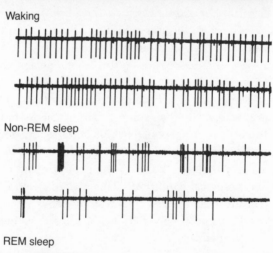

Waking

Non-REM sleep

REM sleep

were our analysis confined to, say, Arab men. Evarts's population of pyramidal cells behaved much more uniformly than an undifferentiated collection of motor-cortex neurons. This finding suggested that not only was his concept of a reorganization of activity in sleep correct, but that specific neuronal systems within the brain change their patterns in uniform and predictable ways.

As in the visual cortex, Evarts found that the rapidly discharging pyramidal-tract cells of the motor cortex also tended to decrease their rate at sleep onset, whereas the slowly discharging cells tended to increase. Studying the motor neurons of the spinal cord, the Harvard physiologist Elwood Henneman had discovered that small cells tended to have higher firing rates at rest than did large cells (1965). Applying Henneman's "size principle" to his sleep data, Evarts assumed that the rapidly discharging cells were small neurons and that the slowly discharging cells were large neurons. Evarts proposed that it might be these rapidly firing smaller neurons that most needed to rest during sleep. Thus, while the net change in cellular activity might be relatively slight in transition from waking to sleep, it might selectively benefit a specific subpopulation of neurons.

But *all* of Evarts's pyramidal-tract neurons increased their bursting property during the REM phase of sleep, having rates as high as those during waking with movement. This finding meant that, during dreaming, motor commands are actually being issued by the cortex but not being enacted, and thus could be related to our sense of constant movement during dreaming. Such "fictive" dream movements have a nonfictive base! This finding also extended Evarts's notion that a change of the organization of information generation within the system might be a functionally important change in sleep.

The most sophisticated technical user of the Evarts-Hubel technique in the study of the cortex in sleep is now the neurophysiologist Mircea

---

FIGURE 7.2
Edward Evarts

To test further the theory that sleep is restful for the brain, Edward Evarts used the Hubel technique to study neurons in the motor cortex of the brain. By restricting his attention to cells that sent long axons to the spinal cord, Evarts was able to obtain more uniform results: even though all cells reduced firing rate in non-REM sleep, they fired as briskly in REM sleep as they did in waking. Evarts was thus able to confirm that brain motor centers are active in REM sleep; and he emphasized the change from the regular pattern of firing in waking to a more clustered pattern in REM sleep, which he attributed to diminished inhibition. These clusters are, in fact, correlated with the muscle twitches and eye movements of REM which in humans, as Helmholtz surmised, are associated with the imagined movement of dreaming. *Source:* Photo courtesy of National Institutes of Health; pyramidal tract cell graph from *Journal of Neurophysiology* 27: (1964).

FIGURE 7.3

Mircea Steriade

By recording specific cells in cortex, thalamus, and midbrain, the Rumanian-born neurophysiologist Mircea Steriade has defined the cellular basis of Moruzzi and Magoun's cortical activation-arousal process. In his Quebec laboratory, Steriade has shown that non-REM sleep is associated with intense inhibition that blocks the transmission of information within the brain; this physiological process may be the basis of the obliteration of conscious awareness that a sleeper experiences early in the night. In REM sleep the brain is reactivated; and all classes of cortical neurons fire intensely, including the interneurons that Evarts thought might fall silent. It seems likely that this wild cortical abandon is part of the physiological substrate of human dreaming. *Source:* Courtesy of Mircea Steriade.

Steriade of Quebec (figure 7.3). Steriade has confirmed Evarts's findings regarding the intense activation of motor output cells and has also shown that the local interneurons, whether excitatory or inhibitory, also fire frenetically in REM sleep. And he has also demonstrated that the most likely source of all this cortical activation is the brain-stem arousal system of Moruzzi and Magoun. So no critical difference has yet been found in the electrical activity of the cortex.

The theory of selective neuronal rest is one of Evarts's lasting contributions. His notion that certain brain cells may rest in sleep preserved the rest theory and gave it a specific character which we have yet fully to appreciate. Even though he may have been wrong about cortical interneurons, it is now clear that the aminergic interneurons do rest in sleep. Here again, he was on the right track.

Conclusion

Hubel and Evarts's findings show a close formal correspondence between the state of the brain and the state of consciousness. Dreams are intensely visual, and visual neurons fire intensely during REM sleep. Their pattern of discharge is pulsatile, just as it is in response to external visual stimuli. Dreams are characterized by a sense of continuous movement, and brain neurons concerned with movement fire intensely during REM sleep. Their pattern of discharge is pulsatile, just as it is when movement is generated in the wake state. As far as the neurons are concerned, the brain is both seeing and moving in REM sleep.

One difference is that we seldom have the experience of willing the movements that occur in our dreams, but instead experience a sense of compelled or involuntary motor activity over which we have little and sometimes no control. This contrast is particularly and strikingly sharp in those dreams in which motor activity becomes a central part of the plot: for example, when one attempts to escape from a pursuer. When the need or desire to escape becomes intense and one's voluntary effort increases, the muscular system is not likely to respond to that command. When dreaming, we experience this inhibition of motor output as heaviness in our legs.

As much as it is the study of vision, the study of REM sleep is thus the study of movement. During this curious state of the brain-mind, motor systems act independent of input and of output. Since output is blocked by inhibition, the operation of the central motor commands is free of feedback from the consequences of movement.

The pioneer work of David Hubel and Edward Evarts has three general implications. First, they gave to sleep physiology the techniques and concepts by which individual neurons could be studied and their contributions to state control evaluated. Second, a subtle and important shift in the understanding of sleep as rest has resulted from Evarts's suggestion that only the cells specifically crucial for normal waking decrease their activity in sleep. And, third, the study of visual and motor neurons in REM sleep is the study of the brain basis of perception and movement.

The Neuronal Activity of the Brain Stem in REM Sleep

We have just seen how visual and motor centers of the cerebral cortex are activated during REM sleep, so as to mediate some visual and motor aspects of our dreams. But how do those cells know when to become activated during sleep? What cells tell them to turn on? And when? And how? And why? We can begin to answer these questions from two major points of view: anatomical and physiological. In the first approach, we look at the location and connections of cells that are capable of affecting simultaneously the visual cortex, which is in the posterior forebrain, and the motor cortex, which is in the anterior forebrain. We know, too, that cells in the spinal cord must be simultaneously affected. So our intuitive attention focuses on the one point in the brain that might coordinate all of these diffuse systems: the brain stem (see figure 7.4).

By following this line of reasoning, we can develop anatomical criteria for neurons involved in the central control of REM sleep. The first criterion is that the location of the cells should be appropriate to the task of coordinating the multiplicity of REM-sleep events in many distant parts of the brain. It may seem obvious, but it is nonetheless logical to suggest that a *center should be central.* After all, it is the state of the whole brain that needs to be controlled. Thus, the evolution of an effective brain center for sleep follows the three rules of real estate value: location, location, and location. And the best location is the brain stem.

Within the brain stem, there are many neuronal candidates. But from a theoretical point of view, it would also be reasonable to suppose that not only location but connection is important. Here the analogy is to the law of politics: It's not who you are but whom you know that counts. With whom do you talk? If you are a neuron, with whom do you synapse? What is your network?

The brain stem is one of the few places in the nervous system where one finds cells that are not only ideally located but ideally connected to control REM-sleep events. The Norwegian anatomist Alf Brodal has emphasized the extensive reach of neurons from the brain stem: upward to the thalamus, and downward to the spinal cord (1956). According to the UCLA anatomist Arne Scheibel, a few of the brain stem's neurons may even send axons in uninterrupted long sweeping trajectories to both the cortex and the spinal cord (1958). Thus, on the basis of both location and connectivity, the brain stem seems to be ideally structured to execute state changes within the brain.

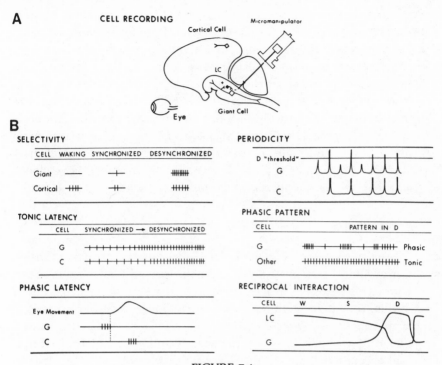

FIGURE 7.4
Neuronal criteria of REM-sleep generation

The Hubel-Evarts micromanipulator can be used to record from different classes of neurons in the pontine brain stem of cats, and the changes in level and pattern of discharge can be studied to create a picture of how REM sleep is engineered. Giant cells (G) of the pontine reticular formation have five properties consistent with an executive role: selectivity, tonic latency, phasic latency, periodicity, and phasic pattern (see pages 174–80). Most important is the finding that the activity level of these giant cells is exactly reciprocal to that of two chemically specific sets of cells: the aminergic neurons of the locus ceruleus (LC) and the raphe nuclei (see pages 180–83). This finding gives REM-sleep generation a chemical basis and is at the heart of the reciprocal-interaction concept (see chapter 8). *Source:* J. Allan Hobson and Robert W. McCarley, "The Brain as a Dream State Generator: An Activation-Synthesis Hypothesis of the Dream Process," *American Journal of Psychiatry* 134, no. 12 (1977): 1341.

Another desirable feature of a state-control center is flexibility. It must be capable of resetting accurately across a wide range of conditions, because behavioral state changes are not rigidly programmed phenomena. Animals that had been suddenly *obliged to sleep* regardless of external circumstances would long since be as extinct as the dinosaur. Although most people living in settled environments do sleep with striking regularity, the property of regularity is flexible and not rigid. The brain takes a running account of the environmental factors that make it safe and propitious (or unsafe and deleterious) to sleep at a given time. At the anatomical level, this flexibility necessitates integrating signals from many outside sources. If the environment is threatening—that is, the stimulus level is too high—the internal control system will summate those signals and say, "Wait, don't sleep now. It's not safe to do so."

In humans, such threats are often internalized as obsessive thoughts, the bogeys of insomnia. By virtue of its location and connections, the brain stem is ideally situated to receive signals from—as well as to send them to—other parts of the brain. These include the cortex, the neural substrate of obsessive ideas, and the probable source of those internally generated signals that lead to the unwanted arousal of our white nights.

Generator Neurons: The REM-On Cells

Using a modified version of the Hubel-Evarts microdrive, Robert McCarley and I began in 1968 to explore the pontine brain stem in search of neurons whose electrical activity might mediate the widespread cortical activation, the motor inhibition, and the rapid eye movements that gave REM its name (see figure 7.5).

By 1977, we knew that compared with the other neuronal populations we had encountered, the reticular giant cells had a unique relationship to REM sleep. This relationship was quantitatively measured as *selectivity* (the tendency to concentrate firing during REM sleep), by *tonic latency* (the tendency to anticipate the REM-sleep period with progressive increases in firing rate), by *phasic latency* (the tendency to fire in bursts which began before the eye movements and the PGO waves), by *phasic pattern* (the tendency to fire in clusters, which were longer and denser than those seen in other cells and in other states), and by *periodicity* (the tendency to activate at REM-sleep frequency whether or not REM sleep actually occurred.

Selectivity. When the action potentials of individual neurons in the pontine reticular formation were recorded in our laboratory during the early 1970s, their activity was at its lowest level during waking, increased progressively during slow-wave sleep, and reached dramatic peaks during REM sleep. While the recording conditions under which these studies were made prevented the animal from moving, Jerry Siegel and Dennis McGinty of the University of California have since shown that the apparent selectivity of pontine reticular formation neurons is not seen in animals that are free to move. Also, our finding that the giant cells fired in association with waking movements indicated both that selectivity was an artifact to the experimental conditions under which we conducted our original studies, and that the selectivity of the reticular giant cells may only be one focal

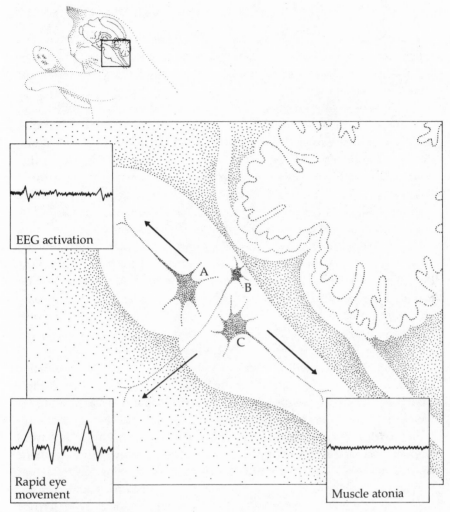

A Midbrain reticular neuron
B Oculomotor neuron
C Medullary reticular neuron

FIGURE 7.5

REM-generator neurons

Each of the three cardinal signs of REM sleep are now known to be generated by
a specific subset of brain-stem neurons. The activation of the EEG is mediated by
the midbrain reticular formation (A), and the rapid eye movements are mediated
by oculomotor neurons (B) in both cases, just as they are in waking. The muscle
atonia—which is unique to REM—is mediated by medullary reticular-formation
neurons (C). In this way the brain-mind is aroused, internal signals are generated,
and motor output is blocked. In dreams, one thus perceives sensation and, without
external stimuli, experiences movement although one is actually paralyzed. *Drawing
by Barbara Haines.*

part of the widespread autoexcitation of the brain that is REM sleep. The selectivity observed under immobilized recording conditions is nonetheless a faithful indicator of the autoexcitatory process that is the essence of REM-sleep generation.

One way to interpret these observations is to say that reticular giant cells are part of an extensive extrapyramidal motor system which becomes activated whenever movements are commanded: in waking, the movements are executed; in REM sleep, they are blocked by inhibition. This concept fits well with our view of dreaming as a continuous sequence of "fictive" movements. In this view, their activation could be considered nonsignificant with respect to any *specific* state-generator function. We know that REM sleep can still occur after the extensive destruction of a cat's pontine giant cells by neuronal poisons, yet humans with shrapnel wounds of the pons may report a loss of dreams. Current evidence thus does not allow us to decide whether reticular activation is normally an essential part of REM-sleep generation. I thus consider it prudent to keep this question open, for there is no doubt that the pontine brain stem is a region somehow critically important to the occurrence of REM sleep.

Another cruel experiment of nature has taught us to exercise caution in interpreting brain-lesion data. An individual suffering from epilepsy may have a well-defined "focus" in the brain: that is, the abnormal electrical activity is seen most prominently at one point in the brain, which is considered to be the starting point for the seizure; hence, the term *focus*. Neurosurgical removal of the tissue in which this electrical focus resides does not necessarily cure the epilepsy: rather, there have often appeared several new foci in the surrounding tissue. This finding suggests that gradients of excitability normally underlie the spread of excitation from one point in the brain to another. The whole system normally undergoes a progressive excitability change so that when one presumed focus is destroyed, others become prominent. Thus, a consequent behavior (as REM sleep) or a disease (as epilepsy) is not eliminated.

The analogy of REM-sleep/dreaming to epilepsy is of more than academic interest. We know that seizures become more probable when REM sleep is prevented; and that epileptic discharges may be released in non-REM and suppressed during REM sleep. These observations indicate that changes in the excitability of the brain are common to both conditions. Dreaming may thus be viewed as the conscious experience of a normal nocturnal brain seizure which helps the brain avoid the excessive excitability that plagues epilepsy victims even during the waking state.

Tonic Latency.   Whether or not they start the war, the giant cells of the pontine reticular formation are in it from the very beginning and, in addition to showing intense increases in firing rate during REM sleep, begin to increase firing rate earlier than any neuronal group so far studied. When their discharge activity was averaged over repeated sleep cycles, we found that the rate increases leading to the REM-phase peaks of firing activity anticipated REM-sleep onset by as much as 5 minutes—well in advance of the activity curves recorded for cortical neurons. It takes the brain a long time to change its mind.

But do the cortical neurons need to be pushed up to speed or do they simply need more time to fall in line? An event that occurs as the first of a pair *may* cause the second, but this possibility has not been proven. All that one can say is that the opposite cannot be the case: the cortex cannot cause the brain stem to turn on in REM sleep. Jouvet had already shown the cortex to be unnecessary for REM-sleep generation: a cortex that was separated from the brain stem no longer demonstrated periodic activation of REM sleep still observable in that brain stem (1962). Thus it seems clear that if unconscious wishes are the cause of REM sleep/dreaming, they must be stored in the cellar of the brain, and not in the attic.

Phasic Latency. The increases in firing by pontine reticular formation neurons are remarkably sporadic in REM sleep. As one listens to the chatter from the microelectrode, one hears staccato runs of activity as the cell revs up for an oncoming REM period. The brain-stem troops are being mobilized for another assault upon the citadel of consciousness. During the REM period itself, these bursts of firing become machinegunlike, similar to those recorded from an epileptic focus. Each fusillade of activity is associated with clusters of PGO waves and with eye movements.

There is, in fact, a strong three-way correlation between the phasic firing of the giant cells, the phasic PGO waves, and the phasic movements of the eyes which give REM sleep its name. When each individual wave and/or eye movement is analyzed, it is further found that the giant-cell firing starts before either of the other two events. And whether or not the waves and the eye movements are correlated with each other, there is a strong, positive anticipatory cross-correlation of each with giant-cell discharge. Here again, antecedence does not prove cause. But it is clear that the giant-cell firing can not be caused by PGO waves or by eye movements. The giant cells seem likely to be causally related to the generation of the eye movements and/or to the PGO waves; at least one internal stimulus generator for dreaming is in the pontine brain stem.

And because the firing-rate increase of giant cells begins as long as a second before each eye movement or PGO wave, probably many other neurons are interposed between the pontine reticular formation and the oculomotor neurons. Excitation must gradually increase in these neurons

FIGURE 7.6
Giant-cell discharge within the REM-sleep period

As indicated in figure 7.4, giant-cell discharge has a clustered, or phasic, pattern in REM sleep. Each dot in figure 7.6 represents an action potential, each line represents ten seconds, and the entire record (which reads from left to right and top to bottom, like the pages of a book) represents one complete REM period. Notice that activity builds slowly and steadily in the beginning of REM sleep but then becomes intensely sporadic, with each of the four horizontal bands of dots corresponding to fifteen-to-thirty-second-long periods of intense rapid eye movement. Awakenings of human subjects at such times yield the most dream reports, suggesting a direct correlation between the neurophysiological and the mental phenomena. This is one foundation of the activation-synthesis hypothesis of dreaming. *Source:* J. Allan Hobson and Robert W. McCarley, "The Brain as a Dream State Generator: An Activation-Synthesis Hypothesis of the Dream Process," *American Journal of Psychiatry* 134, no. 12 (1977): 1344.

during the second before an eye-movement burst and its associated PGO-wave cluster. This build-up of excitation is mediated by interconnections between reticular cells, vestibular neurons, and oculomotor neurons, and all of these brain-stem circuits must be synchronously activated for the REM-sleep pulse generator to work. The pontine reticular formation is known to be a premotor system for eye-movement generation during the waking states. The giant cells may thus play a similar role in generating the eye movements of both waking and REM sleep, and hence their pulsatile activity may not be state-specific. The causes and effects of their firing could, nonetheless, be different in the two states: in waking, they are coordinated with vision, and the perceptual system compares the externally generated images with those stored in memory; in REM sleep, only the internally generated images are available. Thus dreams are composed of fictive visions as well as fictive movements.

Phasic Pattern. *Autocorrelation* is a statistical measure of the tendency of neurons to fire in volleys. This tendency is higher for reticular giant cells than for other cells in the brain stem during REM sleep. The tendency of giant cells to fire in bursts also exists during waking, but the bursts are less sustained, indicating once again that the excitability of the system has been increased during REM sleep. The machinegunner has now lost all restraint; his initial shots were in short bursts; but once the battle is going full tilt, he fires until his magazine is empty. If synapses are like cartridges, it may be that is why REM sleep ends: no more synaptic ammunition. (See figure 7.6.)

Periodicity. When we record from a cell under the most favorable conditions, it is possible to resolve its action potentials continuously for many hours. Often I have gone home for dinner, leaving a well-resolved cell that had been found early on that morning, and come back after dinner to find the cell still present; I then keep on recording until two or three o'clock in the morning. The longest continuous observation of a pontine reticular giant cell is sixteen hours. My co-worker, the American neurophysiologist Ralph Lydic, has since smashed that record by conversing with a single raphe neuron for six straight days (1987a, 1987b).

In addition to the intense peaks of activity that accompanied all full-blown REM periods, there was a tendency for giant cells to activate every thirty minutes, whether or not REM sleep was generated. Pontine reticular giant cells thus fulfilled the periodicity criterion for a causal role in the generation of REM sleep. The observation of periodicity without REM raises the interesting question whether our brains undergo period activation and deactivation throughout the day. It certainly feels that way!

But all of these measures could still be evidence only of correlation and not of cause. How could the causal hypothesis of cause be critically tested? Peter Wyzinski, a postdoctoral student from Mircea Steriade's laboratory in Quebec, implanted stimulating electrodes among the moto-neuronal pools of the spinal cord and checked for antidromic activation of the reticular giant cells. In this way, he demonstrated that the giant cells we recorded in the pontine reticular formation had the requisite connectivity to cause the motor events of REM sleep (1978).*

Turning REM Sleep Off: The Aminergic System

Whether or not the giant cells are specifically and selectively causal of one or another REM-sleep event, they clearly exemplify the activity of a widespread excitatory process in a distributed executive neuronal population. We can thus be confident that the behavior of giant cells is at least exemplary. But the generation of REM sleep events is only one part of the process; we have still to discover how and why the executive network turns on during REM sleep. Neurons, like most soldiers, only do what they are told. Who orders the machinegunners to open fire? (In assassinating President Kennedy, did Lee Harvey Oswald act alone? Or was he part of a conspiracy? Or was he inspired by some remote ideology? Or perhaps disenchanted with a local ethos?) Or do they fire when, their leader wounded, there is no one to restrain them? The neural analogy of such running amok is disinhibition. As inhibition declines, excitation rises.

The idea that giant cells become disinhibited in REM sleep was suggested by the finding that the aminergic cells of the pontine brain stem are turned off at the same time that the giant cells are turned on, and thus show equal but opposite discharge profiles to those of the giant cells. A push-pull dynamic was immediately envisioned.

Since these REM-off aminergic neurons are thought to be mainly inhibitory to the cells that they contact, they could be interacting with the excitatory REM-sleep executive population in a permissive way, so that when they turn off, the giant cells turn on, and vice versa. In other words, the clock that triggers and determines the periodic activation of REM sleep consists of an on-off, excitatory-inhibitory mechanism, characterized by continuous and reciprocal interaction.

*We reasoned that if the giant cells directly trigger REM-sleep eye movements and the muscle twitches, then the axons of the giant cells should project directly to the motor regions mediating those movements. Since, for phasic muscle twitches, the final common-path motoneurons are in the spinal cord, it was of interest to determine whether the giant cells that we were recording in the brain stem did or did not project directly to the motoneuronal pools of the spinal cord.

If the giant cells projected directly to the spinal cord, then it would be possible to stimulate their axons via a spinal electrode and to backfire the cell in the brain stem (just as Evarts had done with pyramidal tract neurons in the cortex).

My co-workers and I found the REM-off cells by accident in 1973 when we were conducting our antidromic invasion studies of reticular neurons. One day Peter Wyzinski called me into the recording room to observe a faintly visible, slowly discharging cell on the oscilloscope screen. Wyzinski (who had sharp eyes then and is now an ophthamologist) was looking for a cell with two properties: it would turn on during REM sleep and be antidromically backfired from the spinal cord. But the cell that caught his attention that morning had neither of these properties. It was, moreover, unique in our experience because it *stopped* firing during REM sleep: it was the first such cell we had ever seen. Histology later revealed that our microelectrode was not in the pontine reticular formation, at which it had been aimed, but in the nucleus locus ceruleus, a millimeter anterior and dorsal to the target area. (In the brain stem, a miss of a millimeter is as good as a mile!) Although Wyzinski was impatient to move on and to find cells that met the criteria of his study, I wondered whether we had accidentally discovered something important.

I instructed Wyzinski to not move the microelectrode but rather to record this anomalous cell as long as possible. In repeated REM-sleep episodes, we found that the cell invariably showed progressive rate decreases during non-REM sleep to a nadir of activity early in the REM period. In contrast to REM-on giant cells, these REM-off neurons had a *negative* selectivity for REM sleep (and hence a positive selectivity for waking). This REM-off property turned out to be shared by two-thirds of the cells in the locus ceruleus, the "blue place" brain-stem nucleus containing cells that manufacture the neurotransmitter norepinephrine in their cell bodies. And it appeared likely that it was the noradrenergic cells in the locus that were the REM-off contingent. Since their noradrenergic influence is distributed throughout the brain via an extensively branching axonal network, whatever synaptic influence they conveyed was thus widely distributed, even to the seats of memory, perception, and thinking in the cerebral cortex.

We soon found that REM-off discharge selectivity was shared by serotonergic cells in the dorsal raphe nucleus—a discovery we made at the same time as Dennis McGinty and Ron Harper at UCLA (1976). Subsequent studies in many laboratories have designated three brain-stem zones containing REM-off cells. All three zones contain aminergic neurons: the noradrenergic nucleus locus ceruleus, the serotonergic raphe nuclei, and the peribrachial pons, which sits beside the locus ceruleus and is related to the control of respiration.

A quantitative comparison of each group's REM-off strength showed that the greatest negative selectivity was in the raphe nuclei. The locus ceruleus was second, and the peribrachial zone third, in consistency and strength of REM-off selectivity. We have interpreted this selectivity gradient as a function of the proportion of cells in each population that were aminergic (as against other chemical types). The dorsal raphe nucleus was the most purely aminergic structure and showed the highest selectivity; the peribrachial zone had the greatest admixture of other cell types and showed the lowest selectivity. There were even a few REM-off cells scattered throughout the midbrain reticular formation, and we expect that further explorations will reveal others. This finding indicates that no neuronal population consists of either pure REM-on or pure REM-off cells. As in any human group, there are always dissenters, and the group mind is the compromise outcome of continuous negotiation: yes versus no; stop versus go; conservative versus liberal. So it goes: we wake; we sleep; and we dream—in cycles that are determined by a statistically shifting consensus.

All of the REM-off cells that we have recorded so far have the same distinctive spontaneous firing pattern during the waking state. Then they discharge slowly, continuously, and monotonously, almost like a metronome. They sound the steady drumbeat of a slow march, not the staccato of a charge. Their firing can be imitated by the sound of a pen tapping slowly on a desk surface. A stimulus increases the rate slightly; and, if it is sufficiently novel, there may even be a burstlike discharge. But the most striking feature is regularity. Thus the REM-off cells differ from the giant-cell population not only in sign of activity (negative versus positive) but in pattern of firing (regular versus irregular).

The aminergic REM-off cells showed a negative tonic latency symmetrical to the tonic latency rate increases of giant cells. The former began to decrease rate immediately at sleep onset, and their rate increase became more and more pronounced until just before the REM period began, when cell firing was sometimes fully cut off. The aminergic cells thus had not only the strongest negative selectivity but also the strongest negative tonic latency. They also had a tonic pattern. In all of their properties, they were opposed to reticular neurons.

The connectivity of the aminergic neurons was ideally suited to a state-regulatory role. Axons of the aminergic neurons are characteristically distributed widely throughout the forebrain: they sweep up into the frontal lobe and then back across the cortex, making perpendicular intersection with the dendrites of millions of cortical neurons. They also send their axons deep into the spinal cord, synapsing as they pass with the dendrites of millions of brain-stem spinal cord neurons. In contrast to sensorimotor systems—which line up in radial vertical channels—the aminergic neurons run a tangential horizontal course. The result of intersection of the two systems in the cortex may be visualized as a grid or screen; the aminergic fibers from a meshlike net, in whose holes the processes of the sensorimotor neurons are caught like so many fish. In REM sleep, the aminergic net is dissolved, and the cortical fish are free to swim. And so we dream.

As our observation of REM-off cell modulation was repeated over and over again, our excitement grew exponentially—like the firing of the giant-cell population prior to the REM period—as we realized we had resolved the paradox (ongoing since Jouvet's work in the late 1950s and early 1960s) of the respective roles of the pontine reticular formation and the aminergic nuclei in REM-sleep generation. Both were equally important but for symmetrically opposite reasons. Lesion and stimulation techniques had simply been unable to discern this interplay: destruction of either system led to decreases in REM sleep; so did stimulation of either system. A whole era of conceptual struggle thus ended with the revelation that an apparent dilemma was false. As is commonly the case with intellectual controversy, it was a *both/and* rather than an *either/or* situation.

This was an exciting breakthrough also because we knew that others who had recorded in these regions had missed the observation: all of us had become so accustomed to seeing REM-on activity that the REM-off property was an unexpected surprise. Furthermore, many others who *had* seen it did not suggest what it might mean. Finally, and most thrilling, the prospect of a new theory of dreaming was implicit in our discovery of a REM-on population in the reticular formation and a REM-off population in the aminergic nuclei.

Conclusion

The brain stem is the nightly battleground of warring neuronal factions, and REM sleep and dreaming are the result of temporary domination of one neuronal population over another. Victorious is a troop of reticular-formation neurons concentrated mainly in the pontine portion of the brain stem; owing to their fusillades of firing in association with REM-sleep events, these pontine reticular neurons are likely to play the executive role in the generation of REM sleep and dreaming. Sharing the white flag of temporary surrender is a population of aminergic neurons located in the locus ceruleus, the raphe nuclei, and the peribrachial regions of the anterior pontine brain stem; hardly a shot is fired by this neuronal phalanx during REM sleep. By virtue of this ceasefire, these aminergic neurons are likely to play a permissive role in the generation of REM sleep. In the next chapter, I shall consider the dynamic rules of continuous nocturnal skirmish as we came to explain it through the reciprocal-interaction model.

8

A War of Nerves: The Reciprocal-Interaction Model of REM-Sleep Generation

Dreams are but interludes which fancy makes
When monarch reason sleeps, this mimic wakes.
—JOHN DRYDEN
"The Cock and the Fox" (1700)

Aside from the general assumption that certain cortical
regions increase while others decrease, let us deduce
from the psychological symptoms . . . [that] the arrest
of functions of certain central influences is related to an
increase in function of certain other influences which
have reciprocal relations with one another.
—WILHELM WUNDT
Grundzuge der Physiologischen Psychologie (1874)

THE RECIPROCAL-INTERACTION hypothesis proposes that the continuous competition between the excitatory reticular neurons and the inhibitory aminergic neurons is the basic physiological process underlying
sleep-cycle alternation. According to this theory, REM sleep and dreaming
occur only when the activity in the REM-off aminergic neuronal population has reached a level low enough to allow the REM-on reticular system
to escape from its inhibitory control. Then the reticular neuronal popula-

tion becomes spontaneously active and switches the state of the brain to the REM mode. While this switching process is "centered" in the brain stem, it is mediated by disinhibition and by consequent excitation of neurons throughout the brain. This neuronal activity is a sort of continuous war whose effects spread from the brain stem throughout the brain, taking the mind hostage. This battle for the mind occurs regularly—and silently—every night in our sleep. And the only outward sign may be the fleeting recollection of a dream as we read the morning newspaper!

THE RECIPROCAL-INTERACTION MODEL

Does some higher law or rule govern the pace and tempo of the war of nerves that we were witnessing in the exchange of fire between the aminergic, waking neurons and the reticular, dreaming neurons of the brain stem? Is the competition observed in their on-off give-and-take merely metaphorical, or were we uncovering a true contest between groups of nerve cells within the Darwinian paradigm of a continuous struggle for survival? Is an underground battle for the mind going on continuously throughout the day as well as all night? The evidence suggests that Nature is indeed economical in her means, and that formal descriptions of population dynamics that hold true for field biology also hold true for neurobiology. One's state of mind is thus the result of a continuous internal negotiation between different parts of the self. Deeper than left brain versus right brain is the contest between the aminergic and the reticular neuronal populations of the brain stem.

In developing the reciprocal-interaction model, we started by observing the reciprocal on-off activity of the two neuronal populations (see figure 8.1). An oppositional or competitive process was immediately sensed. And we knew that opposition in the nervous system is typically expressed by excitation and inhibition. Specifically, we knew that the dynamics of reflex action discovered by Sherrington depend upon the interplay of excitatory and inhibitory neurons. But it was not generally supposed that such long-term alternations in neuronal activity that characterize the states of sleep would obey the same basic rule as the short-term alternations of activity that characterize reflexes. The millisecond duration of synaptic action, while adequate to account for reflex processes, was far too short to account for the occurrence of REM periods every 90 minutes. In fact, the time course of synaptic action was about five million times too

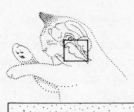

Reciprocal interaction

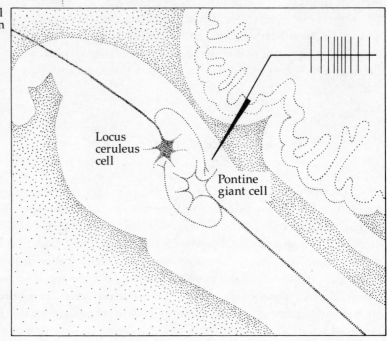

Locus ceruleus cell

Pontine giant cell

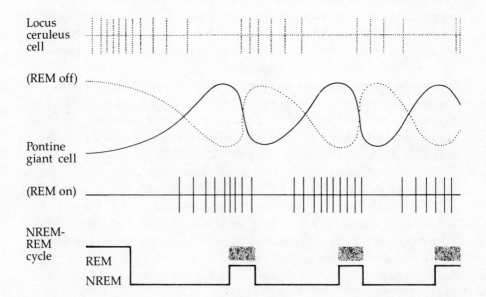

Locus ceruleus cell

(REM off)

Pontine giant cell

(REM on)

NREM-REM cycle

REM

NREM

brief to account for long-term processes involved in state changes. Although it is still incompletely understood how such a long-term process is mediated by neurons, I will suggest several possibilities as I discuss the reciprocal-interaction model.

After it was established that aminergic neurons turn off at the same time that reticular neurons turn on, we had to plot the average activity level of each population as continuous curves in order to determine the precise temporal order of the inverse process we had discovered. Building on the transition data that led to the tonic latency finding, we extended the curves to include the whole cycle. They proved to be very beautiful. The reciprocity of action was indeed continuous across all three states: waking, non-REM sleep, and REM sleep. And the activity was continuously changing in both populations in what appeared to be a precisely reciprocal fashion.

The reciprocal rate levels and the reciprocal rate curves of the aminergic and the reticular populations led us to wonder whether there might be reciprocal connections between the populations. Anatomical evidence suggested that there were impressive inhibitory projections from the aminergic system; and there were impressive excitatory projections from the reticular population. But neither cell group projected exclusively or even particularly strongly to the other—indicating not that the anatomical assumptions of the model were wrong, but only that the model as schematically illustrated was both misleading and incomplete. Misleading, because the interaction might be quite weak; and incomplete, because many other anatomical connections were not represented at all. The interaction of neuronal populations described by the model may nonetheless be exemplary of how the populations of neurons with REM-on and REM-off properties are coordinated.

Conceptual models are aids to scientific progress at two very different levels: at a concrete level, they need to be taken literally and checked out

---

FIGURE 8.1

Reciprocal interaction

The reciprocal anatomical connections and reciprocal activity curves of the excitatory REM-on (e.g., giant cell) and inhibitory REM-off (e.g., locus ceruleus cell) populations are a part of the physical basis of brain-mind state. As long as aminergic cell activity levels are high, one is awake. As they decline, one enters non-REM sleep. When they reach their low point, they have completely withdrawn their inhibitory restraint and the REM-on cells show peak activity as they generate the REM period. Thus, as Wundt surmised (see figure 1.2), dreaming is the conjoint result of increased activity of some brain cells and decreased activity of others, which account for the dreamer's enhanced and impaired cognitive capacities, respectively. *Drawing by Barbara Haines.*

in detail; at an abstract level, they express a concept of a process that can be valid whether or not the postulated underlying details are exactly correct. In this latter sense, a model is said to be *heuristic*. Two heuristic virtues of the reciprocal-interaction model are related to its simplicity. First, the localization studies of the lesion era suggested that the pontine brain stem was the critical zone for sleep-cycle control. It thus seemed unnecessary to specify other populations elsewhere in the brain as potentially causal even though we recognized that they could play a significant contributory role. Second, philosophically, a simple explanation is to be preferred over one more complicated. This rule is called *Occam's razor* after the medieval scholastic Thomas Occam (1285–1347), who cut away redundant theory to reveal the essence of an idea: *Non sunt multiplicanda entia praeter necessitam!* ("Entities are not to be multiplied beyond necessity").

If both the discharge rate curves and the anatomical connections were reciprocal, what about the signs of the interaction? How was the excitation of the REM-on cells chemically mediated? How was the inhibition of the REM-off cells chemically mediated? The aminergic REM-off cell population was thought to be inhibitory to its postsynaptic domain via the long-acting inhibitory postsynaptic potentials generated by norepinephrine and serotonin. The REM-on reticular population was less certainly identified chemically, but much indirect evidence suggested that this system might be cholinoceptive and/or cholinergic. We adopted the working hypothesis that the excitatory actions of the REM-on population are mediated by Otto Loewi's dream transmitter, acetylcholine. We also proposed that the reticular cells could be exciting each other with acetycholine.

Thus, the model also became reciprocally interactive at the level of synaptic neurotransmission: inhibition was mediated by aminergic neurotransmitters; and excitation, by cholinergic neurotransmitters. Little by little, a formally adequate and experimentally testable model was building in our minds. We drew the schematic of possible connectivity patterns and, using Occam's razor, reduced them to their simplest possible formulation. Each population was represented in the model by a single-cell type with a single axonal projection to the other. That projection was either excitatory or inhibitory. Similarly there was a feedback loop to the cell population of origin. Put simply, the model proposed two interconnected populations: one, with feedforward and feedback excitation; the other, with feedforward and feedback inhibition.

The Mathematics of Prey and Predator Fluctuations

Another reason for keeping simple the postulates of the structural model was to enable us to locate and to study a mathematical counterpart. Dr. Robert McCarley, my collaborator in the physiological experiments from 1968 to 1985, was responsible for the quantitative analysis of the neuronal data and for their imitation in the mathematical model (figure 8.2). In reviewing the mathematical models that might account for periodicity, McCarley came upon the classic work of Vito Volterra (1860–1940), a European mathematician who had been hired by the French government to analyze the marked periodic fluctuation in the supply of fur pelts from Canada, an economic enterprise important to the French in the nineteenth century.

The ecological data indicated that the populations of fur-bearing animals underwent a long-term periodic fluctuation. Volterra, together with biologists familiar with the Canadian ecology, suggested that the interaction between prey and predator populations might be determining the economically significant variations in supply of fur. His model is easy to understand since it involves whole animals instead of neurons. Imagine two populations: one of lynx, a small cat predator; and the other of rabbits, the prey of the lynx. These two populations are in a fluctuating balance in the field. If the population of prey, the rabbits, should be plentiful, then the number of lynx that can be supported by them will increase. As a consequence of their increasing numbers, the lynx predators will consume more and more of their rabbit prey and the population of rabbits will eventually diminish. The limits on the number of prey population available has to do with such factors as food supply, and with territorial issues affecting their own reproductive fitness. As the number of lynx begins to outstrip the capacity of the prey population to supply their needs, they will diminish through starvation. As the lynx population diminishes, the number of rabbits will increase. And so on.

As this cyclical process repeats itself, the numbers of the individuals in the two populations will fluctuate periodically and out of phase with one another. The phase delay (or periodicity) of such an interactive system is determined by the respective gestation periods of the animals, because the pregnancies, conceived at peaks of nutritional plenty, take several months to result in population increases. The longer gestation periods of the larger animals (usually the predator population) will have a strong role in determining the periodicity. The longer the gestation period, the longer the phase delay in the interaction of the two populations.

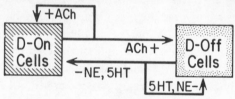

FIGURE 8.2
Allan Hobson and Robert McCarley

The author *(left)* and Robert McCarley, who collaborated from 1968 until 1984, are the architects of both the reciprocal-interaction model of sleep cycle control and the activation-synthesis hypothesis of dreaming (see chapter 9). The synaptic model, shown below, has successfully predicted the results of chemical manipulations of brain-stem neurons so that REM sleep is now under experimental control (see figure 7.4). It was Dr. McCarley who first recognized that anatomical relationships and physiological patterns could be mathematically described by the equations originally developed by Vito Volterra to describe the periodically fluctuating numbers of animals in prey/predator population interactions. In this sense, waking occurs at the expense of REM sleep, and vice versa. The two activated brain states are at opposite ends of a dynamic neurophysiological continuum. *Source:* Photo from Harvard Medical School *Focus;* schema from J. Allan Hobson and Mircea Steriade, "Neuronal Basis of Behavioral State Control," in *Handbook of Physiology—The Nervous System, IV,* ed. Vernon B. Mountcastle (Bethesda: American Physiological Society, 1986), fig. 44, p. 782.

It was gratifying to observe that the two simple nonlinear differential equations of Volterra and Lotka described well the fluctuating levels of activity in two populations in the brain stem. The aminergic and the cholinergic systems of the brain were thus possibly more than casually analogous to the prey-predator situation of the field interaction. After all, waking occurs at the expense of sleep; and sleep, at the expense of waking. And at the cellular level, there is competition between excitatory and inhibitory neuronal populations. In this case they compete not for ecologic niche or space in a concrete sense but for physiological dominance and for temporal sway in the fluctuating states of the brain-mind. Each population rules for a time. It is not easy to say which neuronal population is analogous to prey and which to predator. Since each feeds on the other, they are even more mutually interactive than their counterparts in the ecological model. And of course the analogy breaks down because the neurons do not literally kill each other in order to eat and propagate. Rather, they functionally silence one another for some as yet obscure neurological purpose.

What is the neuronal counterpart of gestation time in the interacting neuronal populations? What determines the 90-minute length of the physiological oscillation, the non-REM–REM cycle in the brain? It will be recalled that the length of time from the onset of one REM period to the next varies both within and across animals, according to brain size. Thus, the size of the brain seems to be the critical spatial variable in determining the duration of sleep-cycle periods. More specifically still, it is the width of the brain stem that correlates best with sleep-cycle length. Creatures with bigger heads have less frequent but longer dreams. This finding suggested the possibility of a spatial determinant of the temporal-time constant in the sleep-cycle model.

Many dynamic metabolic cycles obey this general law. Small animals have faster heart and respiration rates and higher metabolic rates. It takes much more energy per unit weight to keep a small animal going. Just watch a squirrel or a cardinal in winter. It spends all its time seeking, storing, and eating food.

The Periodicity of REM Sleep and Dreaming

The fact that the size of the brain is critical in determining the period length of the sleep cycle suggested that there might be something more than a general metabolic correlation between size and period length. One possibility was that the gestation time of the REM-sleep cycle is the time taken by each neuronal population to translate the rapid pulses of excitatory or inhibitory signals arriving at its collective membrane to a slower intracellular metabolic event. Such a metabolic event could then exert a greatly delayed effect upon the excitability of the target-cell population. If, for example, the excitatory signals arriving at the membrane were translated—via second messengers—to the nucleus of the cell, then that cell would receive instructions to manufacture an enzyme critical to synthesizing its transmitter. The transmitter-synthetic enzyme, manufactured in the nucleus, would then be transported down the axon to the synapse. We know that protein is piped down axons at the very slow rate of 100 millimeters—or 40 inches—a day; this means that a protein can go halfway across a cat's brain stem in 30 minutes, the exact period of the REM-sleep cycle in cats. Thirty minutes after an excitatory barrage, there would be a pulsed arrival of enzyme at the synaptic endings. In this way, reciprocal changes in synaptic efficacy of the aminergic and cholinergic populations can be modeled.

In my analogy to war, the excitatory barrage upon a neuronal population is like a surprise attack upon a country's outpost. Alarmed, the attacked populace prepares itself for reprisal. Central industries are reorganized to produce the materials of war, and a logistical network slowly transports them back to the front. Thus there is a long phase delay between attack and counterattack.

It is not yet known whether protein transport time is actually the basis of the relationship between brain size and REM-sleep period length. The main point of this discussion is to show how initially correlational data can be organized to create a model whose specific dynamic attributes are sufficient to be scientifically useful. The reciprocal-interaction model has theoretical adequacy: a system so designed could produce periodic changes in excitability. It also has empirical testability: the model suggests critical experiments to determine its veracity.

New experimental possibilities include testing the sign of interaction (is it excitatory or inhibitory?) and the intensity of the interconnections of the interaction (how strong is the excitation or inhibition?) by electrically stimulating the REM-on cells or the REM-off cells. The shape of the mathematical curves derived from the Volterra equations may also be checked back against the average activity curves of the actual neurons, and any differences observed may be used to sharpen one's physiological observations. Finally, it is possible to test important metabolic assumptions of the model in sleep: the brain appears to undergo a periodic shift in neurotransmitter ratio, from a predominantly aminergic mode in waking to a predominantly cholinergic mode during REM sleep.

It has already been possible for us to test some assumptions of the model by experimentally instilling chemicals into the brain and thus experimentally increasing (or decreasing) the efficacy of the natural neurotransmitters. Using artificial acetylcholine, we can now produce REM sleep at will in cats. And a variation of this approach has actually been used successfully to intensify dreaming in humans. This is the major experimental consequence of the development of the reciprocal-interaction model.

ARTIFICIAL REM SLEEP AND DREAMING: CHEMICAL ACTIVATION OF THE BRAIN-STEM GENERATOR

Can we fool the REM-sleep generator chemically? And does changing the molecular climate of the brain increase the chance of dreaming? The answer to both questions is yes. The reasoning is as follows: if the reciprocal-interaction hypothesis is correct in its proposition that REM sleep and dreaming are the consequences of the release of cholinceptive neurons from aminergic inhibition, and if there is a focus of excitation beginning in the brain stem, then it should be possible to cause the system to produce REM sleep and dreaming by artificially increasing the cholinergic drive within the brain stem. By symmetrical reasoning, any chemical that *interferes* with the aminergic inhibition of the cholinergic system should have the same net effect. The reciprocal-interaction theory also predicts that both cholinergic antagonists and chemical agents that mimic the inhibitory action of the aminergic system will decrease REM sleep and dreaming if they are injected into the REM-generator network.

These four general hypotheses are the major theoretical predictions of the reciprocal-interaction model. They have allowed sleep scientists to move from the early descriptive correlational phase into a more mature experimental period. This is because experimenters now can *cause* particular brain and mind states to occur and are no longer obliged to sit and wait for their subjects to produce them spontaneously.

The experimental capacity to cause a behavior using cholinergic agonists does not, of course, prove that the behavior is generated by acetylcholine under physiological conditions. In order to develop such proof, a long list of criteria needs to be satisfied. For instance, it would be desirable to measure the actual amount of acetylcholine released in the brain stem during the normal sleep cycle. The reciprocal-interaction model predicts that acetylcholine release will increase progressively over the sleep cycle, and that there will be a peak in REM sleep. Symmetrically and simultaneously, release of the aminergic neurotransmitters, norepinephrine and serotonin, should decrease. And the aminergic and cholinergic release curves should be mirror images of one another. While such studies have been conducted elsewhere in the brain—and with encouraging results for our model—they have not yet been done in the brain stem itself.

According to the reciprocal-interaction model, it should also be possible to cause REM sleep to occur by increasing the spontaneous release of acetylcholine. This is done by blocking the brain enzyme acetylcholinestrase, which normally and rapidly hydrolyzes the spontaneously released acetylcholine and so inactivates it. As a result of blocking the breakdown enzyme, the naturally occurring acetylcholine builds up to a level capable of triggering the generator network. If this test were positive, we could have considerably more conviction about the validity of the theory because the brain's own chemicals would be generating the artificial REM sleep and associated dreaming.

The emerging functional picture is of a tidelike shift of chemical predominance within our brains as we sleep. Underlying—and explaining—the change from our waking orientation (toward external information and externally directed action) to our REM-sleep orientation (toward internally generated information and suppressed action) is a major shift in metabolic orientation. Waking is concerned with information acquisition, catabolic energy expenditure, and action upon the world; REM sleep is concerned with information shuffling, anabolic energy conservation, and suspended animation. Sleep may thus serve development and maintenance of the nervous system, perhaps with reorganization of the nervous system's own information. It appears that our brains and our minds are in a tidal ebb and flow: from concern with the outside world to concern with the internal events that are brain activity itself.

EARLY STUDENTS OF CHOLINERGIC REM-SLEEP GENERATION

The reciprocal-interaction model is not the first to suggest that REM sleep is cholinergically mediated. This idea goes back to the early 1960s when the Mexican neurophysiologist Raul Hernandez-Peon reported that installation of acetylcholine crystals in the brain stem could enhance REM sleep (1965). At the same time Michel Jouvet in Lyon was showing that the REM sleep of cats could be blocked with atropine and increased with the acetylcholinesterase blocker, neostigmine (1962).

Another outstanding proponent of the cholinergic theory was the Pisan physiologist Ottavio Pompeiano (1979), whose work on sleep-related changes in spinal-cord reflex activity is discussed in chapter 9 (see figure 8.3). One of the preparations whose spinal cord reflexes Pompeiano studied was the chronic decerebrate cat. Although their brain stems had been transected above the level of the pons—thus separating the forebrain and cortex from the lower brain stem and the spinal cord—these cats still showed periodic changes in state. Every 30 minutes, and/or in response to a stimulus, their spastic muscle tone melted; and rigidity gave way to flaccidity, just as it had in Jouvet's pontine cats. When Pompeiano administered physostigmine* (an acetylcholinesterase enzyme blocker which leads to a buildup of acetylcholine within the nervous system), his animals entered prolonged periods of atonia. And in association with this experimentally induced atonia, he observed stereotyped clusters of eye movements and PGO waves.

THE CHOLINERGIC MICROSTIMULATION OF REM SLEEP

To increase our capability of interpreting results, I felt that the pharmacological approach was worth taking further. I wanted to know whether increasing the synaptic efficacy of cholinergic synapses at localized sites within the brain stem could also enhance REM sleep in cats.

The first systematic study of the effects of cholinergic-agonist injection was made by Tom Amatruda and a crew of enthusiastic amateurs, including Tom McKenna and Debbie Black. The Amatruda results were encouraging but inconsistent. On some days we saw massive and unequivocal enhancement: genuine orgies of REM sleep! On other days we saw total suppression. Ed Silverman, a physicist-turned-psychiatrist, showed that this inconsistency was related to problems controlling the physical parameters of drug injection. The brain is so sensitive that any

---

*One problem with Pompeiano's work was that it could not precisely localize the pharmacological effects. Since the cholinergic drug was given parenterally, the whole animal was exposed to increased levels of acetylcholine; and Pompeiano could not be sure where in the brain the effective cholinergic enhancement took place. He had to assume that the behavioral consequences were the result of widespread cholinergic enhancement. The same limitations apply to clinical studies in humans, where the usual route of administration of drugs is oral.

increase in pressure, ionic concentration, or other variables associated with directly pumping in a drug can result in suppression of cellular activity and of REM sleep.

Building upon Amatruda's positive findings and upon Silverman's careful analysis of the experimental problems involved with the technique, Ennio Vivaldi, a Chilean physiologist, spent four years firmly establishing the validity of the cholinergic-microinjection technique. Vivaldi was able to show that micropipettes—with tips fine enough to record individual cells—were also capable of ejecting sufficient quantities of cholinergic agonist to induce REM-sleep signs. Vivaldi's results were also the first to suggest that chemical microstimulation could be used to dissect the neuronal systems of the brain stem that generate the several components of the REM-sleep syndrome.

In one of Vivaldi's most dramatic experiments, he introduced a carbachol-filled micropipette into the brain stem, and recorded the activity of single cells at its tip. For sixteen hours he observed clusters of PGO waves and tightly linked bursts of cellular activity that were continuous whether or not the animal was in REM sleep. This dissociation at first troubled us. How could a typical REM-sleep activity, the PGO wave, occur when the animal was wide awake? We later realized that Vivaldi's carbachol was exciting cells that were preferentially related to the generation of PGO waves. His histology showed that the PGO site was in the paribrachial region, several millimeters distant from Silverman's most effective REM-sleep site. The zone that Vivaldi had perfused during those experiments was identical to the zone identified by Jack Nelson's microelectrodes as the PGO burst-cell zone.

Since we had seen REM sleep enhanced from widespread sites in the pons, the question of localization began to worry us. In light of Hernandez-Peon's earlier claims of a diffuse REM-sleep-enhancing system, it seemed that the trigger zone might not be localized at all. Vivaldi thus began a series of experiments to differentiate the functions of various cell zones within the brain stem. Working with two Harvard undergraduates, Mark Goldberg and Dan Riew, Vivaldi began to microinject the midbrain and the medullary reticular formation. This line of work has been recently extended by Helen Baghdoyan, who conclusively demonstrated that the microinjection of cholinergic agonists into either midbrain or medullary brain stem produces increased waking but decreased REM sleep. Only pontine-reticular-formation injections produced increases of REM sleep.

Another line of work that Vivaldi began was pharmacological differentiation between the kinds of cholinergic agonist that were affective. Carbachol activates at least two kinds of acetylcholine receptor: one ace-

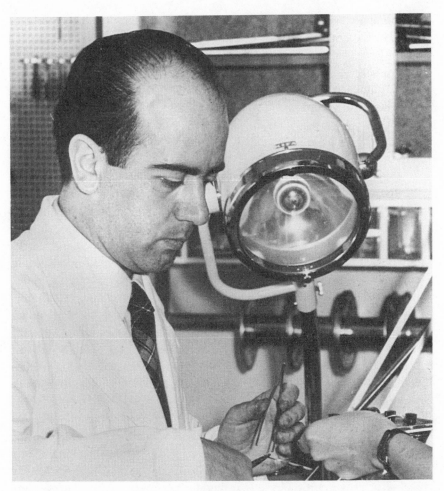

FIGURE 8.3

Ottavio Pompeiano

How the brain suppresses muscle tone during REM sleep so that commanded movements are not enacted was revealed by the experiments of Ottavio Pompeiano. Working in the Pisa Institute directed by Giuseppe Moruzzi (see figure 5.3), Pompeiano applied the classical techniques of spinal reflex analysis introduced by Charles Sherrington (see figure 4.4) to demonstrate that the motor cells leading directly to the muscles are actively inhibited throughout each REM period. Furthermore, stimuli coming from the skin and muscles are also blocked by a second inhibitory process associated with the clusters of rapid eye movement. Both kinds of inhibition were shown to come from the brain stem. *Source:* Courtesy of Ottavio Pompeiano.

tylcholine receptor is turned on by nicotine; the other, by muscarine.* But Vivaldi also achieved spectacular REM-sleep enhancement with the pure muscarinic agonists bethanechol and dioxylane, which are muscarinic but *not* nicotinic. He was thus able to show that activation of the muscarinic receptor alone was as effective in enhancing REM sleep as was activating both classes of receptor.

The Efficacy of Acetylcholine Itself

However encouraging, these REM-sleep-enhancement results were still unsatisfactory because they used synthetic agonist compounds. We needed to know whether the brain's own acetylcholine could produce the same effects. When we microinjected acetylcholine, it did not work, presumably because the degregative enzyme acetylcholinesterase immediately chewed up the externally applied molecules. It was thus possible that all of the REM-enhancing effects we had observed were real but unphysiological.

We began to act on this skepticism by injecting physostigmine, the anticholinesterase drug Pompeiano had found to be effective in inducing a REM-like state when parenterally administered to his decerebrate cats. To our chagrin and disappointment, the effects ranged from only modest enhancement to no effect at all. I relayed this apparently negative result in a pharmacology seminar convened by my colleague Jim Fisher at Tulane University in New Orleans in 1984. In the audience was the pharmacologist Marc T. Alderdice, who informed me that, when administered to the neuromuscular junction, physostigmine had cholinergic-blocking effects as well as the desired increase in the life-expectancy of spontaneously released acetylcholine molecules. It therefore seemed possible that we were inadvertently setting up a chemical competition between the direct anticholinergic effects of the drug and their acetylcholine-enhancing effects. Alderdice had found that neostigmine, a compound that also blocks acetylcholinesterase, did not have the unwanted anticholinergic properties.

Back in Boston, Helen Baghdoyan acted on Alderdice's suggestion and quickly demonstrated that neostigmine was spectacularly successful in enhancing REM sleep. Her studies are significant for several reasons. First, she showed that neostigmine produced a dose-dependent enhancement of

*Cigarette smokers and mushroom fanciers will recognize the names of two active ingredients of their respective addicting plants: nicotine, inhaled with cigarette smoke, stimulates the nicotinic acetylcholine receptor and causes the widespread vascular changes that give the Camel man his jolt; muscarine-like compounds make the beautiful amanita mushroom deadly because they interfere with the normal traffic flow at muscarinic acetylcholine receptors throughout the body.

REM sleep every bit as intense as any of our earlier experiments using mixed or pure synthetic cholinergic agonists. Unless neostigmine itself had a directly cholinergic action, we could be much more secure in our idea that the physiological model was valid. Since the dose-dependent neostigmine REM-sleep enhancement was completely atropine blockable, the effect of neostigmine was mediated via muscarinic receptors.

The shortest times to onset of REM sleep seen with carbachol had been in the range of 2 or 3 minutes. Since it normally takes the cat brain about 5 minutes to produce a full-blown REM-sleep episode, this did not seem unduly long. A vast ensemble of neurons throughout the brain must, after all, be recruited to produce REM sleep. And some cells must be turned off while others are turned on, implying a delicate, dynamic balance. Since the trigger zone in the brain stem had been activated by a pre-emptive excitatory chemical signal, it was not surprising that it might take several minutes to bring the rest of the brain into line. (See figure 8.4.)

But with neostigmine the latencies were never less than 15 or 20 minutes—and sometimes even longer. This delay coincides with that seen under physiological conditions: since the cat normally interposes 20 minutes of non-REM sleep between waking and REM, non-REM sleep could thus be considered to be an incubation period during which the efficacy of spontaneously released acetylcholine is building up. In other words, when neostigmine is microinjected, it immediately inactivates the enzyme acetylcholinesterase, but acetylcholine is released only slowly. It therefore takes a considerably longer time for the released acetylcholine to build up to levels sufficient to pull the brain-stem trigger and begin the recruitment process that results in REM sleep.

ARTIFICIAL DREAMS: CHOLINERGIC REM-SLEEP INDUCTION IN HUMANS

For the clinician looking only at the hundreds of studies of drug effects on human sleep, the interpretive problems are impressive. When Mircea Steriade and I reviewed the literature (1976), we compiled a scorecard of clinical studies: in every category, there were contradictory results. On balance, nonetheless, this scorecard indicated strong support for the reciprocal-interaction hypothesis: drugs with cholinergic-agonist action tended

Human Model

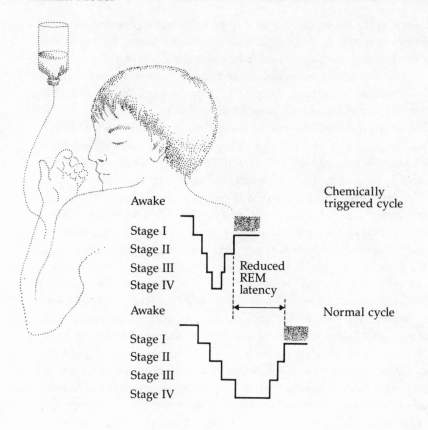

Awake

Stage I
Stage II
Stage III
Stage IV

Awake

Stage I
Stage II
Stage III
Stage IV

Chemically
triggered cycle

Reduced
REM
latency

Normal cycle

Cat Model

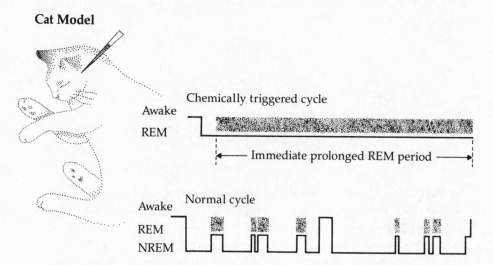

Awake

REM

Chemically triggered cycle

Immediate prolonged REM period

Awake

REM
NREM

Normal cycle

to increase REM sleep, while cholinergic antagonists tended to decrease REM sleep; contrastingly, aminergic-agonist compounds tended to decrease REM sleep, while the antagonists tended to increase REM sleep. An updated discussion of these data, which have become even more convincing in the intervening decade, can be found in the monograph "The Neuronal Basis of Behavioral State Control," by Steriade and myself, which has recently been published in the 1986 *Handbook of Physiology*. Of all the clinical studies, the most exciting to us were those carried out at the National Institutes of Health sleep lab, then led by Christian Gillin (1985). The Gillin studies were of interest for two reasons. First, the experimental design was ingenious: it allowed subjects to fall asleep before the intravenous infusion of cholinergic agonist drugs was begun. Since cholinergic agonists work throughout the brain and peripheral autonomic nervous system, they have an arousing effect which would keep people awake if given before sleep onset. But once sleep has begun, the cholinergically mediated REM phase can be enhanced without producing arousal.

The Gillin group also blocked the peripheral actions of the drug with scopolamine (a cholinergic antagonist that does not cross the blood-brain barrier) so as to be reasonably certain that any observed REM-sleep enhancement was centrally and not peripherally mediated. Subjects who were given intravenous infusions of the cholinergic agonist, pilocarpine, during the first non-REM sleep episode showed a marked reduction in latency to the onset of the first REM period. The first REM period also increased in length and in intensity, there being a greater density of eye movements during the cholinergically enhanced REM sleep. Most exciting of all was Gillin's discovery that subjects aroused from these artificially induced REM periods reported mental activity with all the formal characteristics of dreaming. This was the first scientific evidence for chemically induced REM sleep and dreaming.

FIGURE 8.4
Chemical triggering of REM sleep and dreaming
When drugs that imitate acetylcholine are injected into the blood of a sleeping person, the first REM period occurs earlier than expected. It may also be more intense (have more REMs), and it is associated with dreaming. In a cat, where the same kinds of drug can be introduced directly into the REM trigger zone of the brain stem, the effects are much more dramatic: REM sleep may occur within a few minutes—with no intervening non-REM sleep—and may last for two and one-half hours. These chemically induced REM periods are also more intense—having more REMs and more PGO waves—than normal. *Drawing by Barbara Haines.*

CONCLUSION

The reciprocal-interaction model has incorporated the cholinergic-agonist hypothesis of REM sleep. From the early work of Jouvet and Hernandez-Peon in the late 1950s and early 1960s, this hypothesis was sustained by the Italian physiologist Pompeiano and supported by the human clinical literature. Now it has received its most striking confirmation by the deliberate enhancement of REM sleep and dreaming following intravenous injection of cholinergic agonists in sleeping humans.

These results have powerful implications for our understanding of the brain and the mind. If even a minute imbalance of chemicals in a minute region of the brain can influence the whole system and change its state, our conceptual model is important in understanding not only normal conditions (such as REM sleep and dreaming) but abnormal ones (such as mental illness).

The results would also appear to dispose of the theory that wishes *cause* dreaming, as well as to favor the alternative view that cholinergic brain-stem mechanisms *cause* REM sleep and dreaming. Once REM sleep and dreaming have been cholinergically triggered, wishes may be expressed and may even shape dream plots, but they are in no sense causative of the dream process. The fact that dreaming can now be experimentally caused is one of the strongest points in favor of the activation-synthesis hypothesis, which I will now build upon the physiological foundation provided by the reciprocal-interaction model.

9

The Brain as a Dream Machine:

An Activation-Synthesis

Hypothesis of Dreaming

The master of the school is gone and the boys are in an uproar.
> —THOMAS PAINE
> "An Essay on Dreams" (1795)

I can but give an instance or so of what part is done sleeping and what part awake . . . and to do this I will first take . . . Dr. Jekyll and Mr. Hyde. I had long been trying to write a story on this subject. . . . For two days I went about wracking my brains for a plot of any sort; and on the second night I dreamed the scene at the window, and a scene of turmoil split in two, in which Hyde, pursued for some crime, took the powder and underwent the change in the presence of his pursuers. All the rest was made awake, and consciously.
> —ROBERT LOUIS STEVENSON
> "A Chapter on Dreams" (1892)

ALL SUBJECTIVE EXPERIENCE, including dreaming, tends to be organized by the linguistic faculty of our brain-minds as a narrative-scenario. And we are so intensely involved—and in such peculiar ways—in these story-films that we tend to adopt an interpretive literary stance when reacting to our dreams. But just as literature and film—regardless of their content—may be profitably regarded as particular forms of expression, so may dreams also be profitably viewed as particular forms of mental experience. And it is this formal view of dreaming—as a particular kind of mental experience—that is enlightened by the reciprocal-interaction model of REM sleep physiology.

We begin by asking the most general and—we think—the most fundamental question about dreams: Where do they come from? Why are they so strange? Why are they so hard to remember? And what purpose do they serve? To answer these questions, we have developed the new dream theory called the *activation-synthesis hypothesis* (Hobson and McCarley 1977).

The recognition that the brain is switched on periodically during sleep answers the question of where dreaming comes from: it is simply the awareness that is normal to an auto-activated brain-mind. This causal inference is continued in the term *activation* in the new dream theory's title. The question of why dreams are paradoxically both coherent and strange is in turn suggested by the term *synthesis,* which denotes the best possible fit of intrinsically inchoate data produced by the auto-activated brain-mind.

The original dream theory thus had two parts: *activation,* provided by the brain stem; and *synthesis,* provided by the forebrain, especially the cortex and those subcortical regions concerned with memory. The physiology that is now in hand best supports the first part of the theory; much more work needs to be done on the synthetic aspects of the process. But I now add a third major component to the theory, the concept of *mode switching,* which accounts for the *differences* in the way the activated forebrain synthesizes information in dreaming (compared with waking): for the twin paradoxes of dream bizarreness and insight failure (where the system has lost self-reference as well as its orientation to the outside world) and for dream forgetting.

Brain-Mind Isomorphism

The simplest and most direct approach to the correlation of dream mentation with the physiological state of the brain is to assume a formal isomorphism between the subjective and the objective levels of investigation. By *formal isomorphism* I mean a similarity of form in the psychological and physiological domains. Such an approach begins with the general features (forms) of dreaming mentation and leaves until later consideration the narrative content of the individual dream.

As an example of the formal isomorphism approach, it may be reasonably assumed that subjective experience of visually formed imagery in dreams implicates activation of perceptual elements in the visual system during REM sleep. We may further assume that the visual-system activation of REM sleep must be formally similar to that of the waking state. We could not otherwise account for the clarity of our dream vision. Other details of psychophysiological correlation are assumed to obey the same general law; for example, the vivid hallucinated sensation of moving is assumed to be related to patterned activation of motor systems and of those central brain structures subserving one's perception of where one's body is in space. When we look at the physiological level, for patterned activation of the visual motor and vestibular systems, powerful, highly coordinated excitatory processes are found to be recordable in visual, sensory, and motor centers of the brain.

The Psychophysiology of REM-Sleep Dreaming

To conceptualize how the brain-mind is activated during sleep in such a way as to account for the distinctive cognitive features of dreaming, some of the physiological processes described by the reciprocal-interaction model have been converted into the intermediate language of systems theory. In using electrical-circuit and computer terminology in this section, I aim to facilitate understanding, not to reduce the brain-mind to an electrical circuit or a computer.

Brain-Mind Activation

The brain-mind has to be turned on and kept internally activated to support dream mentation throughout the REM sleep episode. A possible mechanism is the removal of inhibitory restraint upon many brain circuits consequent to sleep-related cessation of activity in a specific subset of neurons.

I propose that the *on-off switch* is the reciprocal-interacting neuronal populations comprising the aminergic neurons and the reticular neurons of the brain stem. While we do not yet know which of the two populations is the initiator, we have reason to favor the aminergic group for this role. Once the reticular system is disinhibited, its own energy will be capable of supplying the *power* to maintain neuronal activation throughout the brain.

The aminergic REM-off neurons are thought to exert a modulatory as well as an inhibitory influence upon the brain during waking. When this modulatory neuronal activity ceases in REM sleep, other brain cells become spontaneously active. Not only are they more active, but the "mode" of their activity is changed: they run free of restraint from both external stimuli and internal inhibition. By such a mechanism, we may not only explain how the mind may be turned on during sleep but also account for its unusual operating properties during dreaming.

Sensory-Input Blockade

Access to the internally activated brain-mind by input from the outside world has to be excluded in order for sleep—and the illusions of dreaming—to be maintained. This appears to be accomplished in at least two ways. First, active inhibition of the nerves denies stimulus signals of peripheral origin access to the central nervous system; such *pre-synaptic* inhibition has been recorded at sensory-relay centers throughout the brain. The physiologist Ottavio Pompeiano, of Pisa, Italy, has shown that the nerve terminals from primary sensory neurons feeding information either into the spinal cord, or into certain brain stem and thalamic sensory-relay nuclei, are depolarized by signals coming from the brain stem (1978). The source of this depolarization is probably the same reticular neurons that constitute the on side of the power switch and include also the pre-motor neurons generating eye movements. Because of their depolarization by internal signals, the primary sensory neurons were rendered less efficacious in transmitting external information: there is simply less transmitter available for each of the externally excited volleys to release at the primary sensory endings.

The second mechanism for excluding external sensory signals is competition, or *occlusion,* by which the higher levels of sensory and associative circuits are kept so busy processing the internally generated messages that they ignore external signals. The net effect of occlusion is the outright neglect of external stimuli or the facile incorporation of them into the internally generated information stream of dreaming. In a REM-sleep dream, I once interpreted the buzzer (which timed our EEG records in the National Institutes of Health sleep lab) as a telephone ringing. Such stimulus incorporation into dreams not only helps preserve sleep, but also provides insight into the temporal aspects of brain-mind interaction in sleep.

Motor-Output Blockade

The internally activated but sensorially disconnected brain-mind must also quell motor output so as to prevent the enactment of dreamed motor commands—lest we all take off on dream walks, dream runs, or even dream flights four times a night! Motor acts appear to be canceled by inhibition of motor-command neurons in the spinal cord and brain stem. This output blockade also prevents the disruption of sleep by the sensory stimulation that such movement would necessarily feed back to the brain.

Here again it was Pompeiano who provided an explanation of this paradox (1978). In an elegant series of experiments, he convincingly demonstrated that the final common-path motor neurons of the spinal cord are actively inhibited via the physiological mechanism of postsynaptic inhibition. Pompeiano's evidence suggested that the origin of these postsynaptic inhibitory signals is, again, the brain stem. Some of the reticular neurons, activated via aminergic disinhibition, are sending "no go" commands down to the final common-path motor neurons in the spinal cord, while others are conducting "go" commands to upper levels of the motor system. This is a "zero-sum" game as far as motor output is concerned: internal motor commands are generated, but their external activation is effectively canceled by concomitant inhibitory signals.

By three processes, the brain-mind in REM-sleep dreaming is thus made ready: (1) to process information (activation); (2) to exclude sense data coming from without (input blockade); and (3) not to act upon the internally generated information (output blockade). (See figure 9.1.) It remains to provide the activated but disconnected brain with internal signals and to make it process them as if they came from the outside world.

Internal Signal Generation

Dream stimuli appear to arise by a process intimately associated with the mechanism of brain activation. In most mammals, including humans, the so-called *PGO waves (P* for *pons, G* for [lateral] *geniculate,* and *O* for *occipital cortex)* present themselves as evidence for an automatic, internally generated information signal which originates in the brain stem. In precise association with the rapid eye movements, strong pulses of excitation are conducted from the brain stem to the thalamus. They are also sent via independent pathways to both the visual and the association cortex. It is now known that these PGO waves are generated by brain-stem cellular activity that faithfully replicates the direction of the rapid eye movements. Thus, not only is internal information generated in REM sleep but that information has a high degree of spatial specificity. According to the activation-synthesis hypothesis of dreaming, the now auto-activated, disconnected, and auto-stimulated brain-mind processes these signals and interprets them in terms of information stored in memory.

REM SLEEP AND DREAMING

A. Systems Model

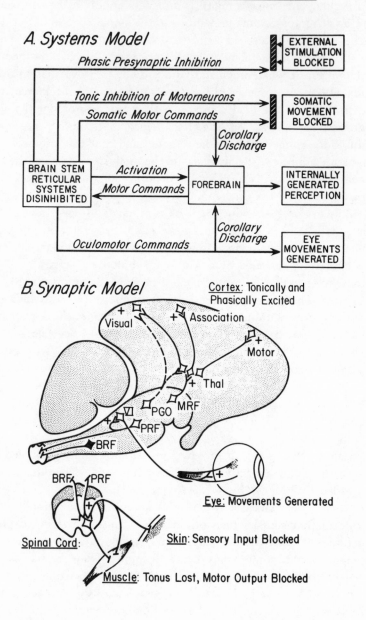

Phasic Presynaptic Inhibition → EXTERNAL STIMULATION BLOCKED

Tonic Inhibition of Motorneurons
Somatic Motor Commands → SOMATIC MOVEMENT BLOCKED

Corollary Discharge

BRAIN STEM RETICULAR SYSTEMS DISINHIBITED

Activation
Motor Commands → FOREBRAIN → INTERNALLY GENERATED PERCEPTION

Corollary Discharge

Oculomotor Commands → EYE MOVEMENTS GENERATED

B. Synaptic Model

Cortex: Tonically and Phasically Excited

Visual
Association
Motor
Thal
MRF
PGO
PRF
BRF

Eye: Movements Generated

BRF   PRF
Skin: Sensory Input Blocked

Spinal Cord:

Muscle: Tonus Lost, Motor Output Blocked

Synthesis: Switching the Mode of Information Processing

Although the precise cerebral basis of the distinctive cognitive disorders of dreaming is not yet fully understood, it is tempting to see these failures as perhaps related to the cessation of activity in the modulatory neurons. This arrest of modulatory neuronal activity would affect the entire brain including the cerebral cortex by depriving it of a tonic influence that may be essential to attentional processes, including the capacity to organize information in a logical and coherent manner and to achieve full self-awareness. This is what I mean by a change in mode of information processing: the brain-mind is active but, for some physiological reason, it lacks the capacity to test both external and internal realities.

During the waking state, the modulatory neurons are active; and the brain is thus set to perform its information-processing functions, including analyzing incoming stimuli, integrating them with the priorities of the day, and producing the appropriate actions upon the environment. In the absence of both external information and the internal modulatory influence,

---

FIGURE 9.1

REM sleep and dreaming

A. Systems model. A schematic representation of the brain processes underlying dreaming. Cessation of aminergic inhibition leads to activation of the reticular formation. The reticular formation turns on the cortex and sends it information about the rapid eye movements that it generates, resulting in visual perception. External stimuli and movement of it are both blocked by inhibition.

B: Synaptic model. Some directly and indirectly disinhibited neuronal systems, together with their supposed contributions to REM sleep phenomena. At level of brain stem, four neuronal types are illustrated.

MRF: midbrain reticular neurons projecting to thalamus that convey tonic and phasic electrical signals rostrally.

PGO: burst cells in peribrachial region that convey phasic activation and specific eye movement information to geniculate body and cortex (dotted line indicates uncertainty of direct projection).

PRF: pontine reticular-formation neurons that transmit phasic activation signals to oculomotor neurons (VI) and spinal cord, which generate eye movements, twitches of extremities, and presynaptic inhibition.

BRF: bulbar reticular-formation neurons that send tonic hyperpolarizing signals to motoneurons in spinal cord. As a consequence of these descending influences, sensory input and motor output are blocked at level of spinal cord. At level of forebrain, visual association and motor cortex neurons all receive time and phasic activation signals for nonspecific and specific thalamic relays. *Source:* J. Allan Hobson and Mircea Steriade, "Neuronal Basis of Behavioral State Control," in *Handbook of Physiology—The Nervous System, IV,* ed. Vernon B. Mountcastle (Bethesda: American Physiological Society, 1986), fig. 44, p. 795.

the REM-sleep-activated brain interprets its internally generated signals as if they were of external origin. Both orientation-in-the-world and self-critical perspective are lost. By a similar mechanism, which we might call *demodulation,* it may be speculated that the synthesized dream product is unremembered. According to this view, the activated forebrain circuits that mediate the dream experience are simply not instructed to keep a record of the dream transactions, unless, of course, the dreamer is aroused and his or her modulatory neurons are turned back on. Thus the "remember" instruction (or mode) is also postulated as being carried out by signals from the modulatory interneurons in waking (when they are active) but not in dreaming (where they are inactive). All current models of learning and memory evoke the intervention of such modulatory interneurons, making the attribution of dream amnesia to the loss of aminergic modulation consistent with state-of-the-art hypotheses regarding learning and memory at the cellular level.

The Form of Dreams Explained

The activation-synthesis hypothesis can now account, in a preliminary but specific way, for all five of the formal aspects of dreaming as I have defined them: visual and motor hallucination; the delusional acceptance of such hallucinoid experience as real; extremely bizarre spatial and temporal distortion; strong emotion; and, finally, the failure to remember.

Hallucination

Mental activity in sleep is different from that in waking in that formed images arise in the absence of external sensory input and motor output: we see clearly, and motion is vividly hallucinated. In the waking state, we can fantasize scenarios; but even the fantasies of a Walter Mitty are not as intense as dream experience. According to the activation-synthesis hypothesis, the sensorimotor hallucinosis of the dream experience is the direct and necessary concomitant of the specific activation of sensorimotor brain circuits. These circuits link the brain stem to other subcortical centers and to the upper motor neurons and analytic sensory neurons of the cerebral cortex. If the higher-level neurons of the visual system are subjected to the same type of phasic excitatory signal that they "see" during the wake state, they will process that signal as if it came from the outside world. Our cortical neurons read the signals as visual sensory inputs. (See figure 9.2.)

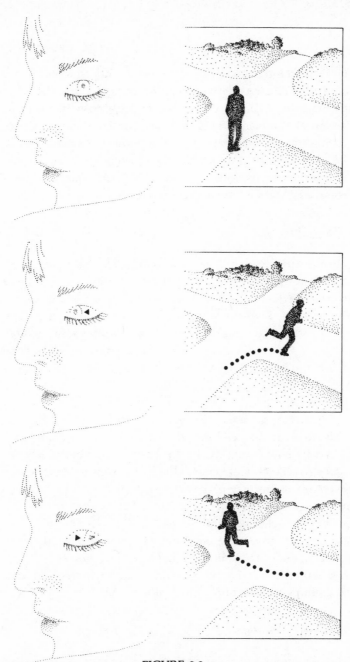

FIGURE 9.2

Visual imagery and REMs

How eye movement information may be related to visual scene construction in dreams is suggested by the change in position of a dream character with each change in eye position. While the data bearing on this specific question are still controversial, there is no doubt either of the strong correlation between eye movement and visual image intensity or that specific information about eye movement does reach the visual centers of the forebrain. Since the existence of an internal signal system has been known since the clinical observation of Helmholtz (see figure 1.1), it seems likely that the visual brain uses its own eye movement data in dream scene elaboration. *Drawing by Barbara Haines.*

The brain-mind knows what state it is in only from its context. Since most organized percepts derive from the waking state, the REM-sleep-activated brain-mind assumes it is awake despite the distinctly different organization of experience. In REM sleep, the brain has no choice but to interpret its internally generated signals in terms of its previous experience with the outside world. According to activation synthesis, the change in mode of information processing caused by an arrest in aminergic neuronal firing contributes to this loss of self-reference.

Dreaming as Delusional

The internally generated signals are not only synthesized into extraordinary stories but are also accepted as experiential reality. The reason is that there is no external input to structure experience, and that only remote memory serves as a reference point. The past is thus interpreted as if it were the present. There are no external cues from which the brain-mind might construct a consistent orientational framework. And because the brain-mind has lost self-reference, it cannot provide internal stability, either.

In using the terms *hallucinoid* and *delusional* to describe dreams, I do not mean to imply that dreaming is psychopathological; it is a normal mental process. But that it is a valid model of psychosis, there can be no doubt. I think that understanding the dream process may better inform understanding of psychosis. Conversely, I believe that the "psychopathology" of these clinical states may probably best be explained by an extension of the kind of functional psychophysiological theory I am proposing here for dreams. While psychotic symptoms, like dreams, have individually specific meanings, it is not those meanings that generate the psychotic experience. Rather, the human brain-mind ascribes meaning to internally generated signals, whether it be normally deluded as in REM sleep, or abnormally deluded as in psychosis during the waking state.

Disorientation: Distortions of Time, Place, and Person

The hallucinoid and delusional mental activity of REM sleep is the more extraordinary for its flagrant violations of natural law. There are discontinuities of all aspects of the orientational domain. Persons, places, and time change suddenly, without notice. There may be abrupt jumps, cuts, and interpolations. There may be fusions: impossible combinations of people, places, times, and activities abound. Other natural laws are disobeyed, and sometimes pleasantly so: gravity can be overcome in the sensational flying dream. We understand these remarkable dream features by adding to previous arguments the notion that the internally generated signals are qualitatively similar to, but quantitatively different from, those that arise from outside the brain. They are different in terms of intensity, of pattern, and of classes of sensory stimuli.

The eye movements of REM sleep in the cat have many oblique and rotational components, which may well generate an unusual sensory code for the forebrain to interpret. Thus, one aspect of spatiotemporal distortion, or dream bizarreness, may reside in the unusual nature of the stimulus source itself. Attentional processes also may be impaired (owing again to mode switching), making it more difficult for the brain to distinguish between different channels of information. In REM sleep, multiple sensory channels are simultaneously activated. Under such circumstances, the kaleidoscopic barrage of all internally generated information must be synthesized into a single plot. And despite the intense bizarreness of these hallucinoid experiences, we accept them as real. The changed mode of the synthetic analytic system may, I think, account for this marked loss of insight.

Intensification of Emotion

Activation synthesis ascribes the intense feelings (such as anxiety, surprise, fear, and elation) characteristic of some dreams to activation both of emotional centers, probably of the limbic brain, as well as of brain-stem "startle" networks. We also know that the autonomic motoneuronal system of the brain stem (which causes the heart to beat fast and the breathing to speed up) may be activated as an integral component of the brain-stem neuronal process responsible for REM. Hence there may be not only intensification of the central components of emotion via forebrain activation but also peripheral feedback from the autonomic mediators of emotional experience.

Amnesia

We can only speculate about one of the most striking cognitive aspects of dreams: that is, the failure to remember most of them. REM sleep is switched on, as I have said, when the firing of the brain stem's aminergic neurons is arrested. These *modulatory* neurons determine the metabolic mode of the brain. One aspect of this notion is that the mode selector (or controller) sends the instruction "Record this experience" (or, "Do not record this experience"). An analogy to a tape recorder is apt if overly concrete. In dreaming, the brain-mind follows the instructions: "Integrate all signals received into the most meaningful story possible; however farcical the result, believe it; and then forget it." The "forget" instruction is most simply explained as the absence of a "remember" instruction.

During REM sleep, the aminergic neurons do not send their "remember" instruction to the forebrain. If not told to remember, the forebrain will forget. I assume that the reason for such dream recall as we do have is that our dream experience is temporarily stored in a fragile short-term memory system, and that it can be more permanently stored only if an arousal occurs so that the aminergic neurons are reactivated. If, and only if, aminergic signals arrive at the many neurons storing that trace memory will the perceptual and cognitive experience of the dream be transferred into intermediate memory.

ACTIVATION SYNTHESIS AND PSYCHOANALYSIS

The activation-synthesis hypothesis assumes that dreams are as meaningful as they can be under the adverse working conditions of the brain in REM sleep. The activated brain-mind does its best to attribute meaning to the internally generated signals. It is this synthetic effort that gives our dreams their impressive thematic coherence: dream plots remain remarkably intact despite their orientational disorganization. And it may be that their symbolic, prophetic character arises from the integrative strain of this synthetic effort. The brain-mind may need to call upon its deepest myths to find a narrative frame that can contain the data. Hence, one can continue to interpret dreams metaphorically, and even in terms of the dynamically repressed unconscious, if one so chooses. But such a practice is no longer either necessary or sufficient as an explanation of either the origin or the nature of dreaming.

I differ from Freud in that I think that most dreams are neither obscure nor bowdlerized, but rather transparent and unedited. They contain clearly meaningful, undisguised, highly conflictual impulses worthy of note by the dreamer (and any interpretive assistant). My position echoes Jung's notion of dreams as transparently meaningful and does away with any distinction between manifest and latent content. While contemporary conservative psychoanalysts continue to defend and apply Freud's dream theory without substantial modification, the more liberal (or hermeneutic) wing of psychoanalysis has explicitly divorced itself from neurology and the causal paradigm of physical science. Both groups may now wish to reconsider their positions in view of the new findings. To maintain their allegiance to Freud and his scientific style, the orthodoxy should welcome an updated dream theory that is compatible with an updated neurobiology (see figure 9.3). Because of its openness, the new theory gives the radicals the interpretive license they seek while offering a return to the safe harbor of classical science. To clarify the contrast, let me review the theory and examine the way in which its components are explained by orthodox psychoanalysis and the way in which we can now understand them.

Energy of the Dream Process

Freud's point of departure in the *Project for a Scientific Psychology* was rigorously scientific. He made it quite clear that his ambition was to establish a theory of the mind that was at one with his theory of the brain. The dream theory was a simple translation of those neurobiologically derived notions that he worked with in the *Project*.

Psychoanalytic dream theory is predicated on the erroneous idea that the nervous system, lacking its own energy, derives energy from two nonneural sources: the external world and somatic drives. We now know that the brain generates its own energy and, in so doing, is not dependent upon either the external world or somatic drives.

Nature of the Energetic Forces

The energy that activates the brain during REM sleep is neuronal, and the neuron is able to create its own information. The power demands of the energy system are relatively low; in Freud's view, they were high. Complementing this shift in emphasis, psychoanalysis sees the shaping of dream content as primarily ideational (the latent dream thoughts); activation synthesis sees it as strongly sensorimotor (there is no difference between latent and manifest content). Freud believed that unconscious wishes and day residues join forces to initiate dreaming. Activation synthesis sees wishes and day residues as two of many shaping forces in the synthetic process of dreaming but as having nothing whatsoever to do with generating the state in which such forces exert their influence.

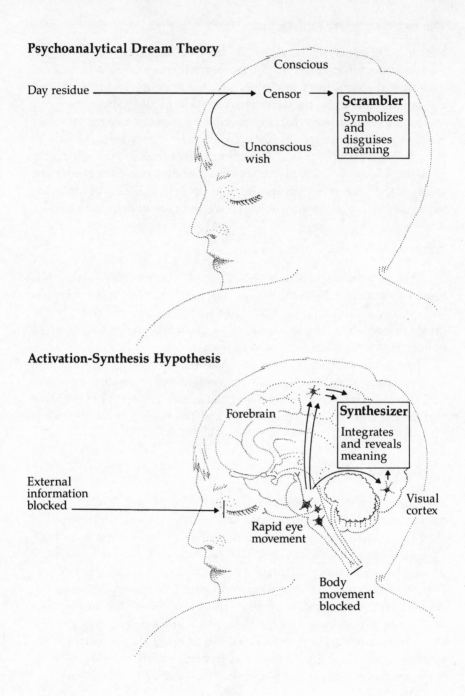

Psychoanalytical Dream Theory

Conscious

Day residue ⟶ Censor ⟶

Scrambler
Symbolizes and disguises meaning

Unconscious wish

Activation-Synthesis Hypothesis

Forebrain

Synthesizer
Integrates and reveals meaning

External information blocked

Rapid eye movement

Visual cortex

Body movement blocked

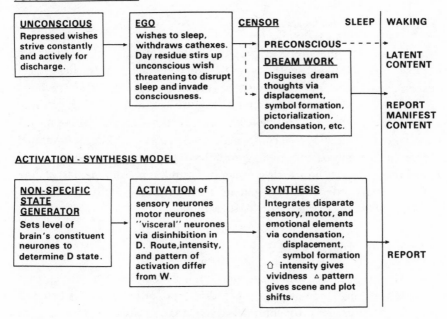

PSYCHOANALYTIC MODEL

| UNCONSCIOUS | EGO | CENSOR | SLEEP | WAKING |

UNCONSCIOUS
Repressed wishes strive constantly and actively for discharge.

EGO
wishes to sleep, withdraws cathexes. Day residue stirs up unconscious wish threatening to disrupt sleep and invade consciousness.

CENSOR

PRECONSCIOUS- - - -

DREAM WORK
Disguises dream thoughts via displacement, symbol formation, pictorialization, condensation, etc.

SLEEP | WAKING

LATENT CONTENT

REPORT MANIFEST CONTENT

ACTIVATION - SYNTHESIS MODEL

NON-SPECIFIC STATE GENERATOR
Sets level of brain's constituent neurones to determine D state.

ACTIVATION of
sensory neurones
motor neurones
"visceral" neurones
via disinhibition in D. Route, intensity, and pattern of activation differ from W.

SYNTHESIS
Integrates disparate sensory, motor, and emotional elements via condensation, displacement, symbol formation ⌂ intensity gives vividness △ pattern gives scene and plot shifts.

REPORT

FIGURE 9.3

Activation synthesis and psychoanalysis

The old psychoanalytic model and the new activation-synthesis model are sketched here to emphasize their differences. It is obvious that the old model has no brain basis: the strangeness of dreams is attributed to the active disguise by the censor of unacceptable unconscious wishes which, together with recent experience ("day residue"), constitute the instigators of dreaming.

The new model is brain-based: the strangeness of dreams is attributed to the distinctive physiological features of REM-sleep generation by which disparate and chaotic internal data must be integrated in the absence both of the structure of external space-time data and of the internal chemical controls necessary for logical thought, attention, and insight. *Drawing by Barbara Haines.*

The differences sketched above are emphasized here by showing, in parallel, the three critical steps in dream construction posited by each model. For psychoanalysis, the dream report is a symbolically encoded transformation of the true dream stimulus, needing interpretation to reveal the latent content. For activation synthesis, the dream as reported is the transparent and directly legible product of an unusual mode of information processing. The sense and the nonsense of dreams are both related to this change in brain-mind mode. *Source:* J. Allan Hobson and Robert W. McCarley, "The Brain as a Dream State Generator: An Activation-Synthesis Hypothesis of the Dream Process," *American Journal of Psychiatry* 134, no. 12 (1977): 1346.

Direction of Information Processing

Since the required energy (power) and the informational sources are of low level, activation synthesis sees dream construction as a *meaning-added process;* whereas for psychoanalysis, it is *meaning-substractive.* This is what I mean by contrasting synthesis with disguise-censorship of information. For psychoanalysis, the motive force of the dream is an idea whose meaning has to be concealed by a complex decoding process. While motivational forces and recent experience may enter into the synthetic construction of the dream, I hypothesize that dreaming builds up from signals of low informational order (the endogenous sensorimotor stimuli) to a higher-order final product (the dream as narrative).

The Sensory Aspects of a Dream

According to activation synthesis, the development of perceptions during dreaming is progressive, proceeding from primordial visual stimuli to perceptual imagery. By contrast, psychoanalysis sees the development of imagery as a regressive function from the ideational motive force of the dream to a perceptual experience: in dreaming, said Freud, we "regress" toward the sensory side. Activation synthesis has no need of a regression postulate: it is an intrinsic characteristic of the dream state to have a primordial sensory character, because the sensory systems of the brain are intrinsically and primarily activated. We view this sensorial aspect as progressive rather than regressive because the system is autoactive and autocreative.

Interpretation

Psychoanalysis sees dream bizarreness as the result of defensive encoding of unconscious wishes. By contrast, the activation-synthesis hypothesis sees the bizarreness of dreams as the unadulterated result of an imperfect integration of internally generated sensorimotor data which is processed under distinctive conditions: the space-time dimensions of the external world are absent; multiple sensory channels are activated in parallel; and attentional processes are impaired. Thus the disguise-censorship notion can be discarded as unnecessary and unwieldy. Discarded as unnecessary, because we have a more plausible alternative that fits with the neurophysiological facts. And discarded as unwieldy, because the new alternative theory achieves the same result by simpler means.

Meaning of Dreams

The brain in REM sleep, like the brain in waking, does its best to achieve a meaningful integration of data, even if it must resort to creative storytelling. The meaning of dreams for the activation-synthesis theorist is thus transparent rather than opaque. The content of most dreams can be read directly, without decoding. Since the dream state is open-ended, individual dreams are likely to reveal specific cognitive styles, specific aspects of an individual's projective view of the world, and specific historical experiences.

The notion that dream meaning is opaque is thus no longer either necessary or sufficient to account for the meaning of dreams; while apparent symbols in dreams may have multiplicity of "meanings," as opposed to many symbols being reduced to one or two instinctual drives or to sexual anatomy. Finally, in activation synthesis, it is not necessary to resort to interpretation via the technique of free association to find dream meanings.

Conflict in the Creation of Dream Plots

For the activation-synthesis theorist, conflict may enter into the plot construction of a dream. But conflict is only one of several factors used in constructing a dream plot and, as such, is neither necessary nor sufficient to account for the dream-fabrication process, as Freud assumed. Conflictual material occurs naturally in dreams, and may contribute especially to repetitive dreams since it may well have a relatively high priority in dream plot formation. Other factors include recency of input (the psychoanalysts' day residue) and what I would call *persistent concern* (the psychoanalysts' unresolved conflict).

When I was under consideration for the professorship I now hold, I had many vividly anxious and humorously absurd dreams of missing airplanes, boats, and trains. Should these dreams be regarded as symbolic translations of my professional self-doubt? Or do they more simply and directly reflect the fact that I was then traveling much more frequently than I had at any previous time in my life? And why should I need to disguise my concern about promotion? It was on my mind night and day, day and night, in undisguised form as evidenced by the many dreams of favorable—and unfavorable—votes on my candidacy that were mixed in, like double features, with the transportation comedies. And if the purpose of the disguise was to guard my sleep, I would be obliged to fire my censor, because having auto-suggested dream interruption in the interest of dream collection, I woke up with equal frequency from each scenario! I realize, of course, that the orthodox Freudian would seek an even deeper source of my travel and promotion dream anxiety. But I am inclined to see them both as realistic and undisguised variations on the theme of "incomplete arrangements."

To summarize, seven major points of difference with psychoanalytic theory characterize the new psychophysiologic model: the source of the energy for the process is seen as internal (not external); the nature of the energetic force, as neural (not ideational); the sensory aspects, as progressive (rather than regressive); the direction of the information processing, as elaborative (rather than degradative); bizarreness, as primary (rather than as the secondary outcome of defensive transformation); meaning, as transparent (rather than opaque); and conflict, as incidental (rather than fundamental to the process).

Mozart at the Museum

The following is the transcript of a dream which I offer as a way of further clarifying the difference between the analytic position of the activation-synthesis hypothesis and Freudian orthodoxy.

My wife, Joan, and I are at the Museum of Fine Arts in Boston to attend a concert in the larger Remus auditorium. It is someone (perhaps John Gibbons) playing a Mozart piano (concerto?) on a large Steinway (no orchestra, but image vague anyway). [The piano is reminiscent of the large Steinway grand in the great hall of the Phillips Collection in Washington, which I visited the previous Saturday.] As is usual on such "museum" occasions, I am restive, feeling like the third wheel on Joan's business bicycle, and hence inattentive.

I decide to explore and go down to the smaller, older theater (near the Egyptian sarcophagi). This theater is now limited to small lectures but was, twenty years ago, the place where, as young members, Joan and I attended museum programs of the type that are now in Remus, and now under Joan's direction.

I hear music and the faint bustle of excitement. Opening the door a crack, I am amazed to realize that Mozart himself is on stage, playing the same concerto (again without orchestra) on an antique harpsichord from the museum collection (not the Mozart pianoforte). Although the door is open only for an instant, I notice Mozart's rich red brocaded frock coat (the curlicues are gold-embossed) and his white powdered wig. He has a beatific smile, and the arpeggios stream through the door into my ear. I also notice that Mozart has gotten a bit overweight, and wonder why.

I close the door with a shhh!, and try to figure out how to tell Joan of my discovery.

Then I wake up.

The following table may help to illustrate the practical differences between activation synthesis and psychoanalysis:

Question	Psychoanalysis	Activation Synthesis
Where does the energy for the dream process come from?	From an external stimulus that could not be discharged as a response because of conflict.	It is intrinsic to the brain.
What is the nature of the energy during this dream?	An unconscious idea: for example, a wish to kill my father so I can have my mother to myself.	From the neurons of the brain, each of which is an electrical generator and capacitor.
What is the cause of the sensory aspects of this dream?	Hearing music and seeing concert halls is a regression, to the sensory side, from the unacceptable ideational dream stimulus (such as a wish to kill my father).	The music I "heard" in the dream is quite familiar to me. I often listen to Mozart piano concertos while driving. The scenes (in the museum) are also familiar. I go there often with my wife, who is a program director. I have just been to the Phillips Gallery.
In what direction does information processing proceed?	The report is only the manifest content, which has been designed to conceal the dream's true meaning.	From low-level neural signals impinging on my mind and auditory cortex, I elaborate the sensations that cohere in a plot around the related themes: concern, Mozart, museum.
What accounts for the bizarreness of this dream; the corpulence of Mozart, for example?	Mozart is an obvious symbol of a powerful, venerated but unapproachable male—that is, my father. The fact that he is overweight clinches the argument (but my father is not overweight!).	Mozart is Mozart. I have seen the film *Amadeus* at a special museum showing, so he fits, although in the dream it was not a film. The body-type file has been opened and incongruous plot features are the result: *my* belly has begun to bulge!
What is the role of conflict in this dream?	I want my mother, but my father is in the way. I have to knock him off, but that's not nice.	I am faintly distressed by the incongruities; no orchestra, wrong instrument; Mozart's corpulence (but my distress is not severe enough to make me doubt the dream's reality).

Question	Psychoanalysis	Activation Synthesis
What does the Mozart dream mean?	Opaque: You hate your father and you want to kill him! But you can't face that base wish, so you turn him into a great man and laud him.	Transparent: I would love to see Mozart, to have my wife "score" by attracting him to the museum, and to discover him there so that I could report her coup to others.

At a deeper level I am prepared to admit that this dream might have a psychoanalytic "meaning": I *am* ambitious. I *do* admire Mozart. I *would*, consciously, like to be as brilliant as Mozart. Some of my most devoted friends have even called me "Mozart." But to propose that Mozart is a stand-in for my father seems less plausible than to assume that, under the suspended cognitive rules of REM sleep, Mozart is Mozart. I saw him and heard him, discovered him even, in an obscure corner of the museum. I found the dream pleasant, surprising, and gratifying. I also enjoyed telling my wife this story. From a social point of view, my dream was a belated wedding present!

The examples just given serve as much to demonstrate the difficulty of deciding between alternative theories of dream interpretation as to convince us that one is better than the other. And in such a literary game, the eloquence and mystique of psychoanalysis are likely to win out over the plain talk and common sense of activation synthesis.

In order to transcend the anecdote and to elaborate an ample and detailed mental status inventory of the dream process, it was therefore necessary to develop a new, formal approach to dream content that would be isomorphic with physiology and share its systematic quantitative and experimental features.

In Part IV, I describe our strategy and preliminary results which support the activation-synthesis view of dreaming as organically driven and organically shaped so as to account for its distinctive cognitive features. Having defined, identified, and measured some of the items in reports that make them dreamlike, I then return to the narrative level and show that by regarding the dream story as transparent—and by looking deeply into it—one can discern significant personal meaning without either free association or the interpretation of putative symbols.

PART IV

DREAM FORM:
THE JOURNAL OF
THE ENGINE MAN

PART IV

DREAM FORM:
THE JOURNAL OF
THE ENGINE MAN

10

The Form of Dreams

Now the study of dreams presents a special difficulty: the fact that we cannot examine dreams directly. We can only examine or talk about the recollection of dreams. Possibly the recollection of dreams does not correspond directly to them. A great writer of the XVII century, Sir Thomas Brown, thought that our recollection of dreams was much poorer than the splendid reality of them. Others, on the other hand, think that we improve our dreams, that is, if we think that dreams are works of fiction (and I believe so) we will probably continue to imagine as we wake up and later when we tell about our dreams.

—Jorge Luis Borges

I am accustomed to sleep and in my dreams to imagine the same things that lunatics imagine when awake.

—René Descartes
Meditations on First Philosophy

WHILE ACTIVATION SYNTHESIS is not the first hypothesis to ascribe the distinctive psychology of dreaming to the distinctive physiology of the brain in sleep, it is the first such theory to build upon a specific, factual account of that physiology, whose details have only recently been discovered. Of course, some of our psychophysiological predecessors did well without the facts we now possess (see Part II), but speculation—whether it be psychological, as with Sigmund Freud, or physiological, as with Wilhelm Wundt—is not true science. In the absence of facts, a theory can be neither solidly founded nor developed.

It is probably no accident that the most prescient nineteenth-century dream theorists focused more upon the general form of dream experience rather than upon the content of individual dream narratives. The dream psychophysiology of the late twentieth century has a similar emphasis. In this and the following four chapters, I will show how a formal psychology of all dreaming—as against an interpretive approach to an individual dream—is the natural outgrowth of new discoveries in human sleep physiology. In the emerging concerto for brain and mind, it is the form of the dream that now best matches the electrical patterns of REM sleep that we can record and measure today.

Sleep Research

Early studies of REM sleep reviewed in chapter 6 immediately suggested a parallel between a distinctive state of the brain (REM sleep) and a distinctive state of the mind (dreaming). But how could we be sure that this correlation was not just a function of the relative ease of arousing subjects from REM sleep? And that the dreams were not, as Freud asserted, compressed into the instant before awakening? Reassuring evidence came from the fact that subjects' estimations of dream duration correlated positively with the time they had spent in REM sleep prior to arousal. When subjects were aroused after only 5 minutes of REM sleep they gave shorter reports; whereas after 15 minutes had elapsed, reports were considerably longer and more detailed. Thus, it would appear that despite intensification and contraction of duration estimates within individual dream scenarios, the overall correlation between time estimation of dream duration and real time elapsed in REM sleep is quite close.

To test the time course of memory loss for dreams, awakenings were performed in the non-REM sleep phase at intervals following the termination of a REM sleep epoch. The incidence of reported dreams dropped to non-REM levels within 5 minutes, indicating the extremely fragile state of memory and highlighting the strong state dependence of dream recall upon arousal from REM sleep.

Most of the early laboratory work on the psychophysiology of dreaming was conducted in an attempt to establish a minute-to-minute relationship between the recorded physiology and the recalled dream narratives. Despite occasionally spectacular predictions (such as, the association of a run of vertical eye movements with a dream of ascending a stair, or a run of horizontal eye movements with a dream of a tennis match), the most successful outcome of this real-time cross-correlation paradigm was to establish beyond doubt the general relationship between physiological and psychological activation levels. The physiological methods are simply not capable of going much farther within this paradigm—at least not yet! But the opportunistic scientist does not grope long for the key in the darkness: one looks where the light is. To explore further the robust brain-mind activation correlation required a shift in focus. Instead of looking at dreams as stories, we needed to establish a quantitative inventory of formal dream features: the sensations, movements, emotions, and thought patterns that distinguish dreaming from waking mental activity in humans. Then we could attempt to explain the observed differences in terms of the neuro-physiological details emerging from the comparison of the REM sleep and the waking states in experimental animals.

In modern laboratory sleep research, the usual technique is to record, by means of a tape recorder, reports of relatively few dreams, from a few nights, and for a relatively large quantity of subjects. On the other hand, most "amateur" studies are characteristically home-based, use paper and pencil reporting, and a sample of many nights and one or a very few subjects.

There are advantages to each paradigm. In the laboratory setting, one achieves control and systematization at the expense of naturalness and openness of expression. In the home, one achieves more ample dream experience and a richer expressive range at the expense of the objectivity and control afforded by the observer-initiated interventions of the sleep lab. The professional paradigm is not necessarily the more scientific, especially when it is a question of the fundamental nature of the dream experience. For example, answers that rely exclusively upon words may miss, distort, or poorly represent essentially visual aspects of dreaming. Although there is no way to record directly the perceptual experience of dreamers, the drawings in dream journals bring us at least one step closer to the visual form of dreams than is possible via verbal reports.

In the Laboratory of Neurophysiology at the Harvard Medical School, my colleagues and I have pursued both paradigms: we have studied, first, dream reports collected in the sleep laboratories of our colleagues in Cincinnati, New York, and elsewhere across the country; and, second, dream reports recorded in journals by individuals sleeping at home.

Dream Journals

One important reason for wanting to develop a valid and reliable method of studying home-based reports is that the longitudinal, in-depth analysis of the vicissitudes of dreaming, in the life of individual dreamers, is easily, cheaply, and naturally obtainable. The laboratory is too cumbersome, too expensive, and too intimidating a setting ever to allow the kind of integration that the new science of dreaming would like to make with the ethological tradition of modern biology (where the study of home-based dream reports is analogous to fieldwork) and the biographical tradition of psychoanalysis (where the journal provides both day-to-day details and ancient psychological structures traditionally studied on the couch).

In emphasizing the importance of home-based methods of increasing dream awareness, dream collection, and what I call *dream discussion* (rather than interpretation), I find myself in methodological sympathy with the Senoi-Malaysian people who discuss dreams every morning and consider their dreams as guides to their current concerns and actions. Like the Senoi, I regard dreaming as indicative of my internal state and take its data into account in my day-to-day self-assessment.

In the modern tradition of laboratory-based dream research, instrumental awakenings have become commonplace. Although it has a constrictive effect upon dream content, this objective approach has proven itself useful in establishing a secure link between the state of the brain and the state of the mind during sleep. Such methods furnish the major substantive data of this book. The richness of recall and awareness of dreams is nowhere more impressive than in instrumental awakenings.* Readers who sleep alone (or who have uncooperative bed partners) can utilize the knowledge of REM sleep timing to set snooze alarms or program wake-up calls. For subjects susceptible to autosuggestion, the pre-sleep command, "I will remember my dreams," repeated nightly, is usually adequate to produce dramatically increased dream recall within three to five weeks of placing a dream journal at one's bedside.

---

*Even though dream content may be colored by the experience of the laboratory and even though dreaming may be rendered somewhat less interesting by its occurrence in that setting, the nature of the recall process is so markedly enhanced under such conditions that anyone who really wants to have an appreciation of his or her own dream experience should have awakenings from REM sleep performed in a sleep lab or by an informed accomplice at home.

Sleep Lab Reports

To establish that the formal features of home-based reports are indeed the mental correlates of REM sleep physiology, we have also studied psychological data collected by our sleep laboratory colleagues. This "laboratory paradigm" is more coarse-grained and more statistical than the journal approach, but helps to establish the generality and validity of its conclusions.

The first study, which was conducted by Robert McCarley and Edward Hoffman using data from the Cincinnati sleep lab (1981), quantified formal aspects of 104 REM-sleep dreams from fourteen subjects in five categories: movement, sensation, affect, bizarreness, and lucidity. These categories were selected because of their potential correlation with REM-sleep physiology, which could provide an initial evaluation of the activation-synthesis hypothesis.

Subsequent studies, with Helene Porte (1986b), utilized the unique data set of John Antrobus at the College of the City of New York (1983). Seventy-three subjects each contributed a report for a REM and a report for a non-REM sleep awakening. This experimental design provided an important internal control for the physiological states within sleep. Porte was able to show that not only were movement perceptions distinctive in REM-sleep dreams, but that such dreaming was characteristically bizarre.

DREAM FORM

In conceptualizing our long-term integrative-research program, we make a distinction between dream *form* (which we suppose to be universal and attributable to physiology) and dream *content* (possibly attributable to specific individual experience), as is sketched in table 10.1.

The "Formal Analysis" column of this table is a compendium of signs of major mental illness. Dreaming is thus a model of psychopathology, a normal functional psychosis whose understanding could provide a key to major psychiatric dysfunctions. Thus dreaming (and REM sleep) reveals the mechanisms of the hallucinations and delusions of the so-called functional psychoses (schizophrenia and the affective disorders) and the disorientation and memory loss of the organic dementias. Like the mental status of schizophrenia, that of dreaming is also associatively loose. Like the

TABLE 10.1

Dream Feature	Formal Analysis	Content Analysis
Sensory Aspects	Predominance of vision over other senses	What is seen?
Motor Aspects	Constancy of movement, character of movement (flying, spinning, etc.)	Where does the dreamer go? How does dreamer use mode of movement?
Orientation	Discontinuity of persons, places, times	Who changes into whom?
Memory	Increased recall during, and amnesia after, dreaming	Who and what is remembered during and after dreaming?
Belief	Delusional loss of critical insight (ad hoc explanations, etc.)	What is unreasonably believed?
Plot	Thematic unity	What defensive compromises are made to preserve such unity?
Emotion	Lability, intensity, and kind of affect (surprise, anxiety, fear, elation)	What are the associations to the feelings?

mental status of the organic of brain disease states, that of dreaming is also impressively confabulatory. In its emotional spectrum, dreaming often mimics mania and a panic anxiety state but rarely depression. Because of the physiological similarities between REM sleep and depression, this difference is exceptional and interesting.

The distinction between form and content, while apparently sharp, does not imply absolute independence of the two processes any more than my emphasis upon physiology denotes independence from psychology. Quite the contrary: dream form and dream content, like physiology and psychology, are inextricably intertwined. I believe that when we have truly adequate descriptions of brain and mind, dualism and all of its dilemmas will disappear. We will speak of the *brain-mind* as a unity, or invent some new word to describe it.

The cardinal features of all dreaming—detailed sensory imagery, the illusion of reality, illogical thinking, intensification of emotion, and unreliable memory—constitute its form, as opposed to and irrespective of the *content* of a particular dream. I aim, in this formal definition, for both simplicity and universality.

Simplicity is necessary because brain research has not yet progressed sufficiently to explain the complex physiological phenomenon of dream content. Only if the psychological question is kept sufficiently simple do we have a chance of finding clues, and even some answers, by examining the nature of the associated brain activity. For example, the question, "How do I see in dreams?" is quite different from "Why did I see my friend M. in my dream last night?" One could answer the first question by saying: "Because the visual system of my brain is activated in a manner formally similar to that of waking," while the second question has no secure answer given today's limited knowledge of the brain basis of motivation and memory.

The modesty of the goal of simplicity is matched by the ambition of the goal of universality. If dreaming has a common form, a simple hypothesis will be universally applicable. Whatever I say about the form of dreams will be generally true of everyone's dreaming.

As the arguments of the book develop, I will show that the simple hypothesis about the form of dreams and their correspondence with the form of brain activity in sleep call into question existing theories regarding the determination of dream content. For example, if it is assumed that dreams are formally strange—or, as many say, "bizarre"—owing to formally distinctive brain activity, then we need not conclude, a priori, that bizarre dream elements have hidden meaning. In other words, the form of dreams is important in *shaping* their content. Thus, even if one's interest is mainly in the meaning of dreams, one must recognize the formal determinants of dream content. I will show that in the long history of dream interpretation, this approach has never before been seriously pursued. One reason is that knowledge of brain activity in sleep was previously too limited to support such theorizing.

PSYCHOLOGICAL STUDIES OF DREAM FORM

To test the activation-synthesis hypothesis of dreaming, my collaborators and I have conducted a series of psychological studies of dream form. In focusing on form, we look below, behind, and within the narrative structure of the dream, at the story told by the dreamer, at the syntax and the context of the dream experience itself: the scene; the characters; the kinds of action; and, most important, the kind of thinking demonstrated by the dramatis personae in the dream scenario. I believe that dream stories are—

like literature—so seductive and compelling that they divert attention from this critically important aspect of the analytic task.

One important reason for choosing this formal level of dream analysis is scientific: at this early stage of our work, it is only there that we have any hope of establishing meaningful correlations between the mental activity of dreaming and the brain physiology of sleep. We know far too little about the brain in any of its functional states to hope to account for the narrative aspects of dreaming. In science we often have to look where the light is. The data now best illuminate the brain-mind interface at the level of their respective global states. By providing an alternative view of dream content, the formal method also allows a new approach to interpretation.

In making this scientific choice, I hope not only to be original and right but to avoid certain clinical traps. As a psychodynamically trained psychiatrist, I have found it easy, knowing a person's history, to account for all psychopathology in developmental terms. But, as many of my patients have repeatedly pointed out, such accounts, while appealing and even comforting, really *explain* nothing in a causal sense, since people with formally similar histories do not necessarily have the same psychopathology. So it is with dreams. Though chockful of nonsense, they also have an impressive coherence: they all make a kind of narrative sense, given a dreamer's recent and past experience. But it would be a fatal error to conclude that their *lack* of coherence and their nonsensical character are also historically and psychologically determined. It is this psychoanalytic mistake that my approach hopes both to avoid and to correct.

Let me introduce a dream of my own to emphasize these points:

I am in Williamstown, Massachusetts, talking to a colleague, Van, who is wearing a white shirt (he usually wears blue) open at the neck (he is normally neck-tied, and even collar-clipped) and khakis (he usually sports flannels). Casual. Van says, as if by the way, that he attended the committee meeting that had yesterday considered my candidacy for an invited lecture series. (I know from his tone that he is going to deliver bad news.) The committee has decided against it because "They don't feel that psychoanalysis should be confronted with laboratory data."

I allowed as to how bad an idea that was. "It's the wrong reason," I said. "And their timing is off, because Adolf Grünbaum is just about to publish his important new book in which he insists that this is precisely what psychoanalysis must do." Van ignores this statement, appearing never to have heard of A. G.

Van then begins a gentle pirouette and tosses me a piece of hardware, something like the lock of a door or perhaps a pair of paint-frozen hinges. It is as if to say, "Here, take this as recompense." Despite my scavenger nature, I think I should refuse this "gift," and so I toss it back to Van on his next choreographic spin. He insists that it is meant for me, and the scene changes without clear resolution of whether or not I will keep it.

We go out a door (which is on the corner of the building) to behold the beautiful Williams campus. A red-brick walk extends down a green lawn to the classic white Puritan buildings.

Van says, "They chose Mary" (or seems to say that), "reflecting their priorities, to attract a speaker who might help them with their fundraising efforts."

"That is why you have such beautiful buildings," I note, "and why there is nothing in them."

The narrative significance of my dream should be transparent. My task is to change the psychoanalytic mind: not only mine, but my colleague's (and, indeed, in this book, my readers' as well). The psychoanalyst, always on the lookout for latent meaning, might be interested in the fact that my father also lives in Williamstown, and wish to see my motives as quixotically oedipal! Also a resident is a mutual friend, Bart, whose first wife was named Mary. Perhaps these are clues to a deeper, formative motive of my dream which is cloaked by the dance with Van (itself a thinly veiled homosexual desire?).

But I think my dream has more clearly and openly to do with my annoyance at my old friend Van, who left me in the lurch at Harvard and went to Williams to take an endowed chair in psychoanalytic psychology. I obviously wonder whether he is friend or foe. Is he a faithful ally or a self-serving turncoat? In view of the latter possibility, I get my revenge by accusing him (via displacement to Williams) of mercenary motives that lead to graceful forms devoid of substance. This all seems very transparent to me. Almost naked. Perhaps I also wonder if my theory of dream form will be architecturally appealing but uninhabitable.

So why is Van dressed incongruously? Why does he pirouette? Why does he suddenly toss me a piece of hardware? Why is the hardware "something like" the lock of a door? Why is it "perhaps" a pair of paint-frozen hinges? Why does the scene change? Why does Van "seem to say" that the committee choose Mary? Answers to these questions, which relate to the only features of the report that make it distinctively dreamlike, are all too easily ascribed to defenses whose meaning is to be sought in my mental associations. But viewed as disguises they are inadequate. And viewed as symbols they are unnecessary.

I suggest that they are more likely to represent the typical incongruities, uncertainties, and discontinuities that often becloud dream thinking, regardless of the narrative content. In table 10.2, an inventory of some formal features of dreaming, some of the items from my Williamstown dream are starred and underlined.

By characterizing these *formal* aspects of dreaming (which are distinctively different from other states of consciousness) and understanding their presence in terms of the altered brain physiology of sleep, activation-synthesis successfully explains the most interesting features of my dream. That my brain, auto-activated during sleep, should cook up such a story is not hard either to accept or to explain, since all the psychological issues and conflicts that are manifest in the dream are enduring, important, and even deep concerns of mine. And with such rich manifest content to work with, why delve deeper? The dreaminess of my Williamstown dream derives from: its subjects' dress; his pirouette; his profferring me a strange piece of hardware; my inability to identify the hardware; the sudden scene change; and the surprising choice of "Mary" as invited lecturer. These features, as I shall show in further detail in the next four chapters in respect to the Engine Man, typify dreaming generally and can be boiled down to three categories: discontinuities (for example, the scene change), incongruities (Van's dress), and uncertainties (the unidentified hardware).

TABLE 10.2

Some Formal Features of Dreaming

Uncertain character (It is not clear who Mary is.)
Fictional character, unidentified
Fictional character, identified
Dead character
Merged character
Dreamer/character displaced in time and/or place
Dreamer/*character performing* impossible/*inappropriate action* (Van does not normally perform pirouettes.)
Dreamer/character has distorted, disfigured, or absent body parts
Dreamer/*character has inappropriate*/absent *clothing*/implements (Van does not normally dress as described.)
Character appears or vanishes
Dreamer/character repeats action not normally repeated
Inappropriate combination of environmental features
Fantastic environmental features
Realistic object in the wrong place (Hardware is not normally proffered as a gift.)
Violation of natural law
Object creation
Object with unusual features
Object changes into another object (Lock becomes hinge.)
Unidentified place
Familiar environment with alterations (Williams College buildings do not normally have doors at their corners.)
Time shift (The normal continuity between the sequential acts of dancing and leaving the building is broken.)
Situational abnormality

THE MENTAL STATUS OF DREAMING

The distinction between dream form and dream content may be simply clarified by considering the strategy of the psychiatrist who wants to know both the history of a patient (so as to establish an alliance and a chronicle for comprehending personal developmental issues) and his or her formal mental status (so as to assess the nature and content of that person's thinking, perceiving, and feeling). It is this latter aspect—the mental status of dreaming—that I wish to emphasize.

The formal mental-status exam by which psychiatrists characterize the mental state of their patients is an essentially unchanged rendition of that part of the physical examination in general medicine once considered integral to the comprehensive evaluation of *any* patient. In modern psychodynamic psychiatry, the mental-status exam is honored more often in the breach than in the observance. Indeed, many psychoanalytically oriented practitioners consider it to be not only dispensable but counterproductive in the evaluation of patients. Against these currents, I propose to make a systematic attempt to characterize the mental status of dream consciousness and to do so through the remarkable dream journal of the Engine Man.

The form–content contrast is further apparent in respect to the differences within the mental-status exam between, on the one hand, such cognitive issues as orientation (time, place, and person), perception (hallucinations), belief (delusions), and intellectual functions (abstract versus concrete thinking); and, on the other, the subject matter or mental content of the patient's disturbed thinking.

Since the first formulation of activation synthesis in 1977, I have sought a body of data ideal to this purpose. I wanted an extensive number of dreams from an individual person who had the drive and the discipline to persist in disinterested descriptions free of interpretation. My own collection of one hundred dream reports was a step in this direction, but it could not help but be biased. I had the same reservation about the famous twenty-two volume dream record of Hervey de Saint-Denis, but could not in any case locate it. Then one day, in 1980, I found the work of my principal dream informant, a fellow scientist who had, in the summer of 1939, turned his bedroom into a laboratory, and his own dreaming mind into a specimen. The meticulous descriptions of the Engine Man provided my colleagues and myself with a radically new view into the dreaming brain.

11

The Form

of Dream Sensation

But I was well
Upon my way to sleep before it fell
And I could tell
What form my dreaming was about to take
Magnified apples appear and disappear,
Stem end and blossom end.
And every fleck of russet showing clear.
—ROBERT FROST
"After Apple-Picking"

Images seen in dreams, not the mere idea of things
conceived in dreams, are phenomena of the same kind
as the phantasms. For the images which remain before
the eyes when we awaken are identical with the objects
perceived in our dreams.
—JOHANNES MÜLLER
Handbuch der Physiologie des Menschen

A TRANSPARENT DREAMER: THE ENGINE MAN

I obtained the dream journal of the individual I call the Engine Man from
an advertisement in a medical book catalogue describing a "manuscript
. . . recording in copious detail . . . dreams between July 15 and October
14, 1939. Illustrated and extremely well written. The manifest content is
reported without interpretation."

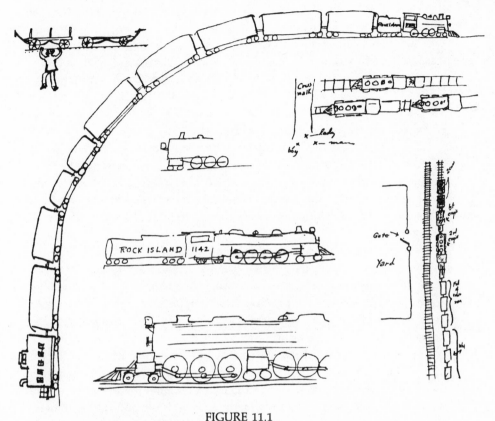

FIGURE 11.1

Railway drawings from the dream journal of the Engine Man

In the scene at the upper left, the Engine Man has drawn himself hanging perilously from the tracks below two station carts of the sort used to move baggage. The other drawings are realistic representations of trains, many of which have unusual features. The long, curved train is going up an unrealistically steep grade. The half-engine below it operates silently, "as if on rubber wheels." And Rock Island Locomotive 1142 has an engineer who speaks only French and therefore (*sic*) denies passengers permission to ride in the engine.

I ordered the manuscript immediately, and shortly thereafter received in the mail a bound laboratory record book of 150 lined pages, 100 of which contain meticulous descriptions—in 233 separate reports varying in length from 1 to 78 lines—of mental activity in sleep. Many of the reports are illustrated, as shown in figure 11.1.

Careful reading of the journal enables one to draw certain conclusions about the dream journalist. He appears to have been a careful and scholarly scientist. At age forty-six, when he wrote his journal, he was economically secure and emotionally reserved. He was close to his mother and two sisters, especially one of them; he had several romances but never married and lived alone as a bachelor.

Like many people of his generation, the author of the dream journal was fascinated by railway trains. Many of his dreams take place on trains, in railway stations, or on train tracks, as indicated by his drawings in figures 11.1, 11.2, and 11.4. It is for this reason that I call him the Engine Man, a pseudonym that also speaks to his interest in developing control of the apparently autonomous dream machine in his brain.

The author described his reason for keeping the journal ("I would like to learn whether the nature, cause, and speed of a dream can be controlled") and his technique ("My method is to place a notebook at my bed-side every night and, on wakening in the morning or during the night, to get down the 'high spots' and sometimes a rough outline of each dream remembered").

Since it is not possible to know the kind of sleep from which the Engine Man's 233 reports are derived, we cannot distinguish between those that fulfill all of the usual formal characteristics of hallucinoid dreams, and those that simply describe thoughtlike activity occurring in sleep. The abundance of vivid details indicate, however, that many of our subject's dreams occurred during REM sleep.

From the dreamer's direct statements and the nature of the reports, we can assume that he had no particular psychological position beyond his skepticism regarding the Freudian theory of dreaming. At the end of the journal is a two-page essay on genetic and environmental determinism, which indicates the author's strong conviction that biological and experiential forces combine to determine individual behavioral outcomes. The author thus seems both psychologically and philosophically rationalistic.

THE SENSORY MODES

Activation synthesis assumes that sensory-channel selection, as well as the nature and intensity of stimulation—as represented in dream consciousness—will parallel the pattern and intensity of REM-sleep sensory-system activation. Thus, if the visual sense dominates dream reports, there is likely to be visual-neuron activation in REM sleep, as well as a pulsatile pattern of internally generated signals that formally mimics the input to which the visual system is most responsive in waking. Other sensory modes are less prominently represented according to the nature and intensity of their activation in REM sleep. If audition is less prominent than vision and sensation of movement, and reports of pain are rare, then we can expect to find correlates of the dream "forms" at the neuronal level.

The Visual Mode: Verbal and Visual Reports

On the night of 14 July 1939, the Engine Man looked into a murky dream pool and saw that "the water became clear, with numerous, rounded stone-like objects on bottom, these apparently something of the nature of corals" (Report 1). From this first report to the last, vividness of visual detail is the norm. On 20 February 1949, he entered a dream clothing store, to be shown, by a clerk, "a light grey suit with some sort of extremely conspicuous design on the sleeves" (Report 233).

These phrases recall the descriptions of psychedelic visual-pleasure seekers like the English author Aldous Huxley (*The Doors of Perception*, 1954), who claimed that his drug-induced visions were sharper than those of normal waking and even were surrealistic. Fresh-water pools that suddenly clear, to reveal coral-like stones on their bottoms, and gray suits with elaborate designs on their sleeves suggest starburst activations of a visual center whose initially abstract geometry becomes integrated (synthesized) with the ongoing dream plot.

In both examples, there can be little doubt that the Engine Man literally saw, even though his descriptions are typically qualified by what I shall later more fully characterize as cognitive uncertainties (*"apparently something of* the nature of corals" and *"some sort of* extremely conspicuous design"*).

What about color? Are dreams, like early films, in black and white? As have all other dream scientists, we have found that reports of color are common in accounts of vividly remembered dreams, and I ascribe to poor recall people's reports of dreaming only in black and white. Here are some colors from the Engine Man's dream palette:

From the upper trunk in the attic, I took a large, *red* apple. (Report 18, 20 July 1939)

The boy with the large face and *tanned* skin seemed to dominate the other. (Report 22, 22 July 1939)

A tall graceful girl dressed in rough suit of *khaki,* over which was a *blue* overcoat, shook all the snow from it, the *color* being impermanent. Some other people across street were in outlandish costumes. These people wait on curb until stop-go signal is *green,* then they all cross. (Report 26, 23 July 1939)

Despite the obvious fact that the sensory mode of dreams is predominantly visual, it is traditional in modern sleep science to represent them as verbal reports. I know of no previous attempt to analyze their direct visual representation in drawings. This is surprising not only from a phenomenological point of view, but also because many intensive students of dream consciousness have naturally resorted to drawing in addition to their narrative accounts. In addition to the lavish illustrations reported to be in the twenty-two volumes of the dream journal of the Marquis d'Hervey de Saint-Denis (see chapter 11), such artists as William Blake, Salvador Dali, Henry Fuseli, and Max Ernst have explicitly and directly documented the unique visual nature of dream consciousness, although their work, too, has remained outside the ken of dream science. Fortunately the Engine Man not only described his dreams in an impeccably legible copperplate hand but also illustrated them profusely with meticulously drawn and labeled pen-and-ink sketches.

There are 110 drawings in the journal, most of which illustrate some detailed aspects of a lengthy report (action scenarios). For example, if the author wished to portray the setting of a dream's action, he might simply present a map of the space as it would be seen from above (a third-person vantage point). Other drawings are multiple images from a single dream (detail sketches) drawn from the dreamer's own perspective (first-person vantage point). Figure 11.2, showing a page of the journal, conveys a direct sense of the author's style. The margin drawings of the pig house and the hairs are typical of his first-person detail sketches, while the map of the railroad station is typical of a third-person action scenario.

In the absence of text, some of these drawings could be mistaken for the unformed free-floating images depicted and described by many authors (including Alfred Maury and Hervey de Saint-Denis) as occurring at sleep onset. But the text indicates that the objects were experienced as embedded in the more elaborate contexts of the long dreams that occur much later in the night.

Most of the subjects of the Engine Man's ninety interpretable dream drawings we described simply: for example, (1) part of engine; (2) engine; (3) tree; or (4) streets. These designations were further subdivided into two classes: sixty were classed as banal, because they represented realistic subjects (using wake-state criteria for realistic); thirty, as bizarre, because they represented unrealistic events or objects. Bizarreness in the drawings was related exclusively to dreamed actions and/or objects, not to characters as it was in so many of the narrative reports.

Examples of these judgments are shown in figure 11.3.

The drawings also represent three categories of movement: twenty-

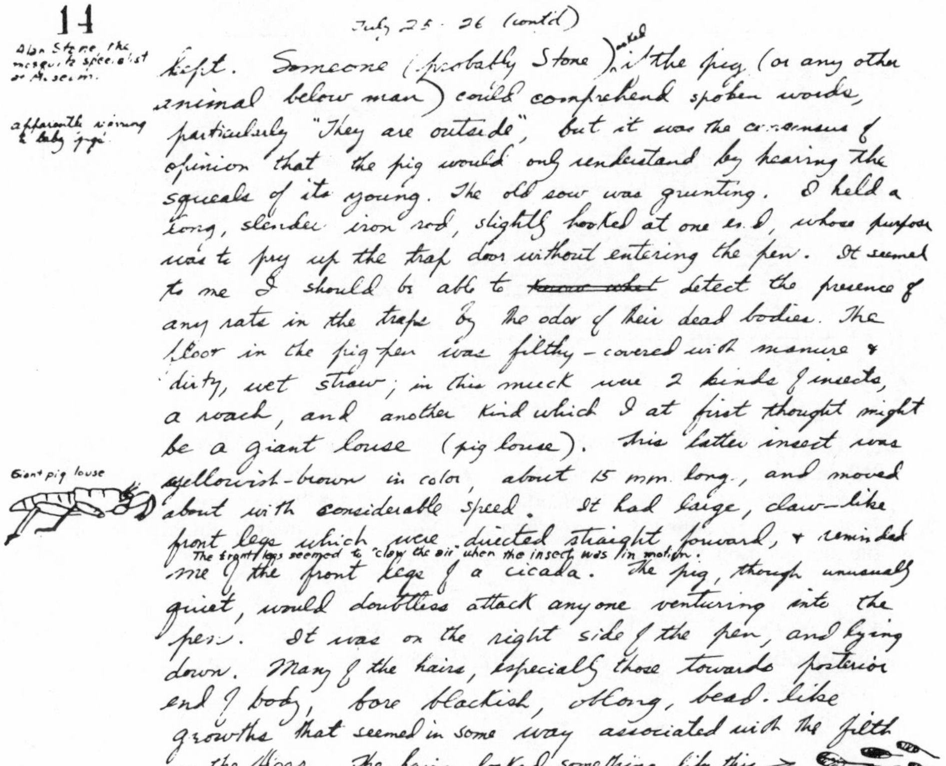

14

July 25 - 26 (cont'd)

Alan Stone, the mosquito specialist at Museum.

kept. Someone (probably Stone) asked if the pig (or any other animal below man) could comprehend spoken words, particularly "They are outside", but it was the consensus of opinion that the pig would only understand by hearing the squeals of its young. The old sow was grunting. I held a long, slender iron rod, slightly hooked at one end, whose purpose was to pry up the trap door without entering the pen. It seemed to me I should be able to ~~know what~~ detect the presence of any rats in the traps by the odor of their dead bodies. The floor in the pig-pen was filthy - covered with manure & dirty, wet straw; in this muck were 2 kinds of insects, a roach, and another kind which I at first thought might be a giant louse (pig louse). This latter insect was yellowish-brown in color, about 15 mm. long, and moved about with considerable speed. It had large, claw-like front legs which were directed straight forward, & reminded me of the front legs of a cicada. The pig, though unusually quiet, would doubtless attack anyone venturing into the pen. It was on the right side of the pen, and lying down. Many of the hairs, especially those towards posterior end of body, bore blackish, oblong, bead-like growths that seemed in some way associated with the filth on the floor. The hairs looked something like this →

apparently viewing the baby pigs

Giant pig louse

The front legs seemed to "claw the air" when the insect was in motion.

July 26-27 and 27-28

Fairly long walk, then sprinkled lawn in evening.

No dreams remembered.

July 28-29

First episode takes place at top of Kent's hill in Solon. I am standing on east side of a cement sidewalk probably watching for a train. A girl or young lady walks up behind me (to my right). She is carrying a child, perhaps 2½ to 3 years old on her shoulder. Sex of child uncertain, but probably male. The lady cranes her neck this way and that, apparently on look-out for some person. The child is now being held by another girl who is standing next to wooden fence several steps or yards to ~~south~~ north of my position. The baby falls from a fence post, head first into the grass of the pasture, its legs sticking straight upward

Solon RR station

Numerous parked vehicles (? buggies or autos) blocking egress to road

Me in buggy or auto

Road

South

Lady with baby

Me

Sidewalk

Road

Wooden fence

Pasture

This should be Nona's child on day of Grand Prix

? Nona's statue - standing on its head.

FIGURE 11.2

A page from the Engine Man's dream journal

This is a typical page from the Engine Man's dream journal, illustrating his detailed descriptions, his drawings, and his margin notes.

FIGURE 11.3

Bizarreness in drawings from the dream journal of the Engine Man

While there is nothing unusual about the truck on the left, its placement in the flower garden is an example of object incongruity. And the building on the right is physically possible, but its roofline and window placement are highly improbable and exemplify object discontinuity.

eight drawings depict explicit movement trajectories. The dreamer or a dream object moved in the space of the drawing along a dotted line. Such trajectories could be traced without reference to other representations in the drawings, as in figure 11.4.

Original   ➜   Tracing

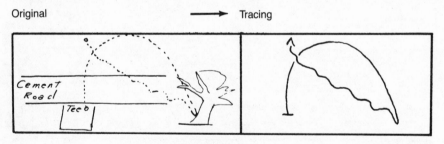

FIGURE 11.4

An explicit movement trajectory from the Engine Man's dream journal

In this example *(left),* the dreamer or a dream object moves in the space of the drawing along a dotted-line trajectory. We in the laboratory traced the trajectory *(right)* without reference to other aspects of the drawing. *Source:* The Engine Man's dream journal, Report 3, 16 July 1939.

A high proportion of drawings is devoted to modes of conveyance. Of the thirty-four instances, figure 11.5 depicts commonplace and unusual dream vehicles.

The Engine Man's dream maps often represent the dream space, whether or not movement is explicitly traced. The space is usually repre-

D83 Truck   D72 Flying Carpet

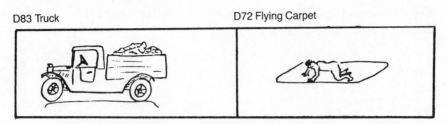

FIGURE 11.5

Commonplace and exotic vehicles in the Engine Man's dream journal

A high proportion of drawings was devoted to modes of conveyance. Shown here are examples of commonplace (D83) and unusual (D72) dream vehicles.

sented as if the dreamer were looking down on his dream from above. Since the texts indicate that the Engine Man experienced his dreams as an actor, not an observer, these drawings must be regarded as a wake-state reconstruction of the setting and action of a dream. Two examples are given in figure 11.6:

D18 No Movement   D47 Movement

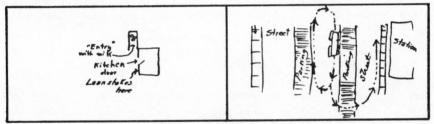

FIGURE 11.6

Maps of dream space from the Engine Man's dream journal

Whether or not movement is explicitly traced, the Engine Man's dream maps often represent the dream space as seen from above (third-person perspective), and were probably a secondary elaboration, or wake-state reconstruction, of the setting and action as perceived within the dream itself.

The Auditory Mode

Hearing has been described in only 65 percent of laboratory REM-sleep dream reports, and the descriptions were more often qualified by perceptual uncertainty than in the case of vision: "Then I heard something in one of the toilet stalls" (Laboratory Collection). But auditory imagery can also be loud and clear. On one of his dream trains, the Engine Man reported that a man "dressed in trousers, BVD's but barefooted and needing a shave . . . called out, 'Hey, do you think one ticket entitles you to hog a whole seat?' " (Report 81, 14 August 1939). There can be little doubt that he clearly heard these sounds.

The Sensation of Movement

Dream movements may be considered as action (see chapter 12); but, to be so reported, they must be sensed and perceived. "Kinesthesis" is thus implied by the presence of action verbs in all REM-sleep dreams. But when it is *explicitly* denoted, it often has a back-and-forth curvilinear or circular character, which McCarley and Hoffman have indexed as "vestibular" in 8 percent of their 104 laboratory reports (1981). Such accounts were often strikingly graphic, signaling intense activation of those brain-stem centers that continuously track body position and program postural adjustment:

I was spinning, my body was spinning around. The circus performers put the bit in their horses, and they spin around. The trapeze was spinning like that. Hands at my sides and yet there was nothing touching me. I was as nature made me, and I was revolving at 45 rpm record [speed]. Had a big hole in the center of my head. Spinning, spinning, and spinning. And at the same time, orbiting. Orbiting what, I don't know. I'd stop for a second, stop this orbit and spinning. [Laboratory Collection]

The Engine Man also flies, magically, as in this account:

I am floating in the air, on a flat stiff irregular piece (?) about 15 or 20 feet from the floor. There is a moderate wind blowing, and this moves me slowly forward. Below me, on the floor, or ground, is a ladder, and I call to a man to set this up against my (? carpet). (Report 72, 10 September 1939)

Having thus rationalized his dream flight and prepared his safe descent (with what we call an *ad hoc* explanation [see page 266]), the Engine Man is somehow impelled to a more acrobatic and more perilous escape:

I start to climb down, but after a step or two I decide *to tumble down* rest of way as I feel sure he will be unable to hold the ladder in place long enough for me to climb down. Accordingly I partially *double up and fall,* apparently with no fear of injury. (Report 72, 10 September 1972)

Did the Engine Man really jump from his carpet? Or was he pushed by the internal activation of his brain motor centers? Whether or not we accept the dreamer's claim of volition in *deciding* to "tumble down," there can be no doubt that he experienced vividly the sensation of being moved, as he floated and as he fell to his typically soft dream landing.

While this report may be reminiscent of astronauts giddily tumbling in the weightlessness of space, dreamers never report nausea or motion sickness.

Little Pleasure, No Pain

In the 104 dreams studied in Cincinnati by McCarley and Hoffman (1981), there were no descriptions of explicitly sexual sensations. Neither did any of the fourteen laboratory subjects ever dream of pain. Are such striking sparings of biologically important sensory channels simply suppressive artifacts of the laboratory, where sleepers always feel watched and never really relax; or are they evidence of physiologically determined omissions, failures of activation, as it were?

The 233 dream reports of the Engine Man, who slept at home and kept his journal for over one hundred consecutive nights, are also devoid of descriptions of physical pleasure or pain. By extreme contrast, visual sensation was reported by all (100 percent) of the 14 Cincinnati dreamers in all of their 104 REM-sleep dreams. For the activation-synthesis theory, this finding means that no amount of experimental suppression is capable of countering what must be the strongly physiological activation of the visual system in REM sleep, an interpretation that accords well with the physiological facts.

Rare Dream Sensations

In the Cincinnati sleep lab, dreamers reported little in the way of explicit thermal (4 percent), touch (1 percent), smell (1 percent) and taste (1 percent) sensations. These sensory channels must not accordingly be as effectively activated in REM sleep as are the visual, the kinesthetic, and the auditory. Some of these underrepresentations, like that of pain, are particularly surprising because the scenarios often provide a context in which such sensations would be expected or even demanded. Consider the following example from my own dream journal:

I am boarding a boat (in France) but my baggage has been left ashore. I run to fetch it but my legs are heavy. I find myself with my friend's mother. She is taking me to the woods to see the wild pigs. She carries two buckets of swill, saying "You must not feed them by hand. Rather, throw out the swill and wait." Sure enough, they come. Great, huge, grunting pigs, loving the swill. The scene shifts to a dinner table with her family present and roast boar (huge, brown, juicy) on the sideboard, but, unaccountably, no wine. I offer to go get some but have no money. The mother gives me some. En route, I realize I should be headed for the boat (or is it a train?)

and go there. My sleeping berth 24 (or is it 41?) is occupied, my baggage isn't there, etc. [27 February 1975]

A garbage feast for pigs is rarely odorless. Yet my "pig" dream had none of those ripe olfactory sensations that I still clearly remember from my hog-feeding jaunts at a Maine summer camp when I was a boy. And when, by a clear associational path, I sat down to dream-dine on a succulent ham, the fragrances of clove, of madeira, and of pineapple were not wafted on the dream air. And my dream wine was neither sniffed nor gargled with my customary wake-state gusto. Sadly, I never recall tasting wine in my dreams. Does this mean there is something deficient with my wish-fulfillment mechanism? Or is my brain's internal-stimulus generator just incapable of finding the right combination to the padlock of my olfactory and gustatory memory bank?

Dreaming is as fascinating for its overrepresentation of visual, as it is for its underrepresentation of visceral, perceptions—contrasts that have parallels in the reciprocal physiology of REM sleep. As those neuronal systems responsible for visceral perceptions decline, so those responsible for visual perceptions increase (a process I discussed in Part III). The match between physiology and psychology is thus not only correlational but may be causal. Given such a straightforward physical basis for dreaming phenomena, it is no longer necessary to entertain convoluted and inherently improbable psychological theories to explain them. The dream stimulus has been found: it is the brain autoactivation of REM sleep.

12

The Form

of Dream Movement

I have made very many attempts to see whether some
particular bodily attitude during sleep would have any
effect upon dream flying. My notes show that lying on
my back, lying upon either side, or as I often lie face
downwards with my head pillowed on one arm, the
sleeping attitude apparently makes no difference whatever to the flying dream.
—MARY ARNOLD-FORSTER
Studies in Dreams (1921)

The nervous signals produced by the motor states go
not only to the motor cortex but also to the visual
centers to produce an image.
—J. MOURLY VOLD
Experiments on Dreams (1896)

THE DREAM TRAJECTORIES OF THE ENGINE MAN

The Engine Man's dream drawings have been particularly useful in answering questions about dream movement. What kinds of movement
occur in dreams? Do dreamers move, or are they moved? Do they move
in particular directions, by one medium or another, or in modes that are
unusual or distinctive? Might specific features of dream movements be
related to specific patterns or motor-system activation in REM sleep?

While many of the Engine Man's 110 drawings (and almost all of his reports) imply or describe movement, I am concerned here only with those 25 drawings that contain *explicit* representation of movement in dream space (see table 12.1). In all these drawings, the Engine Man used the convention of a broken line of dashes to label movement and arrowheads to indicate its direction. We call these two-dimensional records "dream trajectories" (see figures 11.1, 11.3, and 11.5).

Dream Movement Is Active and Transitive.   Twenty-two of the twenty-five drawn trajectories represent the dreamer's movement in the dream space;

TABLE 12.1

Dream Trajectories

Drawing #	Title	Dreamer Moves	Object Moves	Curved	Straight	Circular	#Curves
3	Slice	−	+	+	−	−	6
4	7th & Pa. Ave.	+	+	+	−	−	1
6	Pedestrian & Car	+	+	+	−	−	1
15	Solon RR Station	+	−	+	−	−	(4)
23	Maple trees	+	−	+	−	−	(4)
24	Tennis	+	+/+	+	−	−	(2)×2
25	Const. Ave.	+	−	+	−	−	1
26	Md. Ave.	+	−	−	+/+	−	0
27	3rd Base	+	−	+	−	−	3
34	Barricade	+	−	+	−	−	2
37	Golf balls	−	+/+	−	+	−	0
47	Street	+	−	+	−	+	3
52	Sand hill	+	−	+	+	−	2
58	My course	+	−	+	−	−	3
69	My car	+	−	+	−	−	1
76	?	+	−	+	−	+	1
82	2 trips	+	−	+	−	−	5(×2)
87	4th St.	+	+	−	+	−	0
91	Hooked T shot	−	+	+	−	−	1
81	Large court	+	−	+	−	−	(3)
93	9th St.	+	−	+	−	−	5
95	Fence	+	−	+	−	−	6
100	Tennis Court	+	−	+	−	−	1
109	Md. cop.	+	−	+	−	−	4
111	Slough	+	+	+	−	−	5
N=25	Sports=5 Traffic=11 Walk=7	+22/25	+8/25	+22/25	+5/25	+2/25	≥1=22/25

and the three exceptions involve dream objects whose movement is a function of activity by the dreamer (2 cases) or by another dream character (1 case). Thus twenty-four of the twenty-five depicted movements are a function of activity initiated or guided by the dreamer. There are no dreams of passive movement. This finding demonstrates that the sensation of movement, described in the previous chapter, is tied to activation of motor-command centers in the brain.

Dream Movement Is Purposive and Effective. The Engine Man was always on the go in his dreams. He is operating a motor vehicle in eleven reports, walking in seven, and playing a sport (golf, tennis, or baseball) in five (see table 12.1). In my opinion, these movements are key aspects in the plot definition and in the evolution of dream scenarios. They anchor the dream story in action propelled by the dreamer's movements. One might even suggest, as did Helmholtz (see chapter 1), that movement (or its brain correlate) is a primary event in dream formation. To paraphrase Descartes, my brain-motor centers are activated in a patterned manner, *therefore I think I am* moving!

Dream Trajectories Are Tortuous. A striking feature of the course of dream movement is its tortuosity. To capture and characterize this feature, I made 1:1 scale tracings of the twenty-five explicit trajectories of the Engine Man's dream characters and objects (see figure 12.1).

Twenty-two (88 percent) of the Engine Man's dream trajectories are curvilinear. Of the three trajectories without curves, one involves two objects that move in relation to the dreamer (Report 37); in one, the dreamer moves twice over the same straight course (Report 26), and in the third, the dreamer and other objects move in parallel (Report 87). Thus, the Engine Man's dream trajectories are always curved or, if uncurved, are multiple.

Naive male observers, asked to describe the possible source of the dream trajectories shown in figure 12.1, often guess "football plays," owing to the zigzag routes, the bump-and-go patterns, and the hooks which resemble the moves of an elusive tight-end. Unfortunately the Engine Man left no record of the real or imagined trajectories of his waking-state consciousness, so that it is impossible to decide with confidence whether the curved and complex trajectories are unique to his dream state. It seems unlikely, however, that he would run a post pattern on the way to his laboratory. And even the athletic activity of a great tight end is unlikely to exhibit such constant twisting and turning.

Dream Trajectories Are Bizarre. Internal evidence for the assumption that dream movements are uncommonly complex, and even sometimes impossible, comes from the link, in eleven of twenty-five drawings, between their trajectories and their bizarreness (see chapter 13). I have rated a dream

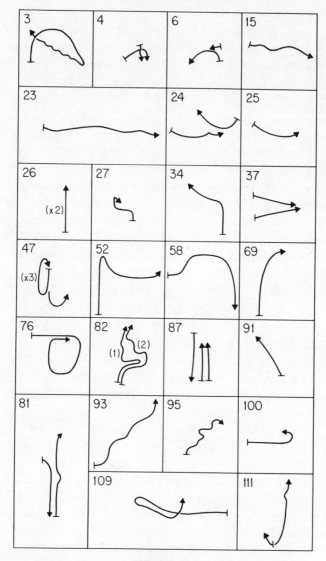

FIGURE 12.1

The Engine Man's dream trajectories

Each drawing representing movement in dream space was traced in the laboratory to create this catalogue of dream trajectories. Notable is the high frequency of curvilinear (all but 26), oscillating (3, 82, 93, 95), circular (47, 76), and reversed (3, 109) paths of movement. Can these dream wiggles and squiggles be related to the automatic activation in REM sleep of Lorente de Nò's vestibular reflex circuits? (See figure 5.1.)

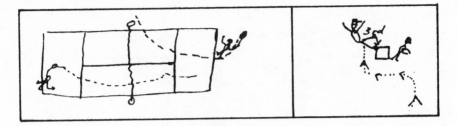

FIGURE 12.2
Bizarre movement trajectories in the dream journal of the Engine Man

Two physically possible but socially unacceptable sports scenarios are shown.

In the dream tennis match, the player at the left baseline served both balls into the wrong court, "apparently intentionally and then asked privilege of reserving the second ball." The serve of the player on the right "curved sharply and struck outside of court before reaching net."

In the dream baseball game, the batter hits a "line drive over first base which goes for triple," but slides into third from behind by running out of baseline in a highly irregular maneuver.

trajectory as bizarre if it was clearly (or, to the dreamer's waking mind, apparently) impossible or highly improbable. For this analysis, we also utilized the Engine Man's narratives to establish the nature of the action.

For example, drawing 3 (shown also as figure 11.3), representing the trajectory of a sliced golf shot, is rated as bizarre because it is impossible for a slice to travel backward and/or bound forward again (from contact with a tree) as far as its original forwardmost point. See figure 12.2 for two other examples.

Dream Vehicles. Vehicles are a common dream subject, appearing in thirty-four of the Engine Man's drawings (see table 12.2). For the most

FIGURE 12.3
Two fantastic vehicles from the Engine Man's dream journal

Bicycle (D107)   Ornate Elevator (D79)

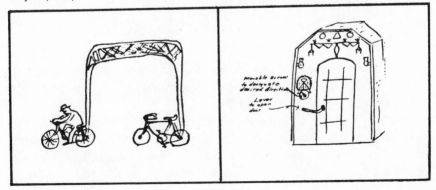

TABLE 12.2

Dream Vehicles in Will Freeman's Journal

Drawing #	Title	Bizarre?/Why
1	Part of Engine	No
2	Engine	No
6	Car	No
15	Cars	No
16	Part of Engine	No
26	Car	No
34	2 cars	No
40	Train	No
42	Cars	No
43	Tractor	*Yes. Unlikely object.
47	Car	No
48	Engine	No
54	Car	*Yes. End of bridge.
55	Top view	No
63	Streetcar	No
67	Car	No
68	Station cars	*Yes. Impossible action.
69	Cars	No
70	Carpet	*Yes. Impossible action.
76	Car	No
79	Elevator	No
80	Cars	No
83	Truck	*Yes. Truck unlikely place.
84	Car	No
86	Car	No
87	Cars	No
88	Car	No
92	2 engines	No
95	Streetcar	No
96	Streetcar	*Yes. Improbable structure.
100	Cars	No
101	Trains	No
107	Bicycle	*Yes. Improbable structure.
N=33	Vehicles	7 bizarre

part, these are banal vehicles: automobiles (17), trains (8), streetcars (3), and trucks (2)—a not unlikely fleet of conveyances for an American born at the turn of the twentieth century.

In five cases, the drawings have been classified as bizarre (although the vehicles themselves are not) because they are in unlikely places (reports 54 and 83); are connected to unlikely objects (Report 43); or have unlikely constituent parts (Report 96). Some are entirely fantastic (see table 12.2, numbers 70 and 101), particularly the creative engineering of the bicycle built-for-two (figure 12.3), the flying carpet (see again figure 11.5), and the ornate elevator (figure 12.3). These latter three items constitute the apogee of the Engine Man's creative dream prowess.

FICTIVE MOVEMENTS

Of course, no actual movement was involved in the dream trajectories and vehicles described by the Engine Man, for the somatic muscles are, in non-REM sleep, inactivated and, in REM sleep, paralyzed. In our laboratory we have freely adapted a term from physiology to conceive of dream movements as *fictive:* that is, they are illusory since they are generated by active motor patterns but are devoid of behavioral expression. We assume that these fictive movements of REM sleep are the cognate images of actual movements that would, in waking, proceed from similar motor-neuron activity.

To test the hypothesis that fictive movement indeed contributes distinctively to mental experience in REM sleep, my colleague Dr. Helene Porte has measured the occurrence of movement in a set of 146 spoken dream reports given by 73 subjects, each of whom was awakened once from REM and once from non-REM sleep (1986).* To score dream movements, a two-stage system was designed. Porte began with the *Oxford English Dictionary* definition of movement as "the action or process of moving (in the intransitive senses of the verb); change of position; passage from place to place, or from one situation to another" (1955). Proceeding from this definition, the first stage of scoring specifies the *agent* of the dream movement. As determined in a pilot study of published and private dream reports, the agent may be the *dreamer or a dream character,* a *dream object,* or the *dreamer or dream character and a dream object* together (Porte and Hobson 1986*b*).

In previous studies of movement in dreams, human movement has also been classified as movement of the *lower limbs* (McCarley and Hoffman 1981) and of the *upper or the lower limbs* (Zepelin 1984). Applied to our pilot collection of home dream reports, these categories proved descriptively apt. In addition, Porte found the subcategory *whole body* movement (as distinct from separate limb movements or simple locomotion) to be useful in describing dream movements in our sample data. Therefore, to the main

*I am grateful to Dr. Porte for allowing me to include this summary of her findings and to Dr. John Antrobus for allowing us access to his data.

scoring category *dreamer or dream character,* we added the secondary scoring options *upper limb, lower limb,* and *whole body* movement.

Dream object movement is often vehicular. The Dream Movement Scale proved highly reliable for the assignment of movement versus no movement to a given report, with the two judges agreeing in 92 percent of cases. Only those reports to which both judges assigned a movement score are treated as scored reports in the data analysis. Under this condition, three times as many REM reports (75 percent) as non-REM reports (18 percent) received a score for fictive movement.

Our data show that REM reports at all report lengths contain more movement than non-REM reports at equivalent report lengths. The incidence of movement in REM reports exceeds that in non-REM reports by 40 percent, 41 percent, 29 percent, and 45 percent, in successively longer reports. In view of the hypothesis that report length itself distinguishes REM from non-REM sleep, the strength of this difference between REM and non-REM in the shortest reports is notable.

The majority of scored movements in both REM and non-REM reports have as their agents either the dreamer or a dream character (86 percent in REM; 82 percent in non-REM). Fourteen percent of movements in REM and 18 percent in non-REM are of dream objects (mostly vehicular) or of the dreamer plus a dream object. Of all fictive movements by the dreamer or a dream character in REM, 55 percent are upper-limb movements, 37 percent are lower-limb movements, and 8 percent are of the whole body or not agreed upon by the two judges. In non-REM, 56 percent of all movements by the dreamer or a dream character are upper limb movements, 33 percent are lower limb movements, and 11 percent are not agreed upon.

Home and laboratory dreams suggest varying degrees of motor activation: moderately paced continuous movement reflecting a "tonic" state, and fast or vigorous movement (particularly when it is discontinuous) reflecting a "phasic" state. This hypothesis could be tested by comparing reports from REM-sleep awakenings during and between the eye movement clusters.

When perception of movement occurs in non-REM sleep mentation, the dreamer's physiological state may in fact be transitional to REM sleep, a conclusion consistent with the incompleteness of physiological measurement in conventional human sleep studies and supported by animal studies. These results confirm McCarley and Hoffman's earlier findings that limb movement is present in a high percentage of laboratory dream reports, and suggest a significantly greater incidence of fictive movement in REM than in non-REM reports. This result is consistent with physiological evidence of high levels of motor activation in REM and lower levels of motor activation in non-REM sleep.

The linear, curvilinear, and up and/or down trajectories are formally similar in both home and in queried laboratory studies. All of these are formally like the stereotyped motor patterns that issue from certain natural and experimental changes in the brain's motor system.

We may conclude, then, that fictive movements occur predominantly in REM sleep dreams, and that such movements likely have a specifiable basis in the activity of the motor system in REM sleep. We do not claim proof of the activation-synthesis hypothesis of dream formation, but we do claim strong support for one of its tenets: that the hallucinatory movements of dreams are related to the patterned activation of the brain's motor-command centers in REM sleep.

IMPLICATIONS FOR THE ACTIVATION-SYNTHESIS HYPOTHESIS

The activation-synthesis hypothesis of dreaming postulates that the conscious correlation of the brain's motor commands form an important part of dream-action construction; these commands would actually move body parts, just as they do the eyes, were it not for motor-output blockade at the spinal level. It is well known that the sensory centers in the brain receive detailed information about movement commands during the waking state; this internal data, called *corollary-discharge* or *efferent-copy information,* allows the brain to anticipate the consequences of its own impending actions. During REM sleep, when actual movement is impossible, the internally generated corollary-discharge information is interpreted by the brain as if the movement has actually occurred. In our dreams, the sense of being moved, as against willing movement, may be one conscious correlate of these internal replicas of the automatically generated but highly organized movement commands of REM sleep.

Let me emphasize the qualification "highly organized," which describes the well-established capacity of the brain stem to produce elaborate behavioral sequences, such as stepping, walking, and running. Activation synthesis assumes that when the brain stem's motor-pattern generator neurons are activated (that is, turned on), whether it be in waking or in REM sleep, they will produce organized command sequences.

In REM sleep, these motor-command sequences stimulate the perception of dream acts. As an apparatus for the performance of reliably integrated and willed actions, the brain stem's motor-pattern generator is in three ways highly compromised: first, no bodily movement is actually possible; second, feedback from such movement is therefore unavailable (and, in any case, sensory input is also blocked); and third, the excitability of the brain stem appears to be enhanced. As a consequence, activation synthesis assumes that automatically generated action sequences run their course despite dreamed volitional efforts to the contrary.

Recall my Williamstown dream (pages 232–34). Beginning with a *conversation* about psychoanalysis and science, the dream is promptly and dramatically animated by Van's Nijinsky-like *pirouette*. After watching him *spin* and *tossing* him back his hardware gift, I *walk* with him out a door and resume *talking*. Activation synthesis suggests not only that each of the imagined movements corresponds to a real motor command, but that the sequence or flow of events in the dream is compelled by such commands. When these commands change suddenly and/or are incongruous as a sequence, a scene change may occur.

In dreaming, as I shall show, many such dream actions are explained after the fact, as if they were both rational and willed when they are clearly, in the light of day, both irrational and involuntary. This *ad hoc* logic is an integral part of the dream form we call bizarreness.

In one sense these motoric impulses may well be the long-sought substrate of dream "wishes" that Freud postulated, but they occur at a very different level from the one he imagined. A possible reason is that the brain normally organizes its motor patterns hierarchically in relationship to what ethologists call *fixed acts,* the behavioral readout of the so-called instincts. Repetitive and stereotyped motor sequences are thus the building blocks of elemental behavior assuring survival and reproduction: defense, including flight from threat (as in the classic chase dream) and attack (as in dreams of motor combat); and appetitive behavior, such as sex (where fictive sexual arousal, approach, and even consummation constitute a not unusual dream sequence). That such dream actions often have a speeded-up, compelled character, accompanied by strong feelings, is, for activation synthesis, the dream-form equivalent of highly organized and strongly driven subcortical neural networks. A gamut of factors, from hormone levels to mental set, could activate and execute one or another of such sequences.

In any case, on all of these grounds, activation synthesis predicts that perceived movement in dreaming will be high in incidence, strong in intensity, stereotyped in course and trajectory, and incorporated into fixed acts of some clearly "instinctual nature." Such elemental motor programs are also available for the enactment of more "sophisticated" repertoires, such as swimming, flying, spinning, and golfing. And, whatever the nature of the dreamed act, it will often seem to just happen to the dreamer, as if one were a wind-up toy! Or an Engine Man.

13

The Bizarreness of Dreams

So long as the dream lasts consciousness is unable to
engage in reflection, it is carried along by its own decline and it continues to lay hold of images indefinitely.
This is the real explanation of oniric symbolism: if unconsciousness can never take hold of its own anxieties,
its own desire, excepting as symbols, it is not as Freud
believed, because of a suppression which compels it to
disguise them: but because it is incapable of laying hold
of what there is of the real under its form of reality. It
has completely lost the function of the real and everything it feels, everything it thinks, it cannot feel or
think otherwise than under the imagined form.
                            —Jean Paul Sartre
                            The Psychology of Imagination

The connections in dreams are partly nonsensical,
partly feeble-minded or even meaningless or partly demented. The last of these attributes is explained by the
fact that the compulsion to associate prevails in dreams.
                            —Sigmund Freud
                            Project for a Scientific Psychology

FOLK WISDOM has it that dreams are not only visually vivid and
motorically animated, but downright strange owing to the presence of
improbable or impossible events, characters, objects, thoughts, and feelings. *Bizarreness* is the term that is often used to denote these peculiar and
distinctive cognitive aspects of dreaming which have been supposed to
distinguish dream consciousness from that of the waking state.

As a formal dream feature, bizarreness has long captured the imagination of laymen and scientists, and various hypotheses have been proposed to explain it. The most popular current view, based upon psychoanalytic investigations, is that bizarre features are introduced by the "dream work" in order to disguise those unconscious "wishes" that are both the true instigators of dreams and unacceptable to consciousness.

The alternative activation-synthesis hypothesis, as I have explained, ascribes dream bizarreness to the unique physiological condition of the brain during the REM phase of sleep when dreaming is most likely to occur. According to this theory, bizarreness is thus the direct consequence of changes in the operating properties of the brain in REM sleep. An implication of the activation-synthesis model is that bizarreness itself has no particular psychodynamic significance; and that its interpretation, as being psychologically overdetermined, is not only gratuitous but even possibly hazardous.

I wish again to emphasize strongly that I am not asserting that dreams are either meaningless or unworthy of clinical attention. On the contrary, as shown in chapters 11 and 14, the meaning of dreams is for me transparent rather than concealed, since fundamentally incoherent cognitive elements are synthesized in a personally meaningful way. This "meaning-added" process is the exact opposite of that envisaged by psychoanalysis, which asserts that fully coherent and deeply meaningful ideas (the latent dream content) must be degraded and disguised (by the dream work), resulting in an incoherent product (the manifest dream content) acceptable to consciousness. For me, the manifest content is the dream: there is no other dream.

In their preliminary study (1981), McCarley and Hoffman enumerated the occurrence of such clearly peculiar elements as physically impossible characters (monsters) and physically impossible acts (flying). In the laboratory we subsequently broadened the definition of bizarreness to include unusual or improbable features of dream plot, character, action, and thinking. It is the discontinuities, incongruities, and uncertainties that make dreaming unique as a mental state; and these are the dream features Freud sought to explain by his disguise-censorship theory. They are thus the most central and the most demanding elements to be explained by any dream theory. Owing to their importance, I devote this and the following chapter to their documentation and explanation.

THE STUDY OF DREAM BIZARRENESS

To formulate an organized approach to the problem of dream bizarreness, we may pose three fundamental questions:

1. What formal definition of bizarreness most descriptively and concisely captures the cognitively distinctive aspects of dreaming?

2. What are the types of bizarre features found in dreams?

3. What is the frequency of different types of bizarreness in dreams?

In identifying and quantifying bizarreness in the reports of the dream journal of the Engine Man, we first made an extensive inventory of many diverse items, and then evolved a simple, two-stage detection system which, while historically independent, is formally similar to that of earlier studies, except that it is both more comprehensive and more concise. In this chapter, I shall first describe this system and then interpret the data with respect to competing hypotheses regarding the possible mechanism and significance of cognitive features of dreams; finally, I shall discuss the activation-synthesis hypothesis in relation to our findings.

Evolution of a Two-Stage Scoring System

We took, as a point of departure, *Webster's New Collegiate* theoretically unbiased definition of the bizarre:

1. *Improbability:* "strikingly out of the ordinary." In our measurement of this quality, we have substituted "significantly" for "strikingly" so as to parallel statistical reasoning in our instructions to judges; an item is improbable if it is estimated to occur in less than 5 percent of real-life situations.

2. *Unusual characteristics:* "odd, extravagant, or eccentric in style and mode." Related to improbability, this feature is further specified as "involving sensational contrasts or incongruities."

Our initial approach was to construct a scale that itemized the various types of dream bizarreness present in the first fifty dreams of the Engine Man's journal. The method used in scale construction was a simple trial-and-error elaboration of categories that described distinctly different types of bizarreness. As the data base was explored, existing categories were refined, and written definitions of each category were formalized. In the first scale we constructed, twenty-three distinct categories were delineated (see table 13.1).

TABLE 13.1

Items in Original Bizarreness Scale

Uncertain character
Fictional character, unidentified
Fictional character, identified
Dead character
Merged character
Dreamer/character displaced in time and/or place
Dreamer/character performing impossible/inappropriate action
Dreamer/character has distorted, disfigured, or absent body parts
Dreamer/character has inappropriate/absent clothing/implements
Character appears or vanishes
Dreamer/character repeats action not normally repeated

Inappropriate combination of environmental features
Fantastic environmental features
Realistic object in the wrong place
Violation of natural law
Object creation
Object with unusual features
Object changes into another object
Unidentified place
Familiar environment with alterations
Time shift
Situational abnormality

We then studied the next sixty dreams (numbers 50 to 110) and expanded the scale to forty-one items. This scale had four major subdivisions:

  I.   Form changes (Mergers, Transformations and Alterations)
  II. Relational Incongruities
  III. Functional Abnormalities
  IV. Uncertainties

Each of the four subdivisions dealt with dream characters, objects, and environments. This expanded scale proved to be unwieldy; and with further examination of the items, it became apparent that items could be grouped according to two broader categories. We thus changed from the inventory approach to a two-stage classification of items: stage 1 identified an item as belonging to one of three domains; stage 2 then assigned it to one of three categories of process abnormality. We used this simple two-stage system for identifying and describing dream bizarreness as the basis for subsequent analyses; it is summarized in table 13.2.

TABLE 13.2

Two-Stage Scoring System for Dream Bizarreness

Stage I identifies items as bizarre if they are physically impossible or improbable (probability of occurrence $\leq$ 0.05) aspects of:
  (a) the plot, characters, objects, or action;
  (b) the thoughts of the dreamer or dream characters;
  (c) the feeling state of the dreamer or dream character.
This stage establishes the *dream domain* or *report locus* of each item of bizarreness.

Stage II then characterizes the item as exhibiting:
  (a) discontinuity (change of identity, time, place, or features thereof);
  (b) incongruity (mismatching features);
  (c) uncertainty (explicit vagueness).
This stage establishes the *character* of each item of bizarreness.

The Engine Man's dream of the "Customs Building" (Report 80) illustrates the varieties of dream bizarreness that we are attempting to identify and characterize and the nature of our approach. Figure 13.1 reproduces a part of this report, which is transcribed in full and discussed in detail in chapter 14. Table 13.3 illustrates the sort of items we considered bizarre.

The dream concerns the author's search for a Customs Building and his discovery of its remarkable features and inhabitants. The most generally bizarre aspect of the dream is the marked and continuous disorganization of the personal and spatial domains. Throughout the dream, there is a vain attempt to reconcile the initial quest with the impressively contradictory findings. Nothing about the Customs Building is consistent with its expected features. Only the dreamer's mind, his own ideas, and his own experience are continuous as the unities of place and person undergo a succession of dramatic and only internally logical changes. The orientation domain is repeatedly fractured as the dream proceeds.

Using the two-stage scoring system, we identified and characterized sixty-five items of bizarreness. In the original, handwritten version of the dream's seventy-seven lines of narrative, hardly a sentence lacks a bizarre item. This report is also illustrated with an intrinsically bizarre drawing depicting the curious ramps on the outside of the building (figure 13.1). Many features reflect disruptions of the ongoing cognitive processes in the dream, along with attempts to repair or maintain the constantly challenged unities.

Plot (A) incongruity (2) was the most commonly scored category of dream bizarreness: almost half the items (44 percent) fall into this class. Mismatching elements were its defining feature. In table 13.3, we find the "no", and I remember thinking that it very probably was in some other part of town. It was at the Customs Bldg where all animals (except small ones such as Cats) must be registered or declared, weighed, and the proper tax paid. Even if the animal were on a train, and the train stopped within the District boundaries, the animals must be brought to the Customs Bldg, weighed & Taxed. Some person we were looking for had brought an animal from the train to the Customs Bldg.

As we wandered aimlessly about we suddenly saw the Customs Bldg straight in front of us. It was a 3-story Bldg of white stone with "ramps" on outside — apparently to enable animals to reach the upper stories (though it later became clear that all weighing was done in the basement). We entered building somehow (not by means of ramps) went to upper stories and looked in several rooms, though signs here & there on the doors & walls indicated that we were in wrong part of building. went from door to door, pushing each open. Usually we saw 2 persons in a room. In one, 2 men at a desk were earnestly talking — at least the attitude (bent over) of one was earnest. It seemed that they were important figures and were discussing weighty matters. In each of 2 other rooms was a girl (young lady) in nurses uniform. Each was talking to small persons — evidently children in years but with aged & deeply lined faces. It dawned on me then that this part of building was house of correction; the aged children were those unfortunates who had grown up on the streets, living by their wits until caught by police. An attempt was now being made to rehabilitate them. One of the children (with extremely peaked & sharp featured face) was asking the nurse some question about a story or picture he was

FIGURE 13.1
The Engine Man's Customs Building dream

TABLE 13.3

Item	Phrase	Scale
1	"buildings *none of which seemed large*" plot (A) incongruity (2)	A–2
2	"*seemed* large" cognitive (B) uncertainty (3)	B–3
3	"a child . . . later turned into Jason" plot (A) discontinuity (1)	A–1
4	"companion . . . who at first seemed like a stranger" plot (A) incongruity (2)	A–2
5	"seemed like a stranger" cognitive (B) uncertainty (3)	B–3
6	"I asked him if he *knew the location* of the Customs Building" plot (A) incongruity (2)	A–2
7	"thinking it was in some other part of town" cognitive (B) discontinuity (1)	B–1
8	"Customs Bldg. . . . where all animals registered" plot (A) incongruity (2)	A–2
9	"except small ones such as cats" plot (A) incongruity (2)	A–2
10	"train stopped . . . animals must be brought . . . weighed" plot (A) incongruity (2)	A–2

following examples: uncommonly small buildings (item 1) in downtown Washington; an adult asks a six-year-old child for directions (item 6); a customs building becomes an animal registry (item 8); an animal registry that excludes cats (item 9); and a train stop that serves as an animal weighing station (item 10).

Cognition (B) uncertainty (2) was the next most frequently observed

TABLE 13.4

Bizarreness Characterization

Category	Percentage of Total Raw Scores (judges 1+2)		Percentage of Agreements of Two Judges		Percent of Time Score Used Similarly by Two Judges
A1	9.30%	(N=110)	8.70%	(N=36)	65%
A2	44.5	(N=525)	44.3	(N=183)	70
B1	0.25	(N=3)	0.24	(N=1)	67
B2	19.3	(N=228)	16.0	(N=66)	58
B3	24.3	(N=286)	29.3	(N=121)	85
C2	2.30	(N=27)	1.45	(N=6)	44

TABLE 13.5

Distribution of Bizarreness Subtypes and Their Reliability

Category		Percent of Time Scored	
1. A1			
a.	Total orientational shifts	89%	(N=32)
	1. Time	36	(N=13)
	2. People (appear/disappear)	36	(N=13)
	3. Scene; location	11	(N=4)
	4. Attention	6	(N=2)
b.	Transformation (occurred *within* dream)	11	(N=4)
2. B2			
a.	Ad hoc explanation—i.e., explanation to resolve or explain strange situation	58	(N=41)
b.	Incongruous quotes	17	(N=12)
c.	Incongruous thoughts and feelings	25	(N=18)

species of bizarreness. In waking life: buildings are either large or small, large ones do not "seem" small (item 1); persons are either known or unknown, familiar ones do not "seem" like strangers. About one third (30 percent) of the scored items reflected this indefinite aspect.

More dramatic examples are the orientational instabilities scored as plot (A) or cognitive (B) shifts (1): a child (who first seems like a stranger) turns into the dreamer's nephew; he suddenly thinks that the building that is his dream destination is in some other part of town. More quantitative data are given in tables 13.4 and 13.5.

Dream Length and Bizarreness

We plotted the frequency of different dream lengths against bizarreness scores and the correlation between dream length and number of bizarreness items per dream. Thus, bizarreness was a constant feature of the dreaming process, not a feature that changed from night to night or from dream to dream.

Figure 13.2 shows the distribution of dream lengths by number of lines. We suppose that the smaller number of short (0 to 5 lines) reports is related to generally poor recall of the dream experience. The second graph shows that the number of bizarre items increases linearly as a function of dream length. Bizarreness thus appeared to be a constant feature in dream reports.

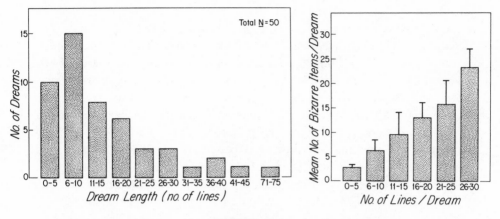

FIGURE 13.2

Distribution of dream lengths for fifty consecutive reports in the Engine Man's journal
Variable memory is probably responsible for the decay in the histogram on the left
(from its peak at 6–10 to its low point at 71–75 lines). Whether long or short, the
Engine Man's reports are consistently bizarre, suggesting that bizarreness is a
constant aspect of dream cognition. *Source:* J. A. Hobson, S. A. Hoffman, R. Helfand,
and D. Costner, "Dream Bizarreness and the Activation-Synthesis Hypothesis,"
Human Neurobiology 6 (1987): 157–64.

The Indefinite Nature of Improbability

Although some features and events of dreams are physically impossible, many others are only improbable. A problem arises here, owing to the
subjectivity of decisions about what in this sense constitutes bizarreness.
Differing knowledge bases about the varied contents of dreams may also
lead to discrepancies in the assessment of what is improbable and/or
unusual.

We have recognized and accepted the impossibility of attaining per-
fect agreement among judges on what constitutes bizarreness when improbability is a defining characteristic. The reason is that we find it unsatisfactory to limit identification of bizarreness to physical impossibility, as
other investigators have done. Since few of our high-agreement items
would have been detected using only the impossibility criterion, we feel
that we have a scale whose increased sensitivity is worth the price of
imperfect reliability. But even with this limitation, our reliability coeffi-
cients are as high as those attained in most other studies.

Verbal reports are not only derivative and secondary to the dream
experience itself but also subject to individual factors, such as an author's
verbal capacities and idiosyncrasies. In using a journal, we also take the

risk of relying upon an unknown subject over whom we exert no experimental control. Our conviction is that this naturalistic method allows us to gain access to an ample dream experience and a rich expressive range that more than compensate for the loss of objectivity and control afforded by the observer-initiated and instrument-assisted interventions of the sleep lab, especially since recall after laboratory awakenings is often poor.

Another rationale for looking at sleep-lab reports is thus to assess the validity of hypotheses concerning dream thought based upon the intensive analysis of home-based dream journals. In her collaboration with Dr. John Antrobus of the College of the City of New York, Dr. Helene Porte applied the bizarreness scale developed in the Engine Man's journal data to a set of seventy-three report pairs, each pair from a single subject awakening, one each from REM and from non-REM sleep (Porte and Hobson 1986*a*). Using bizarreness alone as an index, Porte has successfully predicted that a report came from REM sleep. In this paradigm, we are mapping back and forth not only between REM-sleep physiology and dream mentation but also between the extensive, physiologically controlled conditions of the laboratory and the freer, intensive, and uncontrolled conditions of home sleep.

THE INTREPRETATION OF DREAM BIZARRENESS

Keeping in mind the limitations of our data base, we can begin to form a picture of this most distinctive feature of dream mentation and think about it in a new way. We have seen that many bizarre features are found in the domain of a dream's sensations and actions, and appear to arise from, or be embedded in, the plot of the dream. The domain of dream thought is also significantly involved, but an appreciable portion of these cognitive abnormalities appear to be of the *ad hoc* variety: that is, they are explanations that are clearly secondary to abnormalities in the action domain. In addition, there are cognitive uncertainties that may be due to an inability to describe abnormal or ambiguous dream actions in the language of the waking state. Unlike ambiguities due to poor recall, these uncertainties may arise from an attempt to explain an action that is itself ambiguous, incongruous, or otherwise bizarre but is not recognized as such within the dream. The domain of feeling, at least in most of the dreams we have studied, is relatively untouched by whatever process causes dream bizarreness.

Our findings would seem to locate a major source of cognitive disturbance in dreams on what might be called the input side of the synthetic process that develops dream mentation. In other words, the trouble arises at or near the sensori-motor level, since perceptual and motoric phenomena are much more profoundly perturbed than are affective phenomena. The cognitive domain is dominated by an inability to describe and/or a vain attempt to explain a host of perceptual and motoric abnormalities.

CONTRASTING VIEWS OF BIZARRENESS

Psychoanalysis suggests that these data reflect a defensive and regressive shift in cognition "toward the sensory side." But this theory is at pains to account in an economical way for what seems to be simultaneous disturbance in many sensorimotor areas. For example, if pictorialization is serving a defensive purpose, why should it need to be further amplified by pictorial incongruity? For this cumbersome accumulation of rationalizations, I suggest substituting the simpler assumption that bizarreness and visual autostimulation are both intrinsic to the nature of brain activation and modulation processes in REM sleep, and conclude that they are thus primary and physiologically determined, not secondary and cognitively derived attributes.

Activation-synthesis attempts to model the production of dreams by contrasting the condition of the outside world and the psychophysiological state of the subject in the waking state with that of the REM sleep/ dreaming state. With reference to the feature called bizarreness, three aspects of mental functioning are considered in each condition: the orientational, the contextual, and the conceptual. Waking and dreaming are thus seen to be at opposite ends of three continuums:

1. stability, instability (of orientation);
2. congruity, incongruity (of context);
3. confidence, uncertainty (of concept).

During waking, the external world provides input that our brain-mind orders via orientational unity, feature or figural continuity, and cause-effect linearity. The waking brain-mind achieves orientational stability via a combination of accurate monitoring of these reliably continuous inputs and by the constant updating of recent memory. In dreaming, not only are the external cues lost but recent memory mechanisms are impaired; as a result, the internally generated orientational schemata (as well as object and action features) have neither external nor internal control. The result is the orientational instability that is a major component of dream bizarreness. Deafferentation and amnesia likewise collaborate to account for the change from the contextual congruity of wake-state consciousness to the incongruity that typifies dream bizarreness.

In waking, conceptual confidence is achieved by a simple preservation of real-world event order and by the attendant mirroring of real-world cause-effect chains in the abstract logical operations of the waking brain-mind. During dreaming, the serial ordering and associated domination of thought by verbal processes give way to more parallel processing and to a relative increase in visual and analogical operations. This cognitive shift could find its substrate in a state-dependent change in lateral dominance (from left to right), and the consequent weakening of cognitive control could contribute to the conceptual uncertainty of the dream state (Bertini et al. 1983; Lavie 1982). In this regard, it is significant that the left hemisphere has to be intact in order for dreaming to occur at all (Greenberg and Farah 1984).

In conclusion, two major factors conspire to determine the difference between wake- and dream-state mental features that we have measured as bizarreness:

The first factor is the consequence, in sleep, of the instability of the external stimuli that convey to the wake-state brain-mind such conditions of the outer world as orientational unity, contextual congruity, and linearity of cause-effect relations between events. These constancies are reflected in wake-state mentation as long as attention, memory, and linear-verbal information-processing functions are maintained.

The second factor is the internal change, in sleep, in the state of the brain-mind where arise internally generated stimuli that lack all three features of external-world stability. These internal stimuli are actively organized by the brain-mind into orientational schemata and object-action scenarios which are inherently unstable, possibly because of the sleep-dependent failure of memory and attentional functions. The same failure would be expected to contribute to conceptual uncertainty, while logical failure may result from a loss of the predominantly linear-verbal (left brain) mode of information processing and the ascendance of a predominantly analogical, parallel (right brain) mode of processing. The net result is what we call, and can now to some extent define and measure, dream bizarreness. This is what we mean when we say, "I had the strangest dream."

Now the question becomes: If we were to regard both the sensory and motor hallucinations and the bizarre cognition of dreams as state-dependent features determined by REM sleep physiology—and not of psychological significance, per se—what change would that necessitate in our interpretive stance? To explore that question in a preliminary way, the following chapter looks at the Customs Building dream to see what its narrative reveals about the Engine Man's psychology without recourse to either free association or symbol interpretation.

14

The Interpretation
of Dream Form

I think it is a very good way to examine dreams every
morning when I awake; what are the nature, circumstances, principles and ends of my imaginary actions
and passions in them, to discern what are my chief
inclinations.

> —JONATHAN EDWARDS
> *The Works of President Edwards* (1851)

Certain exceptional dreams, however, are so impera-
tively significant, so vitally important, that it would be
wrong to withhold them from the knowledge of those
that happened not to dream them, and I feel some such
quality in my own dreams so strongly that I could
scarcely forgive myself if I did not, however briefly,
impart them.

> —WILLIAM DEAN HOWELLS
> "True, I Talk of Dreams" (1895)

THE DISCONTINUITY and incongruity of dream plots can be viewed
as contributing to the inconstancy and inconsistency of background aspects of the dream, where *background* is defined as the orientational framework of the dream and the characteristics of its subjects and actions. Both
the fluid shifts in orientation (change without notice of the identity of
persons, places, and times) and the kaleidoscopic or patchwork-quilt quality of dream objects (improbable constellations of disparate characteristics)

contrast with the remarkable stability of the foreground aspects of the dream, where *foreground* is defined as the overall theme and narrative structure of the dream experience.

Narrative-thematic constancy, which Allan Rechtschaffen (1978) has called "the single-mindedness of dreams," is all the more surprising given the high cognitive uncertainty expressed by a dreamer about the logic of the dream experience. In addition to disorientation, the dreamer's insight appears to be markedly impaired: Why does one so seldom recognize the dream for the distinctively bizarre mental state that it is? Put another way, why is one so rarely aware that one is dreaming during the dream itself? These questions are doubly puzzling in light of the ease with which one diagnoses dreaming upon awakening. Surely the answer must be that some critical, self-observing quality of waking consciousness is lost in dreaming. Although we have not yet attempted to measure insight quantitatively, I can report that there was not a single description of dream consciousness* in the Engine Man's entire collection of 233 dreams.

Activation synthesis has not yet attempted to account for the thematic-narrative constancies of dreaming in any systematic way. But these formal dream features must reflect the laws governing the storage, organization, and retrieval of information within the brain, just as do the relatively simpler sensory (chapter 11) and motor (chapter 12) aspects. In this section, I foreshadow an attempt to devise such laws for two important aspects of dreaming—enhanced associations and personally significant plot construction—without depending upon the disguise-censorship assumption of psychoanalysis.

To illustrate the way in which the formal approach to dreaming is distinct from, but compatible with, the content-analytic approach to an individual dream, let me turn again to the Engine Man's "Customs Building" dream (Report 80, 14 August 1939), which I here recount in full. In the following discussion, I assume that the coherence of the story, which is eroded by the deficits of thinking specific to the REM sleep state, derives from the dreamer's biographical experience, and that its manifest content directly reflects the operation of personally significant meaning-attribution processes. My interpretation of this dream is thus broadly psychodynamic without being narrowly psychoanalytic.

---

*"Dream consciousness," or "lucidity," refers to the awareness, during the dream, that one is dreaming. It can be accomplished by some subjects using autosuggestion, as in the work of Hervey de Saint-Denis (1867), Mary Arnold-Forster (1921), and Stephen LaBerge (1985).

THE ENGINE MAN'S "CUSTOMS BUILDING" DREAM

Walking South on 14th St., just south of Pennsylvania Ave. Street was very muddy. A few blocks (about 3) south of the avenue (Pa. Ave.) I turned east, passing behind various buildings none of which seemed large. No one in sight except my companion, a child of perhaps 6 to 8 years, who later turned into Jason but who, at first, seemed like a stranger.

Fourteenth Street and Pennsylvania Avenue is two blocks from the White House and, even in 1939, was downtown governmental Washington. That the street is very muddy was a point that we judged not improbable enough to be scored as bizarre. That "none" of the buildings "seemed large" in such a heavily built up part of town seems, however, distinctly incongruous. The word "seemed" also reflects the dreamer's uncertainty, as if he knows there is something wrong. That there should be "no one in sight" is, again given the locale, distinctly abnormal. Each of these items, taken alone, is debatable; but together they contribute to the sort of vacuous mystery so beautifully depicted in Giorgio de Chirico's dream paintings.

With the transformation of his companion, "who, at first, seemed like a stranger," into Jason (his nephew), we are unequivocally in dream country. How can a companion be a stranger? He cannot. Therefore the dreamer corrects the situation by turning him into a known person:

I asked him if he knew the location of the Customs Building; he said "no," and I remember thinking that it very probably was in some other part of town. It was at the Customs Bldg. where all animals (except small ones such as cats) must be registered or declared, weighed, and the proper tax paid. Even if the animal were on a train, and the train stopped within the District boundaries, the animals must be brought to the Customs Bldg., weighed, and taxed. Some person we were looking for had brought an animal from the train to the Customs Bldg.

Asking the location of the Customs Building seems to be an attempt to give the dream an orientational goal or anchor. It is as if the dreamer has said to himself: "Here I am walking in downtown Washington; therefore I must be going somewhere (could it be the Customs Building?); and with someone (could it be Jason?) and we are here for some reason (perhaps we are looking for someone)."

But this orientational anchor drags a bit. Since Jason does not know the location of the Customs Building, the dreamer thinks that it is likely "in some other part of town"—a non sequitur that accounts for Jason's

ignorance but does not help the dream's stability. I suggest that there is something wrong in the brain's map room. If the dreamer cannot locate the dream's Customs Building, maybe he can at least find a function for it. Paying a tax seems appropriate enough. And trains make associational sense, too, since goods (transported across boundaries) may be subject to customs taxes. But on animals? Large animals? Surely, sir, you must be in the wrong memory file. The Engine Man's memory search for spatial orientation appears to proceed as follows: Downtown Washington → official building → customs building → animal pound. But even at a pound, small animals, like cats, *should* be registered. To tie together these loose ends and give his dream walk a purpose, the Engine Man's brain-mind creates "some person [unidentified] we were looking for" who had "brought an animal from the train to the Customs Bldg."

All of this preamble seems to serve the purpose of fixing the dreamer's orientational bearings. Where am I? What am I doing here? Who is with me? What is my relationship to that person?

Having decided that he is in downtown Washington with Jason (a familiar locale with his favorite nephew), and looking for the Customs Building (a specific place), the dreamer is still not clear either about the function of the Customs Building or (by implication) why he should be looking for it. These latter uncertainties invite the speculative creations that constitute the balance of the dream plot.

But already a key question arises: Are we to assume that all of this confusion is really in the service of obscuring an unconscious wish? Might it not, rather, reflect the undistorted efforts of the brain-mind to perform one of its most essential functions: to establish orientational stability? Since we have no evidence for the first possibility, we leave it aside. But we take seriously the abundant evidence for the second possibility: that is, as I described in Part III, the orientational brain-mind is indeed operating at a severe disadvantage in REM sleep.

As we wandered aimlessly about we suddenly saw the Customs Bldg., straight in front of us. It was a 3-story bldg. of white stone with "ramps" on outside apparently to enable animals to reach the upper stories (though it later became clear that all weighing was done in the basement). We entered building somehow (not by means of ramps), went to upper stories and looked in several rooms, though signs here and there on the doors and walls indicated that we were in wrong part of building.

The inadequacy of the dreamer's tentative motives is reflected in the adverb *aimlessly:* the Engine Man and his nephew are just wandering about (lower-extremity movement). But "suddenly" (scene change) the Customs

Building appears: it is a fabulous creation, not quite physically impossible but certainly highly improbable.

In designing outside ramps (curvilinear trajectories) to enable the animals to reach the upper stories (a *post hoc* explanation of plot incongruity), the dream architect has gone wild. Even the dreamer himself does not accept the ramps: it makes more sense to do the weighing in the basement; and his own entry to the building's upper stories (not explained) is specifically *not* via the ramps. So the ramps are gratuitous elements that we might consider to be symbols—but whether concave (vaginas?) or convex (penises?) depends on one's point of view. Why not say, on the other hand, that they are curvilinear tracks (that might respond creatively to an internally generated sense of movement) and let it go at that? The dreamer himself is happy enough to leave them behind. A Freudian would contend that, by protecting the dreamer's prudish mind from frank genital exhibitionism, the dream work has succeeded in preserving sleep. But, however entertaining it may be to so speculate, we can never get closure on this point.

So let us return to the dream. Now that the Engine Man and his nephew have found the Customs Building, they see signs "here and there on the doors and walls" indicating that they are in the "wrong part" of the building. What is the *right* part of the building? What could these signs of erroneous location be? What are they looking for, anyway?

Jason went from door to door, pushing each open. Usually we saw two persons in a room. In one, two men at a desk were earnestly talking, at least the attitude (bent over) of one was earnest. It seemed that they were important figures and were discussing weighty matters. In each of two other rooms was a girl (young lady) in nurse's uniform. Each was talking to small persons, evidently children in years but with aged and deeply lined faces.

How about the social aspect of all of this? "Jason went from door to door" (lower-extremity movement), "pushing each open" (upper-extremity movement). Isn't this unusually intrusive behavior for a civil servant and his nephew? "Usually" (not always?) "we saw" (visual hallucination) "two persons" (unidentified characters) "in a room." First, a pair of men talking earnestly. How does the dreamer know their talk is earnest? Because at least one of them assumes an earnest, "bent over" attitude. Surely, "bent over" could mean many things besides "earnest": it could mean crippled or tired, or even condescending; or it could mean curved posture, which satisfies the dreamer's uncritical criteria for seriousness of purpose. "It seemed" (explicit vagueness) "that they were discussing important matters." There *must* be a good reason for them, and us, to be here, but what is it?

The purpose of the Customs Building now switches from animals to people: There are two girls "in nurse's uniform." Are they nurses, then? Why not say so? Because it's not yet clear? Why follow "girl" with "(young lady)"? But if they seem like nurses, of whom are they taking care? Are the "small persons" dwarfs? Gnomes? Rumpelstiltskins? Likely any of the three: "evidently children in years but with aged and deeply lined faces" (identified characters with incongruous features).

What are we to make of these senile orphans? A fusion of the dreamer (who is forty-six) and of Jason (who is between six and eight)? Or do they blend the dreamer's parents (probably in their sixties or seventies) with the grandchildren he never gave them? Either alternative is possible, but cannot be known. Why not, however, simply say that the dreamer is still disoriented, and delving ever more deeply into the orientational memory file? That file is organized as follows:

1. Governmental Washington (14th Street and Pennsylvania Avenue): implies official buildings.
2. Customs Building: implies taxes, transportation.
3. Large animal facility: like a zoo, or a pound.
4. Human-care facility: like a hospital or correctional institution (as we shall see).

In other words, the dreamer is lost (disoriented) but also stuck (associatively) in a related set of orientational memory frames. The simplest explanation for this obvious disorientation is not defensive disguise but disorientation itself, pure and simple. We need not assume a defensive purpose but only that external orientational cues are absent (because the dreamer is asleep and cut off from the world), and that his own brain compass is spinning (because the brain mechanism serving memory, attention, and insight are disabled).

It dawned on me then that this part of the building was a house of correction; the aged children were those unfortunates who had grown up on the streets, living by their wits until caught by police. An attempt was now being made to rehabilitate them. One of the children (with extremely peaked and sharp featured face) was asking the nurse some question about a story or picture he was examining in a book. The nurse's voice, in answering him, though kind enough, was perfunctory: clearly this was merely part of her job, there was not that extra eagerness to explain to and interest the child, no real attempt to implant in his mind the desire to learn and improve; and I meditated, "Nothing will take the place of good home training."

Our "orientational frame" theory has gained further support from the dreamer's dawning recognition that "this part of [the] building was [the] house of correction"; and now we know why it was the wrong part (with respect to its designation as the Customs Building in which he was seeking "some person [who] had brought an animal from the train"). The "aged children" discrepancy is explained away as the metaphorical street wisdom of vagabond youth "living by their wits until caught by police": they are old beyond their years.

Now we clearly enter, via the institutional door, the dreamer's own file of social and behavioral theories. His dream house of correction is supposed to have a rehabilitative function, but this service is "perfunctory": witness the nurse's unenthusiastic response (it is now settled that the girl, or young lady, is a nurse) to one of the children with extremely peaked and sharp-featured faces. This indifference prompts the dreamer to observe that "nothing will take the place of good home training." The orientational quest is over. We are finally home, as it were:

Then we entered a room containing a large, cradle-like bed in which were a fully dressed nurse, and a baby. Jason crawled up on one end of bed, got hold of a water glass, and reached into the glass for a piece of ice. I suddenly decided this called for disciplinary action, grasped him firmly by fore-arm, pulled him down to floor, and led him out of room, saying I couldn't stand for such rambunctiousness. Jason was very reluctant to leave, but I remained firm. (About this time I realized that the animal weighing doubtless took place in basement.)

No question about it, civil servant caretakers are no match for real parents. The Engine Man now enters his dream nursery and assumes a paternal role. There is a cradle containing "a fully dressed nurse, and a baby." When Jason crawls aboard and grabs a piece of ice, the Engine Man decides to take disciplinary action and physically removes his nephew from both cradle and nursery.

"Just because there are babies present, you are not allowed to act infantile," he seems to say to the child-nephew of his dream. Is he really talking about himself (displacement)? Has he regressed, via the dream's disorientational hall of mirrors, to his own childhood? Why should he point out that the mother-surrogate nurse is "fully dressed"? Does this action "cover" an oedipal sexual motive at the same time that it maintains the institutional orientational frame? Perhaps. Now he lays his previous orientational hypothesis to rest by realizing that the animal weighing "doubtless" took place in the basement. No more uncertainty on this point! And the dream continues to unearth the deep strata of the Engine Man's

fundamental behavioral assumptions. The Customs Building dream ends with a Last Judgment:

Next we entered the room of a judge. This worthy was reclining full length (dressed) on a couch. He had a big, jutting nose and a coarse grained skin, like the skin of a man who has lived a hard or fast life. Like most judges he stunk of superiority. By this time Jason had vanished, and there seemed to be two adults with me, probably my sisters Dorothy and June. They left the room as the judge was saying, "Honor is found only in women but does not exist in men." This seemed incomprehensible to the two ladies, but I recognized it as a sentiment expressed by Duff in "This Human Nature," and I asked the judge whether he had read the book. He answered "Yes, of course"; he also said it was fairly good but had two very serious faults (which unfortunately were not explained).

Has the dreamer done right to discipline Jason? He is not sure. So he decides to submit this question to judgment. The scene changes to another room. Is this the fourth, the fifth, or is it the sixth dream chamber? The judge, continuing the prudish tradition of the nurse in the cradle, is dressed while lying "full length . . . on a couch" (is this a psychoanalytic consulting room or a male brothel?). The dreamer's ambivalence about the judge's judgment is expressed in the latter's incongruous physiognomy: "like . . . a man who has lived a hard or fast life." Apparently the Engine Man did not like those smug judges who "stunk of superiority."

Jason has by now "vanished." Was he destroyed by the dreamer's disciplinary action? His replacements—significantly, I believe—are female family members: the dreamer's sisters, Dorothy (Jason's mother) and June. The narrative logic of this double discontinuity is clear enough. Having decided that there is no substitute for home training, and having seen Jason act up with both a baby and a nurse—and all in the same bed—the associational dream stage is set for mother's entry. Enter *two* mothers. Exit the son. The associative path is transparent, not opaque. If this cast reshuffling is in the interest of disguise and of censorship, the dream work is a failure.

And now we hear the judge opine that "Honor is found only in women but does not exist in men," a quote that seems aptly to express the dreamer's growing emphasis upon good mothering and his attachment to his sisters, as well as his doubts about his own ability to be paternal. But, like the good scientist that he is, he cites the bibliographic source: Duff's *This Human Nature.* Then he ends on an oneirically skeptical note, with the judge's opinion that the book "was fairly good but had two very serious faults (which unfortunately were not explained)." I suggest that one fault could be that it was not true!

ANALYSIS OF FORM VERSUS ANALYSIS OF CONTENT

To elucidate further the distinction between analyses of form and of content, and to show that they can be used together to explain both the bizarreness of this dream and its remarkable associative coherence, I shall organize by topic some of the detailed points made in the previous discussion. While the formal orientational categories of persons and places are disorganized, they are nonetheless held together in a narrative frame by their intrinsic associative relations.

Orientational Disturbances: Persons and Places

Members of the dreamer's family contribute to the dream's bizarreness through their appearance-disappearance and their interchangeability. Since Dorothy is Jason's mother, this substitution could be rationalized as associative, especially since, at the point in the narrative when the boy vanishes, the emotional tension concerns discipline and mothering (see tables 14.1 and 14.2).

There is also a succession of scene changes that is, simultaneously, bizarre and associatively logical. Back, back, back (into his memory file) goes the dreamer until he reaches rooms that are formally adequate to the universal twin themes of authority and nurturance. Note that the orienta-

TABLE 14.1

Persons/Family Characters

Character	Action	Bizarre Process
Jason (the Engine Man's nephew)	A stranger "turned into Jason"	uncertain identity/ change of identity; unexplained appearance
	"Jason vanished"	suspension of identity; unexplained disappearance
Dorothy and June (the Engine Man's sisters)	"seemed to be two adults" *"probably* my sisters"	unexplained appearance uncertain identity

Other more "incidental" characters contribute to the dream's bizarreness largely through their uncertain identity and ambivalent, quasi-symbolic qualities. The overlay of two aspects of these characters—one gentle, the other harsh—I shall discuss in due course.

TABLE 14.2

Persons/Incidental Characters

Character	Bizarre Process
"Some person we were looking for"	vague identity
"two persons in a room"	unidentified characters
"earnestly talking, at least . . . one"	uncertain attributes
"It seemed"	uncertain attributes
"girl . . . in nurse's uniform"	incompatible features
"children . . . with aged and deeply lined faces"	incompatible features
"one [child] with extremely peaked and sharp featured face"	incompatible features
"nurse . . . perfunctory"	incompatible features
"nurse, and a baby"	unlikely features
"judge . . . reclining"	unlikely characteristic
"two adults . . . probably"	uncertain identity

tional progression of the whole dream has an associative logic that parallels the shifts in dramatic personae, so as to create a striking harmony of persons and place, as in table 14.3.

TABLE 14.3

Places, Real and Imaginary

Phrase	Bizarre Process
"South on 14th Street, just south of Pennsylvania"	specific locus
"A few blocks south . . . turned east"	uncertain direction
"location of the Customs Building"	change in locus
"some other part of town"	change in locus
"animals" (the building becomes a pound)	change in function
"suddenly saw the Customs Bldg."	change in locus
"ramps . . . to reach the upper stories"	improbable structure
"weighing was done in the basement"	inconsistent feature
"entered . . . somehow"	uncertain access
"wrong part of building"	uncertain locus
"door to door"	inappropriate action
Room 1: "two men at a desk . . . earnestly talking"	uncertain action
Rooms 2 and 3: two girls "in nurse's uniform . . . talking to small persons"	change in function
"this part . . . house of correction" (rehabilitation)	change in function
Room 4: "cradle-like bed," with nurse and baby	change in function
"animal weighing . . . in basement"	change in function
Room 5: "judge . . . reclining . . . on a couch"	change in function

Associative Themes

Examination of the progression of changes reveals, in fact, that these two symmetrical associative themes serve to give the dream *coherence.* One major theme concerns *authority* and involves males; a second major theme concerns *nurturance* and involves females, shown in table 14.4.

TABLE 14.4

Chains of Association in the Customs Building Dream

Authority Theme	Nurturance Theme
official, institutional Washington	girls "in nurse's uniform"
the Customs Building	"attempt . . . to rehabilitate"
the animal pound	the nurse's "perfunctory" voice
the "important figures"	desire to learn, improve
the "house of correction" (delinquency)	"good home training"
Jason's "rambunctiousness"	"cradle-like bed"
the judge's room	"nurse and baby"
the judge's sanctimoniousness	Dorothy and June
males are dishonorable	"Honor is found only in women"

Under the umbrella of thematic consistency, however, the sex-role domain is as subject to oscillation as are the realms of person and place. It is as if the discriminating, decision-making, and value-attributing functions of the brain-mind were as loosely organized as the orientation and the attentional functions. Rather than assuming that a particular and individual logic compels the dream action, I believe instead that only superficial but sturdy sectors of experience and information constrain the dream. Within each sector, the play of orientation and value is without limit. Anything (and everything) goes in the dream state, as long as it connects in some way with the narrative.

The ambivalence between the male (authority) principle and the female (nurturance) principle is split by the judge who condemns himself (male honor does not exist) with the quote from Duff which is, however—according to the judge—unreliable.

The contrapuntal play of the themes is characterized by an oscillation within each of them as well as between them both—a feature that could be described as an abnormal fluidity between opposites, resulting in a heightened ambivalence that amplifies the ironies of human existence (see table 14.5). It is in this sense that we may share with psychoanalysts a fascination with the dream as a mirror of our concerns. But for me the

TABLE 14.5

Associative Connections and Contrasts

	Between Themes	Within Themes
Official place	Customs Building officials	Pound
Nurse	girls in nurses' uniforms	(but perfunctory voice)
Official place	house of correction nurse is perfunctory	rehabilitation center contradiction in terms: *aged babies*
Nurse	nurse and baby in cradle vs. (Jason's rambunctiousness)	hyperbolic image of technical maternality (reaction formation)
Official person	Judge	hard or fast life (decadent)
Nurse	sisters	can't understand (honor exists only in women)

dream mirror reflects its deep structures accurately—and without distortion.

This admittedly anecdotal exercise in dream interpretation is presented to suggest one of the many directions that future dream research might take (see also chapter 15). As in all retrospective speculations, it will be important to verify biographical surmises in living subjects whose dreams are interpreted within the transparency framework of the activation-synthesis hypothesis. We need to study many more dreams from many more subjects to bring the science of dream interpretation into line with the systematic status of dream description we have achieved. Echoing the Engine Man's parental concerns, I believe that we may thus be able to avoid throwing out the psychodynamic baby with the psychoanalytic bathwater.

PART V

THE FUTURE OF DREAM SCIENCE

15

The Functions of REM
Sleep and Dreaming

Sleep is a state in which a great part of every life is passed. No animal has been yet discovered, whose existence is not varied with intervals of insensibility; and some late philosophers have extended the empire of sleep over the vegetable world.

Yet of this change so frequent, so great, so general, and so necessary, no searcher has yet found either the efficient or final cause; or can tell by what power the mind and body are thus chained down in irresistible stupefaction; or what benefits the animal receives from this alternate suspension of its active powers.

—SAMUEL JOHNSON
The Idler (1758)

The wildness of our dreams seems to be of singular use to us, by interrupting and breaking the course of our associations. For, if we were always awake, some accidental associations would be so much cemented by continuance, as that nothing could afterwards disjoin them; which would be madness.

—DAVID HARTLEY
Observations on Man (1801)

THE $64,000 question regarding sleep is "What is it all for?" A behavior as complex as sleep—with its highly differentiated component non-REM and REM phases—is unlikely to be dedicated to any one particular function, yet folk wisdom has tended to collaborate with scientific reductionism in supposing that one, and only one, function is served by sleep. The universal favorite candidate for this function is rest. This is probably the carryover—in the functional domain—of the naive subjectivist notion that in sleep our brains are at a low and monotonous level of activity. We have already seen how wrong subjective experience can be in this regard. Yet, in spite of years of research, science has not definitely established even *one* function for sleep.

In asking functional questions, we must distinguish between levels of discourse just as we must distinguish between such levels in asking mechanistic questions. Although we seek a unifying functional hypothesis— one that encompasses all levels of discourse—we may discover that different functions are served at each level. Thus functional questions asked in the language of one level of analysis must be answered only in the language of that same level. A typical error would be to answer the question "What are dreams for?" in physiological terms, such as "to conserve those neurotransmitters that are necessary to efficient waking." Dreaming is a psychological state; and if dreaming *per se* has a function, it is at the psychological level.

To illustrate this problem, let me point out that those who accept the Freudian functional theory of dreams as the "guardian of sleep" are accepting a physiological answer to a psychological question. Freud's idea that dreaming serves to discharge instinctual energy is similarly problematic. A physiological process might discharge instinctual energy but a psychological process cannot. Freudian theory shifts semantic level. Dreaming is a psychological state, while sleep is a behavioral state. Both are reflections of physiology. One cannot ascribe physiological and behavioral functions to psychological events without risking semantic chaos and, what is worse, confusion of correlation with cause.

It is at least logically appropriate to assume, as our mothers did, that sleep is necessary to health since we subjectively experience sleep as restful and restorative. These commonsense functional statements have the virtue of grammatical agreement between subject and predicate: both are physiological. And so overwhelmingly clear is the sense of restoration following a good night of sleep that no one in his or her right mind would abandon the rest theory despite the deafening silence of physiology on this question. In this sense, subjective experience should more powerfully motivate us to seek physiological or behavioral explanations, just as the experience of dreaming should have motivated scientists to look for evidence of brain activation during sleep.

But the rest theory is likely to require a more specialized answer in the case of the kind of sleep we humans share with our fellow mammals. The reason is that rest does not require sleep. Inactivity alone should suffice to provide us with rest. And many organisms already spend a good deal of their wake-state time at rest. Rest is thus likely to be a fundamental, cellular-level phenomenon that is functionally independent of central nervous system complexity.

The rest function may well be further elaborated in higher animals with complex brains so as specifically to restore efficiency to such crucial wake-state functions as attention and memory. According to this view, the capacity to concentrate upon and to retain new information would be enhanced by sleep. Such rest is likely to be associated with other more active processes than the simple passive version the rest theory would imply. For example, while the brain-mind is freed of the task of monitoring and remembering new information in sleep, it can review and reorganize its own already acquired data. It is in this sense that most of the new hypotheses arising from modern sleep research distinguish themselves from Freud's contributions and from those of his contemporaries and predecessors.

One reason it has been difficult to establish convincing functional hypotheses is, as usual, methodological. The most obvious experimental approach to functional questions is to deprive people of sleep and then observe any behavioral deficits. But anyone who has undergone a night of self-imposed sleep deprivation will know that this approach is not only painful but difficult. So many things need to be done in order to keep oneself awake that it is virtually impossible to control for nonspecific and unintentional effects of the deprivation procedure itself. These nonspecific procedural factors may cause the deficits in performance. And despite all efforts to stay awake, we doze off anyway!

Preferable to sleep deprivation would be some measure of brain function (or behavioral capability, or psychological process) that could be tested around the clock and be found to (1) deteriorate as the wake period was prolonged and (2) recover dramatically following an epoch of sleep. This positive functional model, in which sleep would be shown to reverse a process that declines progressively in waking, has never been successfully applied to any functional question.

Even today, sleep researchers persist in expecting the deprivation approach to help them understand the function of sleep. But just as it is unlikely that the lesion approach could ever have helped us understand sleep mechanisms in adequate detail, I regard it unlikely that the sleep-deprivation approach will answer functional questions definitively. Even if one were successful in completely preventing sleep and effectively controlling the inadvertent side effects of deprivation, one would then have to move to a molecular or cellular neurobiological approach to understand the positive effects of such deprivation. Allan Rechtschaffen and his coworkers in Chicago have convincingly demonstrated that sleep loss can be fatal. Sleep-deprived rats fail to regulate their energy and literally consume themselves metabolically. Now the question is, How are such effects mediated? This example shows clearly that sleep deprivation *per se* is only an instrumental tool; it is not an analytic probe. It may help us to ask the right question but it can never, by itself, give us the answers we seek.

Put another way, we can fairly assume that it will be difficult to establish any functional hypothesis convincingly because the mechanisms of sleep are only beginning to be understood at the cellular and molecular level. Once the cellular and molecular changes that occur within sleep are detailed, it seems likely that functional hypotheses will suggest themselves directly at the level of cells and molecules. Ideally, such hypotheses would be tested without using the deprivation procedure at all.

And it would be surprising if such hypotheses were not isomorphic with the psychological experience of feeling rested and restored following sleep. I thus conclude that the best way to get a fix on functional questions is to go step by step from phenomenology—through mechanism—to function. Since no functional hypothesis can be considered adequate unless the cellular and molecular mechanisms of sleep are understood, this approach is not only strategic but obligatory.

Neuronal Hypotheses

The balance of this chapter is frankly speculative, but the speculations I offer are informed by empirical evidence. Specifically, each of the functional hypotheses to be discussed is based upon mechanistic evidence underlying the reciprocal-interaction hypothesis of sleep-cycle control and the activation-synthesis hypothesis of dreaming.

At the outset, I would like to state emphatically that I have no confidence in the idea that sleep is a functionless state. Nature is much too economical to waste hours of biological time doing nothing but simply saving energy and idling the brain. My conviction is, rather, that a multiplicity of functions may be served by each of the states of sleep.

Sleep as Rest for the Neurons

Many twentieth-century neurobiologists have been convinced that sleep subserves neuronal rest. Both the English neurophysiologist Charles Sherrington and the Russian physiologist Ivan Pavlov assumed that neuronal activity ceases during sleep. Sherrington's image of the brain as a magic loom—with its shuttle jumping from light point to light point—was mirrored in his image of sleep as the progressive attenuation of those glimmers (1955). Pavlov thought that the cortex, used for learning during the daytime, must be inhibited (1960).

I have earlier reviewed the pioneer studies of the electrical activity of nerve cells by Jasper and his co-workers in Montreal (1958), which were conducted in this tradition. When microelectrodes were inserted into the cerebral cortex, these investigators, and later Hubel (1959) and Evarts (1960), observed that as many neurons turned on as turned off during sleep, and that almost all the cells in the brain were spectacularly active during REM sleep. Clearly, a general theory of neural rest during sleep can be only partially correct and is particularly controverted.

When Steriade and I averaged all of the studies of neuronal activity in sleep, there was, roughly, a 5 to 10 percent decrease in neuronal activity when slow-wave sleep was compared with waking; but this difference was reversed during the REM phase (1976). Surely we are not immobilized for eight hours a day to effect a savings of 5 to 10 percent in the energy necessary for generating action potentials.

The brain-energy–conservation theory is also weak for theoretical reasons, because the energy necessary for generating the action potentials is relatively trivial. The brain runs effectively on 20 watts of power, the amount used by an icebox light bulb. Furthermore, conduction failures at the electrical level are unlikely to be the neural basis of fatigue.

Neurotransmitter Repletion

It seems far more likely that those metabolic events responsible for synthesizing and supplying neurotransmitters to the neural endings may be fatigue-sensitive. Small neurons with large postsynaptic domains are more vulnerable to transmitter depletion than are larger cells. If a small neuron discharges regularly and continuously, it is more vulnerable because it never rests during the waking state. In other words, a small cell with a large postsynaptic domain which discharges regularly during waking is the best candidate for transmitter depletion—the very physical characteristics of the aminergic neurons of the brain stem. These cells, as I have said, show the most consistent and dramatic decreases in firing rate during sleep: they fire less even at sleep onset, slow further during the non-REM phase, and then fall to their lowest levels of activity during REM sleep.

These experimental findings allow us vigorously and immediately to resuscitate the rest theory with new selectivity and specificity. The neurons that appear most consistently to rest in sleep are precisely those that theoretical consideration would lead us to believe might need to rest. Furthermore, the functional significance of activity by these neurons is specifically related to the critical state-dependent features of waking: the capacity to attend to the world and to learn about it. In its modern garb, our rest theory comes to have particularly attractive features, ones that are positively correlated to the "braininess" of the animal possessing those neurons. The more the animal is involved in critical attentional and learning tasks, the more likely it is to require adequate maintenance of the synaptic efficacy of its aminergic neurons.

What better way to conserve a neurotransmitter than simply to stop its release? At the same time that its generation of action potentials is quelled, such a cell can still be induced to manufacture synthetic enzymes in its nucleus by being bombarded with, say, cholinergic pulses. This cell might also continue to pump the manufactured enzymes down its axons and into its large postsynaptic domain. After a sleep bout, there would thus be more transmitters available for release at each of the nerve endings.

One of the most attractive aspects of this theory is its positive aspect. It looks at a night of sleep as much as preparation for the subsequent day's activity as recovery from that of the previous day. This change in emphasis may seem slight or even trivial, but it is not: in calling attention to the preparatory action of sleep, we shift our thinking from a catabolic or excretory model to an anabolic or storage model.

Here again we must recognize that the truth is likely to be a "both/ and" and not an "either/or" situation. Other body systems may well take advantage of the period of brain-induced repose to rest and recover. As an example, consider Rechstschaffen's rats, whose fatal failure to regulate energy metabolism could well be ascribed to failure of those central integrative mechanisms already known to involve aminergic neurons. Sleep (in animals with complex brains) could promote those processes that were previously related to rest (in lower organisms). But for such "higher" animals a more specifically brain-related theory is also needed.

After a day of intense intellectual cogitation, we may experience difficulty concentrating; we may feel bored or tense and not want to read any more. A day's work in the pasture produces quite a different result. We are unable to concentrate because sleep invades our brain while fatigue invades our body. After intense physical effort, we can actually feel fatigue in our tired muscles, which will not even respond to our commands. Muscular fatigue is probably the most primitive of many sleep-inducing factors. We know that decreasing muscular tension mentally, as part of the relaxation response, facilitates sleep onset. All motile animals have muscles, and their fatigue may be the energetic basis of sleep for the body. In this regard, it is of interest that when the aminergic neurons are turned off during REM sleep, mammalian muscles are also actively inhibited. In other words, the motor systems that may be subject to primitive sorts of bodily fatigue are actively rested at the same time as are those central neurons subserving our "higher" functions—attention and memory.

THE FUNCTIONAL ROLE OF RECIPROCAL INTERACTION

Reconstructive Implications

If the aminergic neurons are resting and recovering their synaptic efficacy, why is the rest of the system buzzing phrenetically, especially during REM sleep? If, as I have suggested, most of these "sensorimotor" circuits of the brain are relatively nonfatiguable, then we must imagine an even more active and positive function for REM sleep than we have previously imagined. One important feature of REM-sleep neuronal activation is its redundancy, its capability of affecting almost every neuron in the brain in a stereotyped way. The high levels of activity of this redundant firing are just what one would want if one function of REM sleep were actively to maintain basic circuits of the brain. Since our daytime repertoires are not always comprehensive in calling forth a complete set of neural actions, these circuits might otherwise suffer through disuse.

REM sleep would thus guarantee rest for those neurons most sensitive to fatigue—the small ones that are critically necessary for efficacious arousal; simultaneously, there is stereotyped, high-level activation of non-fatiguable brain circuits, assuring their daily use in a safe setting. Our brain may thus be a little bit like the car that sits in a garage and needs to be turned on at least once a day. REM sleep allows us to rev our cerebral motor and actively to test all our circuits in a reliably patterned way. According to this view, REM sleep is an active maintenance program.

Developmental Implications

An antecedent of the concept of sleep as functionally reconstructive is the corollary postulate of sleep as anatomically constructive, especially during the early development of the brain. The function of REM-sleep activation during the period of development of sensorimotor circuits may actually be to perform activation tests that lead to structural change. This idea fits with the fact that REM sleep is overrepresented during early intrauterine life. It appears to peak at about 30 weeks of gestational age when it is the predominant state of the human infant. Exact figures are not available, but estimates of nearly 24 hours per day have been made (Parmelee et al. 1967).

This has led Howard Roffwarg and his colleagues to suggest that REM sleep plays an active role in the structural development of the brain (1966). My idea is that early in neural development a necessarily limited set of genetic instructions would be complemented by an active functional program that elaborated the genetically determined organization of the brain into a more versatile repertoire of response capabilities. To understand this developmental concept better, consider the concept of trophic function. There are metabolic consequences of neural action. A leg that is used gains mass and strength. A leg that is not used withers and limps. Cells fail to differentiate in tissue culture. In a paralyzed limb, muscles that are not electrically stimulated fail to develop normally. How does the developing brain avoid such problems and, instead, steadily gain in both mass and capability? Early in development, REM sleep could provide the brain with a highly organized program of internal action. This program is stereotyped, redundant, and reliable—all features useful to a developing system.

For example, REM sleep could help prepare the organism's reflex repertoire. Imagine the startle reflex that the newborn infant dramatically demonstrates. From a genetically programmed division of cells into excitatory and inhibitory subpopulations, all with locations specified, how could the organism advance to an organized system that could produce startle reflexes? One way might be to begin by establishing a large pool of central excitatory neurons capable of emitting spontaneous motor commands. The reticular formation would be a good location for such an excitatory cell pool. By firing phasically, such reticular cells could command reflex motor activity and also stimulate the oculomotor and vestibular neurons with which they make excitatory synapses.

It would make sense at first for such a system to be overprogrammed. And the human infant is remarkable at birth for its inability to habituate the startle reflex. Because of its unfocused all-or-none character, it is called a "mass" reflex. Such mass reflexes have probably developed in utero. If the system were quiescent while humans were waiting to be born, they would be even more helpless at birth than they already are.

Charming evidence of the high level of reflex activity of which the newborn human infant is capable is the sequence of grimaces, smiles, and other evocative facial gestures babies emit during the REM sleep that typically terminates feeding. I once had the pleasure of sitting next to a nursing mother on a long airplane trip. I observed silently and somewhat jealously as the infant tugged the life-giving fluid from his mother's breast. I also watched the mother's beatific, if soporific expression of pleasure as she gave her infant what he needed. But when the infant was sated, and the sucking movements began to abate, their previously insistent driving rhythm declined. At a crucial point suction was lost, and the nipple popped out of the child's mouth.

At exactly this moment, rapid eye movements were clearly visible beneath the half-closed lids of the baby. There shortly followed a sequence of smiles, which the mother returned with billing and cooing. So as not to spoil this social dialogue, I waited a full five minutes before asking the mother what she thought was going on. She calmly informed me that the baby was pleased to have been fed and was smiling in order to thank her. This attribution of volition, and even good will, to a completely reflexive behavioral sequence from a sleeping baby struck me as the kind of adaptive projective belief that ought not to be challenged, at least in a mother who is still of child-bearing age. She wouldn't have believed me anyway!

Another consideration regarding the developmental hypothesis in its relation to the reconstructive theory is its safety. The fact that the infant is floating in an amniotic bath means that its poorly aimed kicks, stretches, pulls, and contortional twists are performed without risk. Like an astronaut-acrobat, the fetus is virtually weightless.

Thus, among other things, REM sleep is a reliable, stereotyped, redundant, and highly organized means of providing programmed excitation to the immature brain. While the infant floats in an amniotic bath, the eyes dart back and forth, as has been demonstrated by the echographic studies of Jason Birnholz (1983). As development proceeds, the motor readout of these internally generated stimulus sequences are damped by inhibition, so that the safety of interuterine life is carried forward into adult life by the clutch control provided by inhibitory restraint of the centrally programmed motor acts.

Significance for Behavior

The American experimental psychologist Wilse Webb has offered the entertaining notion that one function of sleep is to keep us off the streets (1986). According to Webb, the quelling of behavior during times of the day that are unfavorable to finding food or a mate is likely to be one of the functions of sleep. I like this idea but, like the rest theory, it may be derived from those circadian rhythm processes that affect all cells and thus do not depend upon higher functions of the nervous system.

What *is* necessary—for both lower and higher animals—is that reflex processes become elaborated and coordinated into organized behavior. Since any form of behavior is a complex sequence of reflex acts, the difference between this and the previous level of organization is only one of degree. Even in the fully developed adult human animal, when behavior is (more or less) under voluntary control, particular behavior has the quality of a fixed act when adequately triggered and permitted to run its course. Behavior of this type is feeding, fighting, fleeing, and fornication, the so-called four F's of fixed action. Curiously left out of this inventory is sleep, a fixed-action pattern if there ever was one. And sleep behavior is special in that it appears to include all of the other fixed actions in the fictive mode we experience as dreaming.

This quasi-ethological notion is related to Michel Jouvet's functional concept of REM sleep as a genetically determined behavior rehearsal. It makes sense for the organism to know how to do everything essential to its survival before such acts are elicited. According to this view, the neural program for behavioral acts must therefore be put in place before certain behavior is demanded.

We must be ready to defend ourselves and even to fight, whether or not we have ever been trained as pugilists. Three men once cornered me in the parking lot where I had parked my car. It was early one spring morning, and I was going to the lab to monitor a sleep-lab experiment. All of my wit and wile were unsuccessful in protecting me from assault. Only after I had been knocked to the ground unconscious, and was being kicked and pummeled, did some primordial urge rise up within me. I remember feeling what seemed at the time to be inhuman strength, probably surges of adrenal hormone. I threw the three men off and, with two of them chasing me, ran with Olympic speed up an alley. I recall that, at the peak of my aggressive strength, I thought, "These men want to kill me."

Where did this primordial surge of aggressive energy and strength come from? This particular set of behaviors had never before emerged, yet I was somehow capable of it. I certainly did not have time to learn it on the spot! I would not deny the value of childhood and adolescent play and the ritualized aggressive games of boyhood; but to look back even further, my guess is that the brain basis of many of these acts had been put in place and maintained over time for just such an occasion. It did not save my nose (which was broken into smithereens), but it did save my life.

As with aggression, sexual experience cannot be counted on to guarantee the readiness of the central circuitry underlying that important behavior. In even the richest of sexual lives, there are fallow periods; yet one does not grow incapable of performing sexually when the opportunity arises. Desire may play its role in increasing susceptibility to the releasing stimuli for sex, but the fixed-action patterns that constitute the sexual act itself have a life of their own. They are, apparently, in constant readiness. REM-sleep erections and wet dreams are the outward sign that at least part of this theory must be correct.

I cannot leave a discussion of this behavior-rehearsal theory without noting that our dreams tell us clearly that the repertoires for these "instinctual" acts are indeed represented within the central nervous system. The extraordinary plasticity of the dream experience includes a rich overrepresentation of significant behaviors: fear, aggression, defense, and attack; approach-avoidance; and sex. At the level of our psychological experience, we find evidence of the whole repertoire. By the principle of isomorphism, this denotes a substrate for behavior at the level of neural programming.

INFORMATION-PROCESSING THEORIES

Even before Otto Loewi claimed to have solved intellectual problems in dreams, it has been suggested that REM sleep may have an information-processing function. In its strong form, this theory implies an active and progressive elaboration of existing information. A related, weaker form of the theory states that sleep plays an active role in the consolidation of previously learned experience.

Human subjects recall stimulus words better if they are presented just before sleep than before a period of wakefulness of equal length. New information may thus be more firmly and structurally encoded within the brain during sleep.

There may also occur during sleep a comparison of old and new information. It is possible, for example, that our daily experience is compared with our memory repertoire so as to accomplish two purposes. One purpose is efficiency of storage. If the information is already there, it need not be additionally stored. The second purpose is a comparison between the expectancies programmed by the genetic code and the experiential input. In both cases a match/mismatch process could be carried out, with registration of important discrepancies. This higher-level cognitive version of the constructive theory is analogous to a computer model. And it has even been proposed that programming may be developed during the REM stage of sleep.

The latest variation on this theme is the theory of Francis Crick and Graeme Mitchison published in *Nature* in 1983. Turning the tables on all traditional views, they suggested that the psychological function of REM sleep is to *eliminate* unwanted information: "We dream in order to forget." Crick and Mitchison based this "erasure" theory on the abstract but compelling concept that a system as elaborate as the brain is in danger of dyscontrol via intensification of its oscillations. This is especially true if there were what they called "parasitic resonance" in the circuitry. Parasitic resonance is a condition that is most likely to occur when a system is changing state, as during periods of development or of intense novel experience.

For Crick and Mitchison, it makes sense for Mother Nature to get the brain off-line, to pull out the clutch and to provide an internally generated set of "bangs" or thumps, to allow the system to rid itself of its parasitic oscillations. In its detoxifying, excretory aspect, this is a bit like Freud's drive-discharge theory. Along with the parasitic oscillations would go unwanted memories, especially those of a potentially pathological nature such as obsessions, hallucinations, and delusions. This and other variations of the information-processing theory are difficult to test, but some simple clinical studies can be imagined. Seizure threshold should be lower following a night of sleep than before; the tendency to hallucinate should be lower in the morning than before the night of sleep; and so on.

Specific Functional Theories

Creative Capability

During REM sleep, the brain and its mind seem to be engaging in a process of fantastic creation. It is obvious that our dreams are not simply the reliving of previous experience. On the contrary, we are often actually fabricating wholly novel ones. Thus new ideas and new feelings, and new views of old problems, can be expected to arise within dreams. These may be carried forward into the conscious mind or remain unconscious as part of our deeper creative repertoire. This apogee of the new positive functional theory of REM sleep is related to our recognition that the nervous system is more than a mere copying machine. While it is true that the nervous system is dependent upon external information to form its picture of the world, it also clearly uses that information to create pictures of the world against which it can test reality.

Thus the brain of one and all is fundamentally artistic. We know this when we see the drawings of our children, but tend to discount it in our adult selves. So highly socialized are we to accept our given wake-state role that we fail to recognize the clear-cut evidence of our dreams that each of us possesses creative capability. Each of us is a surrealist at night during his or her dreams: each is a Picasso, a Dali, a Fellini—the delightful and the macabre mixed in full measure.

The Experience of Dreaming

Why can't dreams include the function of being entertaining? Why should we always be looking below decks, fore and aft, to understand in only derivative terms the purpose of these delightful home movies? Why can't we accept the autocreative function of dreams as something given to us, among other things, for our own pleasure? And might not such enhancement of our pleasure—and our self-esteem—even contribute to more successful functioning as human beings? To all these questions, the puritan ethic—now shot through with neo-Judaic authority—says no! We have to cart them off to be sanitized via confession and analysis.

But anyone who has kept a dream journal will understand the sybaritic and delight-enhancing function of dreaming. Dreams are truly marvelous. Why not simply enjoy them? It is in this tradition that the work of the Marquis Hervey de Saint-Denis, and of his followers who experimented with dream lucidity, belongs. Following their techniques, we not only appreciate dreams as they happen to us, but can actively enter into our dream experience. We can enhance recall and even change plots so that they become more enjoyable. Thus, as we still use dreams in psychotherapy, let us recognize that they are plastic as much as they are overdetermined. It seems to me irreverent and inappropriate to reduce this pleasurable function of dreams to the derivation of an instinct. Dreaming may reflect instincts, but it also reflects creative imagination: both serve science as well as art.

Theories of Human Nature

A perhaps even more facetious suggestion, at the end of this highly speculative chapter, is that dreaming not only is worthy of participatory enjoyment but has the function of providing us with an opportunity to understand ourselves better. In this view, dreaming is, after all, a message from the gods in the most prophetic sense. By heightening certain aspects of brain and mental function and by demonstrating the relationship between the two, the correlation between REM sleep and dreaming is uniquely informative. The discovery of REM sleep and its relation to dreaming thus has an impact on theories of human nature.

The change from a psychoanalytic perspective, in which all behavior is derived from a few simple instincts, to the more realistic view of human behavior as based upon, but not reducible to, instinctual life gives us a naturalistic base for a richer humanism. Thus, a New Machine Model of Man is suggested by modern sleep and dream research: the brain is seen as more than a reflex apparatus; and the mind, as more than instinctually bound. Because it can be controlled, such a system is capable of misdirection. Because it has a random aspect, it is capable of spontaneous error. And, for this very reason, it is also capable of imagination—including even self-understanding.

Conclusion

Whatever the general methodological problems involved in determining the function of sleep, we have gone beyond previous approaches, which have tended to see functional possibilities as mutually exclusive rather than mutually enhancing. Although understanding the probably multiple, probably positive functions of sleep will depend upon more detailed studies of the specific cellular and molecular mechanisms revealed by the brain during its elaborate sequence of sleep states, we can nonetheless draw the following conclusions about the function of sleep from consideration of the reciprocal-interaction and activation-synthesis models:

1.   It has been shown that, while most cells of the brain do not rest during sleep, one group of cells, the aminergic neurons of the brain stem—related to attention and memory—do rest during sleep, especially during REM sleep.

2.   While the aminergic cells rest, the sensorimotor neurons are disinhibited and caused to fire in such a manner as to provide a program for the active maintenance of many brain circuits.

3.   Such a program of active maintenance is significant to development not only in assuring continuing function, but in actually changing functional capability through its trophic effects on programmed action.

4.   Building up from the level of reflexes, it is possible to imagine sleep, and especially REM sleep, as providing a means of converting the

necessarily limited genetic program into a functional program for the development of fixed-action patterns underlying crucial behavior.

5.   The active aspects of brain physiology during REM sleep allow us to postulate that certain phases of the learning process—such as the consolidation of memory traces and comparison of old and new information—may take place during sleep.

6.   Carrying this notion a step further, it is possible to suggest that the brain is actually creative during sleep. New ideas arise and new solutions to old problems may be consciously or unconsciously derived during sleep.

7.   Since dreams may occur, in part, to amuse us, we ought at least to take advantage of that possibility.

8.   Dreaming in its relation to REM sleep provides us with a remarkable mirror of our inner selves.

TOWARD A UNIFIED BRAIN-MIND

In the controversies that divide the field of sleep and dream research even after thirty years of intense scientific effort, psychologists and psychiatrists accuse physiologists of being reductionistic, while physiologists accuse psychologists and psychiatrists of being dualistic and mystical. Although it may be tempting, under the circumstances, to conclude that not much has been learned after all, this would be a mistake. Much has been learned, and the field is still ripe with promise.

And we must not turn away from these disputes but, rather, look more deeply into the reason for their continuing existence: our still unclear and inadequate picture of the human mind. This battle for the mind will be won no more easily by the forces of pure materialism than by those of pure idealism—and maybe, as it is now enjoined, will not be won at all.

Instead, a clear and adequate picture may emerge only through a progressive and liberal extension—upward—of materialistic knowledge to the level of information processing, so as to lay bare the creative, multileveled, open-loop nature of the brain-mind. At the same time, psychology must become much more detailed, clear, and precise, so that it can be fitted—downward—upon the schemata of the material structures and dynamics. I believe that the study of dreams is moving simultaneously in these two directions.

BIBLIOGRAPHY

ABRAHAM, KARL

1922. "Die Spinne als Traum symbol," *International Zeitschrift feur Psychoanalyse, Psychiatria et Neurologia* 8:40.

ALDERDICE, MARC T.

1982. "Further Comparison of the Effects of Physostigmine and Neostigmine on Frog Neuromuscular Transmission." *Clinical and Experimental Pharmacological Physiology* 9:35–42.

AMATRUDA, THOMAS T., III; BLACK, DEBORAH A.; McKENNA, THOMAS M.; McCARLEY, ROBERT W.; AND HOBSON, J. ALLAN

1975. "Sleep Cycle Control and Cholinergic Mechanisms: Differential Effects of Carbachol at Pontine Brain Stem Sites." *Brain Research* 98:501–15.

ANDERSON, JOHN R.

1985. *Cognitive Psychology and Its Implications.* New York: W.H. Freeman. Second edition. (First edition, 1980.)

ANTROBUS, JOHN

1983. "REM and NREM Sleep Reports: Comparison of Word Frequencies by Cognitive Classes." *Psychophysiology* 20, no. 2: 562–68.

ARNOLD-FORSTER, MARY

1921. *Studies in Dreams.* New York: Macmillan.

ASERINSKY, EUGENE, AND KLEITMAN, NATHANIEL

1953. "Regularly Occurring Periods of Eye Motility and Concurrent Phenomena During Sleep." *Science* 118:273–74.
1955. "Two Types of Ocular Motility Occurring in Sleep," *Journal of Applied Physiology* 8:1–10.

BAGHDOYAN, HELEN A.; RODRIGO-ANGULO, MARGARITA L.; ASSENS, F.; McCARLEY, ROBERT W.; AND HOBSON, J. ALLAN

1984. "Microinjection of Neostigmine into the Pontine Reticular Formation of Cats Enhances Desynchronized Sleep Signs." *Journal of Pharmacological and Experimental Therapeutics* 231:173–80.

BAGHDOYAN, HELEN A.; RODRIGO-ANGULO, MARGARITA L.; McCARLEY, ROBERT W.; AND HOBSON, J. ALLAN

1984. "Site Specific Enhancement and Suppression of Desynchronized Sleep Signs Following Cholinergic Stimulation of Three Brainstem Regions." *Brain Research* 306: 39–52.
1987. "A Neuroanatomical Gradient in the Pontine Tegmentum for the Cholinoceptive Induction of Desynchronized Sleep Signs." *Brain Research* 414:245–61.

BAILLARGER, JULES

1846. *Des Hallucinations.* Mémoires de l'Académie Royale de Médecine.

BARD, PHILIP, AND RIOCH, DAVID MEK

1937. "A Study of Four Cats Deprived of Neocortex and Additional Portions of the Forebrain." *Bulletin of Johns Hopkins Hospital* 60:73–147.

BELL, CHARLES

1811. *Idea of a New Anatomy of the Brain Submitted for the Observation of Friends,* privately printed. Reproduced in J. F. Fulton, ed., *Selected Readings in the History of Physiology.* Springfield: Thomas, 1930.

1836. *The Nervous System of the Human Body as Explained in a Series of Papers Read Before the Royal Society of London.* Edinburgh: Black.

BERGER, HANS

1930. "Über das Elektrencephalogram des Menschen. Zweite Mitteilung," *J. Psych. Neur.* 40:160–79.

BERTINI, M.; VIOLANI, C.; ZOCCOLOTTI, P.; ANTONELLI, A.; AND DI STEPHALO, L.

1983. "Performance on Unilateral Tactile Tests During Waking and Upon Awakening from REM and NREM." In *Sleep 1982.* Edited by W. P. Koella. Basel: Karger, pp. 383–85.

BETLHEIM, S., AND HARTMANN, H.

1924. "Über Fehlreaktionen des Gedächtnisses bei Korsakoffschen Psychose," *Archiv für Psychiatrie und Nervenkrankheiten* 72:278.

BINZ, CARL

1878. *Über den Traum.* Bonn: Adolph Marcus.

BIRNHOLZ, JASON

1983. "The Development of Human Fetal Learning." *Science* 222:516–18.

BLEULER, EUGEN

1950. *Dementia Praecox or the Group of Schizophrenias.* Translated by Joseph Zinkin. New York: International Universities Press.

BONATELLI, F.

1880. "Del Sogno." *La Filosofia delle Scuole Italiane.*

BREMER, FREDERIC

1935. "Cerveau isolé et physiologie du sommeil," *C. R. Soc. Biol.* 118:1235–41.

1977. "Cerebral Hypnogogic Centers." *Annals of Neurology* 2:1–6.

BROCA, PIERRE PAUL

1861. "Perte de Parole, Ramollissement Chronique et Destruction du Lobe Antérier Gauche du Cerveau." *Bulletin du Social Anthropologie* (Paris) 2:235.

BRODAL, ALF

1956. *The Reticular Formation of the Brain Stem.* Springfield, Ill.: Charles C Thomas.

BROOK, STEPHEN

1983. *The Oxford Book of Dreams.* New York: Oxford University Press.

BURDACH, KARL FRIEDRICH

1838. *Die Physiologie als Erfahrungswissenschaft.* Second edition, vol. 3, 1832–40. Leipzig: Voss.

CALKINS, MARY

1893. "Statistics of Dreams." *American Journal of Psychology* 5:311.

CATON, RICHARD

1875. "The Electric Currents of the Brain." *British Medical Journal* 2:278.

CLARK, EDWARD H.

1878. *Visions: A Study of False Sight.* Boston: Houghton.

CRICK, FRANCIS, AND MITCHISON, GRAEME

1983. "The Function of Dream Sleep." *Nature* 304:111–14.

DAHLSTROM, ANICA, AND FUXE, KJELL

1964. "Evidence for the Existence of Monamine Neurons in the Central Nervous System. I. Demonstration of Monoamines in the Cell Bodies of Brain Stem Neurons." *Acta Physiologica Scandinavia* (Supp.) 232:1–55.
1965. "Evidence for the Existence of Monamine Neurons in the Central Nervous System." *Acta Physiologica Scandinavia* 64 (Supp. 247): 1–36.

DALE, HENRY H.

1914. "The Action of Certain Esters and Ethers of Choline, and Their Relation to Muscarine." *Journal of Pharmacology and Experimental Therapy* 6:147.

DELBOEUF, I.

1855. *Le Sommeil et les Rêves.* Paris: Baillière.

DEMENT, WILLIAM

1958. "The Occurrence of Low Voltage, Fast, Electroencephalogram Patterns during Behavioral Sleep and Their Relation to Eye Movements, Body Mobility and Dreaming." *Electroencephalography and Clinical Neurophysiology* 10:291–96.

DEMENT, WILLIAM, AND KLEITMAN, NATHANIEL

1957a. "Cyclic Variations in EEG during Sleep and Their Relation to Eye Movements, Body Mobility and Dreaming." *Electroencephalography and Clinical Neurophysiology* 9:673–90.
1957b. "The Relation of Eye Movements during Sleep to Dream Activity: An Objective Method for the Study of Dreaming." *Journal of Experimental Psychology* 53:89–97.

DERBYSHIRE, A. J.; REMPL, B.; FORBES, A.; AND LAMBERT, E. F.

1936. "The Effects of Anesthetics on Action Potentials in Cerebral Cortex of the Cat." *American Journal of Physiology* 116:577–96.

DU BOIS-REYMOND, EMIL

1849. *Untersuchungen über Thierische Elektricität,* vol. 1. Berlin: Reimer.

ECONOMO, CONSTANTIN VON

1926. "Die Pathologie des Schlafes." In *Handbuch der Normalen und Pathologischen Physiologie.* Edited by A. Bethe, G. V. Bergmann, G. Embden, and A. Ellinger, pp. 591–610. Berlin: Springer.

EISLER, M. J.

1919. "Beiträge zur Traumdeutung," *International Zeitschrift für (arztl.) Psychoanalyse* 5:295.

ELLENBERGER, HENRI F.

1970. *The Discovery of the Unconscious: The History and Evolution of Dynamic Psychiatry.* New York: Basic Books.

ELLIS, HAVELOCK

1899. "The Stuff That Dreams Are Made Of." *Popular Science Monthly* 54:721.

EVARTS, EDWARD V.

1960. "Effects of Sleep and Waking on Spontaneous and Evoked Discharge of Single Units in Visual Cortex," *Federation Proc. Supplement* 4:828–37.

304   Bibliography

FECHNER, GUSTAV THEODOR

    1860. *Elemente der Psychophysik,* vol. 3, pp. 468–526. Leibzig: Druck.

FERENCZI, S.

    1921. "Die Symbolik der Brücke," *International Zeitschrift für (arztl.) Psychoanalyse* 7:211.

    1922. "Die Brückensymbolik und die Don Juan–Legende," *International Zeitschrift für (arztl.) Psychoanalyse* 8:77.

FICHTE, MANUEL HERMANN VON

    1864. *Psychologie: Die Lehre von Bewussten Geiste des Menschen.* Leipzig: Brockhaus. 2 vols.

FONTANA, FELICE

    1765. "Convulsive Movements in Sleep of Cats and Dogs." *Dei Moti Dell'iride.* Giusti: Lucca.

FOULKES, DAVID

    1978. *A Grammar of Dreams.* Hassocks: Harvester Press.

FREUD, SIGMUND

    1895. "Project for a Scientific Psychology." In *The Origins of Psychoanalysis: Letters to Wilhelm Fliess, Drafts and Notes: 1887–1902.* Edited by Marie Bonaparte, Anna Freud, and Ernst Kris. Translated by Eric Mosbacher and James Strachey. New York: Basic Books (1954), pp. 347–445.

    1900. *The Interpretation of Dreams.* Translated by James Strachey. New York: Avon (1965).

    1933. "New Introductory Lectures on Psychoanalysis." *Standard Edition* 22:3–182.

    1974. *The Freud/Jung Letters: The Correspondence Between Sigmund Freud and C.G. Jung.* Edited by William McGuire. Translated by Ralph Manheim and R.F.C. Hull. New Jersey: Princeton University Press (1974).

GALL, FRANZ JOSEPH, AND SPURZHEIM, JOHANN CASPAR

    1819. *Anatomie et Physiologie du Système Nerveux en Général et du Morales de l'Homme et des Animaux, par la Configuration de Leur Têtes.* Vols. 1 and 2 by Gall and Spurzhein; vols. 3 and 4 by Gall. Paris: Schoell, 1810–19.

GILLIN, J. CHRISTIAN; SITARAM, N.; JANOWSKY, D.; RISCH, C.; HUEY, L.; AND STORCH, F. I.

    1985. "Cholinergic Mechanisms in REM Sleep." In *Sleep: Neurotransmitters and Neuromodulators.* Edited by A. Wauquier, J. M. Gaillard, J. M. Monti, and M. Radulovacki. New York: Raven Press.

GOLGI, CAMILLO

    1886. *Sulla Fina Anatomia Degli Organi Centrali Del Sistema Nervosa.* Milan: Hoepli.

GORDON, H. W.; FROOMAN, B.; AND LAVIE, P.

    1982. "Shift in Cognitive Asymmetries between Wakings from REM and NREM sleep," *Neuropsychologia* 20:99–103.

GREENBERG, M. S., AND FARAH, M. J.

    1986. "The Laterality of Dreaming." *Brain Cognition* 5:307–21.

GRÜNBAUM, ADOLF

    1984. *The Foundations of Psychoanalysis: A Philosophical Critique.* Berkeley: University of California Press.

HAGEN, F. W.

    1846. "Psychologie und Psychiatrie." In *Wagner's Handwörterbuch der Psychologie.* Brunswick: Friedr und Sohn.

HARTLEY, D.

1801. *Observations on Man, His Frame, His Duty, and His Expectations.* London: Johnson.

HELMHOLTZ, HERMANN VON

1863. "Sensations of Tone." In *Helmholtz on Perception: Its Physiology and Development.* Edited by R. M. Warren and R. P. Warren. New York: Wiley (1968).

HENNEMAN, ELWOOD G.; SOMJEN, G.; AND CARPENTER, D.O.

1965. "Functional Significance of Cell Size in Spinal Motoneurons." *Journal of Neurophysiology* 28:560–80.

HERNANDEZ-PEON, RAUL

1965. "A Cholinergic Hypnogogic Limbic Forebrain-Hindbrain Circuit." In *Neurophysiologie des États du Sommeil.* Edited by Michel Jouvet. Lyons, France: CNRS, pp. 63–88.

D'HERVEY DE SAINT-DENIS, JEAN MARIE LEON (LE MARQUIS)

1867. *Les Rêves et les Moyens de les Diriger.* Paris: Amyot.

HESS, WALTER R.

1931. "Le Sommeil." *Comptes Rendus de Biologie* 107:1333–64.

HEYNICK, FRANK

1983. *Theoretical and Empirical Investigation into Verbal Aspects of the Freudian Model of Dream Generation.* Thesis, Rijksuniversitet Te Groningen.

HILDEBRANDT, F. W.

1875. *Der Traum und Seine Verwerthung fürs Leben.* Leipzig.

HOBSON, J. ALLAN

1974. "The Cellular Basis of Sleep Cycle Control." In *Advances in Sleep Research.* Edited by Ed. Weitzam. Vol. 1, pp. 217–50. New York: Spectrum.

HOBSON, J. ALLAN, AND HOFFMAN, STEVEN A.

1984. "Picturing Dreaming: Some Features of the Drawings in a Dream Journal." In *Psychology of Dreaming.* Edited by M. Bosinelli and P. Cicogna. Bologna, Italy: CLUEB.

HOBSON, J. ALLAN; HOFFMAN, STEVEN A.; HELFAND, RITA; AND KOSTNER, DELIA

1987. "Dream Bizarreness and the Activation-Synthesis Hypothesis." *Human Neurobiology,* 6:157–64. Data presented at the Symposium on Dreaming, Fourth International Congress of Sleep Research, Bologna, Italy, July 1983.

HOBSON, J. ALLAN, AND MCCARLEY, ROBERT W.

1977. "The Brain as a Dream-State Generator: An Activation-Synthesis Hypothesis of the Dream Process." *American Journal of Psychiatry* 134:1335–68.

HOBSON, J. ALLAN; MCCARLEY, ROBERT W.; AND WYZINSKI, PETER W.

1975. "Sleep Cycle Oscillation: Reciprocal Discharge by Two Brainstem Neuronal Groups." *Science* 189:55–58.

HOBSON, J. ALLAN, AND STERIADE, MIRCEA

1986. "Neuronal Basis of Behavioral State Control." In *Handbook of Physiology,* vol. 4, The Nervous System. Edited by Vernon B. Mountcastle. Bethesda: American Physiological Society, pp. 701–823.

HUBEL, DAVID H.

1959. "Single Unit Activity in Striate Cortex of Unrestrained Cats." *Journal of Physiology* 147:226–40.

1960a. "Electrocorticograms in Cats during Natural Sleep." *Archives Italienne de Biologie* 98:171–81.
1960b. "Single Unit Activity in Lateral Geniculate Body and Optic Tract of Unrestrained Cats." *Journal of Physiology* (London) 150:91–104.

HUBEL, DAVID H., AND WIESEL, T. N.

1959. "Receptive Fields of Single Neurons in the Cat's Striate Cortex." *Journal of Physiology* 148:574–91.

HUXLEY, ALDOUS

1954. *The Doors of Perception.* New York: Harper and Brothers.

JASPER, H.; RICI, G. F.; AND DOANE, B.

1958. "Patterns of Cortical Neuron Discharge during Conditioned Responses in Monkeys." In *Neurological Basis of Behavior.* Edited by G. E. W. Wolstenhdine and C. M. O'Connor. Boston: Little, Brown, pp. 277–94.
1971. "Acetylcholine Liberation from Cerebral Cortex during Paradoxical (REM) Sleep." *Science* 172:601–602.

JESSEN, PETER WILLERS

1855. *Versuch Einer Wissenschaftlichen Begründung der Psychologie.* Berlin: Viet und Comp.

JOUVET, MICHEL

1962. "Recherches sur les Structures Nerveuses et les Mécanismes Responsables des Différentes Phases du Sommeil Physiologique." *Archives Italiennes dê Biologie* 100: 125–206.
1969. "Biogenic Amines and the States of Sleep." *Science* 163:32–41.

JOUVET, MICHEL, AND MICHEL, FRANÇOIS

1959. "Correlations Electromyographiques du Sommeil Chez le Chat Décortiqué et Mésencéphalique Chronique." *Comptes Rendus de la Société Biologie* 153:422–25.

JOUVET, MICHEL, AND MORUZZI, GIUSSEPPE

1972. *Neurophysiology and Neurochemistry of Sleep and Wakefulness.* Heidelberg: Springer-Verlag Berlin.

JUNG, CARL G.

1965. *Memories, Dreams, Reflections.* Recorded and edited by Aniela Jaffé. Translated from the German by Richard and Clara Winston. New York: Vintage. Originally published as "Erinnerungen Träume Gedankan."
1974. *Dreams.* Translated by R. F. C. Hull. From *The Collected Works of C. G. Jung,* vols. 4, 8, 12, 16. Bollingen Series XX. New Jersey: Princeton University Press.

KANT, IMMANUEL

1764. *Versuch über Die Krankheiten des Kopfes.*
1798. *Anthropologie In Pragmatisher Hinsicht.* Konigsberg: F. Nicolovius.

KLEITMAN, NATHANIEL

1939. *Sleep and Wakefulness as Alternating Phases in the Cycle of Existence.* Chicago: University of Chicago Press.
1963. *Sleep and Wakefulness.* Chicago: University of Chicago Press.

KRAUSS. A.

1958–59. "Der Sinn im Wahnsinn." *Allgemeinsche Zeitschrift Psychologie* 15:617, 16:222.

LaBERGE, STEPHEN

1985. *Lucid Dreaming.* New York: J. P. Tarcher.

LADD, G. T.

1892. "Contribution to the Psychology of Visual Dreams. *Mind* 1:299.

LAVIE, PERETZ

    1974. "Differential Effects of REM and Non-REM Awakenings on the Spiral Afteref-
fect." *Physiological Psychology* 204:1326–28.

LAVIE, PERETZ, AND HOBSON, J. ALLAN

    1986. "Origin of Dreams: Anticipation of Modern Theories in the Philosophy and
Physiology of the Eighteenth and Nineteenth Centuries." *Psychological Bulletin* 100,
no. 2: 229–40.

LEIBNITZ, GOTTFRIED WILHELM

    1896. *New Essays Concerning Human Understanding.* New York: Macmillan.

LING, G., AND GERARD, RALPH

    1949. *Journal of Cellular and Comparative Physiology* 34:383. See also 9 (1946):191.

LOEWI, OTTO

    1921. "Über Humorale Übertragbarkeit der Hertznervenwirkung." *Archive feur die Ge-
samte Physiologie des Menschen und der Tiere* 189:239.

LOOMIS, A. L.; HARVEY, E. N.; AND HOBART, G. A.

    1937. "Cerebral States during Sleep as Studied by Human Brain Potentials." *Journal of
Experimental Psychology* 21:127–44.

LORENTE DE NÒ, RAFAEL

    1933. "Vestibulo-Ocular Reflex." *Archives of Neurology and Psychiatry* 30:245–91.

LYDIC, RALPH; MCCARLEY, ROBERT W.; AND HOBSON, J. ALLAN

    1987a. "Serotonic Neurons and Sleep: I. Long-Term Recordings of Dorsal Raphe Dis-
charge Frequency and PGO Waves." *Archives Italienne de Biologie* 125:317–43.
    1987b. "Serotonic Neurons and Sleep: II. Time Course of Dorsal Raphe Discharge, PGO
Waves, and Behavioral States." *Archives Italienne de Biologie* 126:1–28.

MCCARLEY, ROBERT W., AND HOBSON, J. ALLAN

    1975. "Neuronal Excitability Modulation Over the Sleep Cycle: A Structural and
Mathematical Model." *Science* 189:58–60.
    1977. "The Neurobiological Origins of Psychoanalytic Dream Theory." *American Journal
of Psychiatry* 134:1211–21.

MCCARLEY, ROBERT W., AND HOFFMAN, EDWARD

    1981. "REM Sleep Dreams and the Activation-Synthesis Hypothesis." *American Journal
of Psychiatry* 138:7.

MCGINTY, DENNIS J., AND HARPER, RON M.

    1976. "Dorsal Raphe Neurons: Depression of Firing during Sleep in Cats." *Brain Research*
101:569–75.

MAGENDI, FRANÇOIS

    1825. "Mémoire sur la Liquide Qui se Trouve Dans le Crâne et Canal Vertébral de
l'Homme et des Animaux Mammifères." *Journal de Physiologie Expérimentale et Pa-
thologique* 5:27.

MAURY, ALFRED

    1861. *Le Sommeil et les Rêves.* Paris.

MORUZZI, GIUSEPPE, AND MAGOUN, HORACE

    1949. "Brainstem Reticular Formation and Activation of the EEG." *Electroencephalographic
and Clinical Neurophysiology* 1:455–73.

MÜLLER, JOHANNES

    1826. *Über Die Phantastischen Gesichtserscheinungen.* Coblenz: Jacob Hölscher.

MYERS, F. W. H.

  1892. "Hypermnesic Dreams," *Proceedings of the Society for Psychological Research* 8.

NELSON, J.

  1888. "A Study of Dreams," *American Journal of Psychology* 1:367.

PALUMBO, STANLEY

  1978. *Dreaming and Memory*. New York: Basic Books.

PARMELEE, ARTHUR H., JR.; WENNER, WALDEMAR H.; AKIYAMA, YOSHIA;
  SCHULTZ, MARVIN; AND STERN, EVELYN

  1967. "Sleep States in Premature Infants." *Developmental Medicine and Child Neurology* 9, no.
      1: 70–77.

PAVLOV, IVAN

  1960. *Conditioned Reflexes: An Investigation of the Physiological Activity of the Cerebral Cortex*.
      Translated by G. V. Anrep. New York: Dover.

PFAFF, EMIL RICHARD

  1868. *Das Traumleben und Seine Dentung Nach den Prinzipien der Araber, Perser, Griechen, Inder
      und Ägypter*. Leipzig: L. Denicke.

POMPEIANO, OTTAVIO

  1967. "The Neurobiological Mechanisms of the Postural and Motor Events during
      Desynchonized Sleep." *Proceedings of the Association for Research of Nervous Mental
      Disorders* 45:351–423.
  1979. "Cholinergic Activation of Reticular and Vestibular Mechanisms Controlling
      Posture and Eye Movements." In *The Reticular Formation Revisited*. Edited by J. A.
      Hobson and M. A. B. Brazier. New York: Raven, pp. 473–572.

PORTE, HELENE, AND HOBSON, J. ALLAN

  1986a. "Bizarreness in REM and NREM Reports." Abstract in *Sleep Research*. Edited by
      Michael H. Chase, Dennis McGinty, and Gwen Crane. Los Angeles: University
      of California, p. 81.
  1986b. "Fictive Movement in Sleep: REM vs. NREM Sleep Reports." Abstract in *Sleep
      Research*. Edited by Michael H. Chase, Dennis McGinty, and Gwen Crane. Los
      Angeles: University of California, p. 82.

PURKINJE, JAN EVANGELISTA

  1846. "Wachen, Schlaf, Traum und Verwandte Zustände." *R. Wagner's Handwörterbuch der
      Physiologie* (Brunswick) 3:412.

RADESTOCK, P.

  1879. *Schlaf und Traum*. Leipzig: Breitkopf und Hartel.

RAMÓN Y CAJAL, SANTIAGO

  1909–11. *Histologie du Système Nerveux de l'Homme et des Vertébrés*, vols. 1 and 2. Translated by
      S. Azoulay. Paris: Maloine.
  1937. *Recollections of My Life*. Cambridge: MIT Press, 1937.

RECHTSCHAFFEN, ALLAN

  1978. "The Single-Mindedness and Isolation of Dreams." *Sleep* 1:97–109.

RECHTSCHAFFEN, ALLAN; GILLILAND, M. A.; BERGMANN, B. M.; AND WINTER,
  J. B.

  1983. "Physiological Correlates of Prolonged Sleep Deprivation in Rats." *Science* 221:-
      182–84.

RECHTSCHAFFEN, ALLAN, AND KALES, ANTHONY

  1968. *A Manual of Standardized Terminology, Techniques and Scoring System for Sleep Stages of*

Human Subjects. Washington, D.C.: Public Health Service, U.S. Government Printing Office.

REIK, THEODORE

1915. "Gold und Kot." *Int. Z. Psychoanal.* 3:183.
1920. "Völkerpsychologische Parallelen zum Traumsymbol des Mantels," *International Zeitschrift für Psychoanalyse* 6:350.

RENSHAW, BIRDSEY

1946. "Central Effects of Centripetal Impulses in Axons of Spinal Ventral Roots," *Journal of Neurophysiology* 9:191.

ROBERT, W.

1886. *Der Traum als Naturnotwendigkeit Erklärt.* Hamburg.

ROFFWARG, HOWARD P.; MUZIO, J. N.; AND DEMENT, W. C.

1966. "Ontogenetic Development of the Human Sleep-Dream Cycle." *Science* 152:604–19.

SCHEIBEL, M. E., AND SCHEIBEL, A. B.

1958. "Structural Substrates for Integrative Patterns in the Brain Stem Reticular Core." In *Reticular Formation of the Brain.* Edited by H. H. Jasper, L. D. Proctor, R. S. Knighton, W. C. Noshay, and R. T. Costello. Boston: Little, Brown, pp. 31–55.
1965. "Periodic Sensory Nonresponsiveness in Reticular Neurons." *Archives Italiennes de Biologie* 103:300–316.

SCHERNER, K. A.

1861. *Das Leben des Traumes.* Berlin.

SCHOPENHAUER, A.

1862. "Versuch über das Geisterschen und Was Damit Zusammenhängt." *Parerga und Paralipomena* (Essay 5), vol. 1:313, second edition. (First edition, 1851).

SCHRÖTTER, K.

1912. "Experimentelle Träume," *Zentralblatt für Psychoanalyse und Psychotherapie* 2:638.

SHERRINGTON, CHARLES

1906. *The Integrative Action of the Nervous System.* New Haven, Conn.: Yale University Press.
1955. *Man on His Nature.* New York: Doubleday.

SILBERER, HERBERT

1909. "Bericht über eine Methode, Gewisse Symbolische Halluzinations-Erscheinungen Hervorzurufen und Zu Beobachten." *Jahrbuch für Psychoanalytische und Psychopathologische Forschungen* 1:513.

SILBERMAN, EDWARD K.; VIVALDI, E.; GARFIELD, J.; HOBSON, J. A.; AND McCARLEY, R. W.

1980. "Carbachol Triggering of Desynchronized Sleep Phenomena: Enhancement via Small Volume Infusions," *Brain Research* 191:215–24.

SIMON, P. M.

1888. *Le Monde des Rêves.* Paris: Baillière.

SPITTA, H.

1882. *Die Schlaf und Traumzustände der Menochlichen Seele.* Tübingen: F. Fues. (First edition, 1878.)

STERIADE, MIRCEA

1984. "The Excitatory-Inhibitory Response Sequence of Thalamic and Neocortical Cells: State-Related Changes and Regulatory Systems." In *Dynamic Aspects of Neo-*

cortical Function. Edited by G. M. Edelman, W. E. Gall, and W. M. Cowan. New York: Wiley, pp. 107–57.

STERIADE, MIRCEA, AND HOBSON, J. ALLAN

1976. "Neuronal Activity During the Sleep-Waking Cycle." *Progress in Neurobiology* 6:155–376.

STRACHEY, JAMES, AND KRIS, ERNST

1965. "Introduction" to *Interpretation of Dreams*, by Sigmund Freud. New York: Avon.

STRÜMPELL, A. VON

1883. *Lehrbuch der Speciellen Pathologie und Therapie der Inneren Krankheiten*. Leipzig.

STRÜMPELL, L.

1877. *Die Natur und Enstehung der Traüme*. Leipzig.

SULLOWAY, FRANK

1979. *Freud, Biologist of the Mind*. New York: Basic Books.

SULLY, J.

1893. "The Dreams as a Revelation." *Fortnightly Review* 53.

VAN BOGAERT, L., AND THÉODORIDES, J.

1979. *Constantin von Economo* (1876–1931): The Man and the Scientist. Verlag der Oster-richischen Alcademie der Wissenschaften Wen.

VASCHIDE, NICHOLAS

1911. *Le Sommeil et les Rêves*. Paris: Flammarion.

VIVALDI, ENNIO; McCARLEY, ROBERT W.; AND HOBSON, J. ALLAN

1979. "Evocation of Desynchronized Sleep Signs by Chemical Microstimulation of the Pontine Brain Stem." In *The Reticular Formation Revisited*. Edited by J. Allan Hobson and M. A. B. Brazier. New York: Raven Press, pp. 513–29.

VOLD, J. MOURLY

1896. "Expériences sur les Rêves et en Particulier sur Ceux D'Origine Muscularie et Optique," *Rev. Phil.* 42:542.
1897. "Einige Experimente über Gesichtsbilder im Traume." *Report of 3rd Psychiatric Congress* (Munich) and *Zeitschrift fuer Psychologie und Physiologie der Sinnesorgane* 13:66.

VOLTERRA, VITO

1931. *Leçons sur la Théorie Mathématique de la Lutte pour la Vie*. Paris: Gauthier-Villans.

WEBB, WILSE

1986. "An Objective Behavioral Model of Sleep," personal communication.

WUNDT, WILHELM

1874. *Grundzuge der Physiologische Physchologie*. Leipzig: W. Engelman.
1890. *Compendium of Psychology*. Translation of third edition. Torino: Clausen.

WYZINSKI, PETER; McCARLEY, ROBERT W.; AND HOBSON, J. ALLAN

1978. "Discharge Properties of Pontine Reticulospinal Neurons during Sleep-Waking Cycle." *Journal of Neurophysiology* 41:821–34.

ZEPELIN, HAROLD

1984. "Motor Activity in Dreams and the Activation-Synthesis Hypothesis," abstract in *Sleep Research*, vol. 13. Edited by Michael H. Chase, Dennis McGinty, and Gwen Crane. Los Angeles: University of California Press, p. 103.

INDEX